THE MODEST ART

THE MODEST ART

A survey of
the short story in English

T. O. BEACHCROFT

'No one would ever have guessed that
that little black box could have held
such a quantity of beautiful things.'
'The Two Caskets'
from Andrew Lang's *Orange Fairy Book*

LONDON
OXFORD UNIVERSITY PRESS
NEW YORK TORONTO
1968

Oxford University Press, Ely House, London W.1

GLASGOW NEW YORK TORONTO MELBOURNE WELLINGTON
CAPE TOWN SALISBURY IBADAN NAIROBI LUSAKA ADDIS ABABA
BOMBAY CALCUTTA MADRAS KARACHI LAHORE DACCA
KUALA LUMPUR HONG KONG TOYKO

© Oxford University Press 1968

Printed in Great Britain
by Richard Clay (The Chaucer Press) Ltd,
Bungay, Suffolk

CONTENTS

ACKNOWLEDGEMENTS

I should like to thank a number of friends with whom I have discussed some of the ideas in this book over the course of years; in particular Professor Bonamy Dobrée, Mr. Laurence Brander, Mr. Francis Dillon, and Mme M. C. Larrière. I should like to express my gratitude to the late Mr. James Langham whose work at the B.B.C. gave encouragement to short-story writers for many years. I am grateful to Mr. Maurice Edelman for permission to quote from an article, and to Mr. Kushwant Singh for a quotation from a speech. I should like also to thank Miss Anne Pasmore for her editorial care, and Miss Elizabeth Ziman of the University of London Library and Mrs. M. R. Perkin for their help in tracing books and sources and checking quotations.

I am grateful, also, to Mrs. Patterson of the Royal Society of Literature, and the Staff of the London Library, The National Book League, and the Welwyn Garden City Library for help in various bibliographical queries.

Mrs. Joan E. Youle has given much help in the process of typing, adding many useful suggestions to her skill in reading a tangled manuscript.

I also thank the following publishers for permission to quote from the works mentioned: George Allen & Unwin Ltd. and Houghton Mifflin Company for *Elizabethan Tales* by E. J. O'Brien; Jonathan Cape Ltd. for *Country Tales* and *The Stories of Flying Officer X* by H. E. Bates; and Macmillan & Co. Ltd. and Mrs. Michael O'Donovan for *The Lonely Voice* by Frank O'Connor.

I
The Modest Art:
Some Problems

Telling short stories must be one of the most ancient practices of mankind. Yet it is a paradox and also a commonplace that the writing of short prose stories is a comparatively modern art. Paradoxically again, the novel has fewer and less remote prototypes in antiquity than the short story, yet it developed in the Western world far more rapidly once it came. The short story has in fact been more influenced by its own antiquity than the novel.

H. E. Bates, in his book *The Modern Short Story*, asks where we should begin our inquiry and replies, 'The paradoxical answer is that the history of the short story is not vast but very brief.' Elizabeth Bowen writes in her Preface to *The Faber Book of Modern Stories*, 'The short story is a young art, a child of this century.' Somerset Maugham agrees that it is modern, but puts the date rather further back, connecting it with the spread of magazines. He says in *Points of View*, 'It was not until the middle of the nineteenth century that the short story acquired a currency that made it an important feature of literary production.' He then proceeds to examine the work of two typically modern story-writers, Chekhov and Katherine Mansfield. In *A Study of the Short Story* the American authors H. S. Canby and A. S. Dashiell say that, 'It is from the early nineteenth century onwards that the short story becomes most significant in English literature.' R. West, in his book *The Short Story in America, 1900–1950*, says the short story is the only form of literature in which the Americans have been able to participate since its beginning, referring especially to the work of Washington Irving and Edgar Allen Poe.

We can continue to push the inquiry back through the eighteenth century, the Elizabethans, and beyond. E. J. O'Brien, well known as the editor of *The Best Short Stories of the Year* on both sides of the Atlantic in the 1920s and 1930s, conceives the short story not as a new but as an ancient and continuous art. 'It is a common and general belief,' he writes in his Introduction to *Elizabethan Tales*, 'that the English short story is a modern literary form, although it can actually show a continuous development from King Alfred to the present day. It reached one of its highest points in Chaucer and his successors.'

Chaucer is certainly a 'gateway ancestor', as the genealogists call it. Matter of fact, yet poetical, realistic in his presentation of human nature, yet deeply imaginative in his insight, he stands on the threshold of modern fiction. Yet if we look past him we can see lines of descent which vanish far into antiquity.

The modern short story, that is, the prose narrative of up to 10,000 words or so, seems so obvious a literary form that it is only reasonable to suppose that it must have existed for centuries; and that so many Chekhovs, Kiplings, Somerset Maughams, and Salingers of the past have all been composing stories that give us brief, vivid pictures of the daily life, the feelings, and problems of their times. However, the facts are surprisingly different. It was usually stories of epic length, the more formal compositions of the bard and poet, that were preserved in manuscript. Short stories that have survived in written form from the antique world are rare, and those that have been handed down by word of mouth, and recorded in later centuries, such stories as we may find in the *Gesta Romanorum* of medieval times or in the collections of the brothers Grimm, are full of magic, myths, and wild farce. Very few of them, in fact, have much resemblance to the modern art of the short story.

It is curious, indeed it is mysterious, that a form that seems so obvious today should have taken so long to develop. At times in the literature of the past one seems to feel a void, a missing element. Where are the natural short stories? Where amidst all these saintly miracles, talking animals, petulant gnomes, knock-about farces, patient Griseldas, and Roman fathers who snatch up butchers' knives and plunge them into their daughters to save them from dishonour—where are the stories of the joys and sorrows of ordinary life? They are so few and far between that one is inclined to say with Prince Hal, 'Oh monstrous; but one halfpenny worth of bread to this intolerable deal of sack!'

Nevertheless, short stories from the past abound, and if we look at them historically we see that they seem to be moving slowly towards the modern art. It is the aim of this book to take a rather longer look than has been customary at the gradual changes that lie behind the short story of today; developments not only in technique but in truth, and insight. The study must be confined to one language, English, but it is hoped to show the leading influences of other nations. Gradually the modern short story becomes differentiated from other literary forms, and brings its own kind of understanding: a new short story can be 'a raid on the inarticulate' not in terms of poetic or philosophic meditation, but in terms of an unpretentious narrative. Coppard tells us that some of Hardy's stories struck him 'with the same startling enchantment as Keats's poem "La Belle Dame sans Merci" '.[1]

The difference between the antique and the modern stories stems largely from the difference between reading and listening. If a story is told, the child or adult listener is bound to be affected by the physical presence of the teller, whose personality becomes part of the experience of hearing the story. Moreover, the professional story-tellers of the past, in the bazaar or great hall, were usually telling traditional stories which most of the audience already knew and trusted. The modern writer, on the other hand, is not only unable to meet his audience face to face, but he is trying to interest them in an entirely new story, written by an author whom they may never have heard of before. Again, in addressing an audience face to face there is bound to be a certain amount of playing up to the group response. The effects are broader, less intimate, achieved in a different way; the solitary

[1] A. E. Coppard, *It's Me O Lord* (Methuen, 1957), p. 63.

reader feels and thinks more deeply. It is interesting that both
Chekhov and Katherine Mansfield could stand up before an
audience and give extremely amusing impersonations. However,
they were not at these moments practising their written art.

It is then the literary short story, the printed short story, that
is the modern art. The Elizabethan author Barnabe Rich tells us
in the Preface to *His Farewell to Militarie Profession* (1581)
that his stories are 'fitter to be presented on the stage'. Three
centuries later Scott remarks at the beginning of 'The Tapestried
Chamber' (1828) that a ghost story really should be told in person
and not 'committed to print'. The words 'committed to print'
sound like some form of imprisonment. The personal narrator
style has lingered: it applies far more to short stories than to
novels, because their origin in speech is so much more obvious.
Their roots are found in ordinary conversation; but no one would
ever think of *Middlemarch* as a story to be told at the end of a
dinner party.

People, and perhaps English people especially, are apt to take
fright at the very phrase 'the literary short story'. It suggests to
them a self-conscious, overwrought production, as opposed to
the strong human yarn of the good old-fashioned type. One often
encounters the feeling that a good story can and ought to be put
across without literary skill. Some short-story writers have themselves thought that the best down-to-earth way to go about their
task was simply to simulate a spoken story in print. In his address
to the Royal Society of Literature Somerset Maugham said in a
much quoted passage that his kind of story could be told after
dinner in a ship's smoking-room. Often enough he appears himself as a personal narrator telling the story.

Somerset Maugham is one of the most subtle masters in com-
municating this kind of story, but the fact remains that his
stories are written and printed stories and not told stories. They
are a skilfully devised literary form designed to be read. They are
not in the least like the stories that reach us from the old folk
collections. The sophisticated narrator and his style of speech are
a device, necessary perhaps to Maugham's chosen method but
only at times inherent in the substance of the story itself. In fact

some of Maugham's best stories are told without any personal narrator; they would be most unlikely to be told verbally and certainly not by a smoking-room raconteur.

Other modern short-story writers, such as Chekhov, have tended to eliminate the narrator. Somerset Maugham was apt to put himself in one camp and Chekhov in another; and he was at times very unappreciative of Chekhov. This makes it all the more interesting that in 1917 when Maugham was in Russia he wrote a passage which appeared later in his *A Writer's Notebook*:

But with Chekhov you do not seem to be reading stories at all. There is no obvious cleverness in them, and you might think that anyone could write them, but for the fact that nobody does. The author has had an emotion, and he is able so to put it into words, then you receive it in your turn. You become his collaborator. Yet if you try to tell one of his stories there is nothing to tell.

This is exactly the reverse of the story that is cleverly told, yet fades away in print. In fact there is an antithesis, at times almost a battle, between the two approaches and this is seen no-where more clearly than in Somerset Maugham's own changeable view of Chekhov, which we shall examine in chapter XVI.

Somerset Maugham tells us that he often likes to narrate in the first person, because the fact that the narrator has seen the events for himself gives the story greater verisimilitude.[2] Yet this cuts both ways. While it might apply with great force to any one story, it begins to go beyond the bounds of common sense to believe that Somerset Maugham observed so many excellent dramatic and ironic stories and simply wrote down what had come his way. Besides, he himself tells us that the narrating 'I' is not necessarily quite like himself; but if the narrator is partly invented, one assumes the same of the stories. He seems, in fact, to be telling us that this is a method, a device, rather than the essence of the matter. The essence of the matter is the truth of the story itself.

Plenty of story-writers of very different kinds state, and at

[2] W. Somerset Maugham, *Complete Stories* (Heinemann, 1951), Preface, vol. II.

times insist fervently, that it is the truth they are seeking and nothing but the truth. 'Truth's elder sister—fiction', says Kipling. 'Lord, make me crystal clear', says Katherine Mansfield, and she struggles to eliminate all trace of herself. And here is Chekhov, when he was mature and famous, talking to Alexander Tikhonoff, a young admirer, who had visited him: 'First of all my friend, we must get rid of lies. Art is so good, just because it does not tolerate a lie. You can tell lies in love, politics, medicine—you can deceive men as much as you like, and even deceive God Himself—such cases have been known—but you cannot practise deception in art.'[3] People may well ask how many meanings and non-meanings, how many misunderstandings may arise from any of the above quotations, and the use of the word 'truth'. Yet Kipling or Chekhov in their contrasting styles and moods are good enough guides to the intention of short-story writers.

Fiction, the whole body of the modern novel, and the modern short story, has been working towards a kind of truth which was not even in the sights of many of the story-tellers of antiquity. That fiction has its own kind of truth, that the inventions of poets are in a sense 'more philosophic and of graver import' than history, is supported by Aristotle, but it is certainly not a notion that has been held at all times and places. Let us look very briefly at some conceptions of the truth of story-telling.

Caxton, in his well-known Preface to Malory's *Morte Darthur*, says that one need not take the stories as true in a literal sense. They are written 'for our doctrine'; they are true to inner hopes and needs of knighthood; they are true in Herbert Read's phrase, to 'the sense of glory'. Yet Caxton himself seems to put the attraction of reading them on a considerably less exalted plane. 'And for to pass the time this book shall be pleasant to read in, but for to give faith and belief that all is true that is contained therein ye be at your liberty.'[4] The crude facts of Malory's own life have a very curious appearance, when they are seen against the entrancing tapestry of knighthood that he wove when he was in prison.

---

[3] D. Magarshack, *Chekhov* (Faber & Faber, 1952), p. 371.
[4] Malory, *Le Morte Darthur* (Macmillan, 1912), Caxton's Preface, p. 2.

If we turn to another medieval work, *The Canterbury Tales*, we have numerous striking comments on the whole conception of legendary and magical fiction. It is well known that Chaucer puts into his own mouth some foolish jingling verses which are a debased version of a romantic story, and that the Host of the Tabard Inn breaks in and stops him from talking such nonsense.

No more of this for Goddes dignitee!

Scholars of medieval literature say that *The Canterbury Tales* give us a compendium of every kind of story that was current coin in the fourteenth century, from the saintly to the obscene. Yet it must strike the modern reader, who is not particularly well acquainted with medieval thought, that it is the wonderful presentation of the pilgrims themselves at the Inn and on the road that is 'true', in the sense that Chekhov intended. Nothing vouches for them except the creative life that the author gives them, and it is they who show up that the tales they tell do not exist on the same plane of truth as the tellers.

In Elizabethan times authors were still apt to contrast 'the pleasant delights of a witty pretty tale' with the severities of truth. The land of euphuism was a long way from the harsh affairs of Henry VIII's Court. Professor Bonamy Dobrée has pointed out in *Modern Prose Style* the startling differences between Sir Philip Sidney's language in writing *Arcadia* and his violent words in writing about an affair which affected him closely in the world of fact. Bacon would hardly have equated the world of Elizabethan fiction with life as he knew it: and he says of storytelling, 'A mixture of a lie doth ever add pleasure.'

In the seventeenth century the attacks on the stage are apt to represent fiction as mere lies, while the long theoretical arguments that support heroic poetry, such as Davenant's Preface to Gondibert, talk of the truth of poetry as a more noble version of everyday life. This view itself could deteriorate into escapism.

Yet already a change was at hand. With Sir Roger de Coverley, early in the eighteenth century, with the more stolid middle-class merchants whom we meet in short anecdotes in Defoe's *Journal*, the whole notion of fiction is moving towards a truth seen in everyday life. Charles Lamb's essay on Defoe dwells especially on this point.[5] Thackeray says of Fielding, 'O, wondrous power of genius! Fielding's men and women are alive, though History's are not.'[6]

These are merely a few of the commonplaces of an age-old discussion of truth in fiction—of verisimilitude, symbolic truth, archetypal truth, truth in apologetics, and truth to the terms of daily life. The discussion has, however, a special relationship to the short story as distinct from the novel. As we have seen, the tradition of the personal narrator who vouches for the truth of his story is strong. Yet, on the other hand, the short-story writer has practically no space to chat, to establish his own authority, and his attempts to do so may well interfere with the story itself. Again, some novels can entice one into an acceptance of their world by sheer length, but a short story has no surrounding acreage of the provincial town or the cathedral close. It must be remembered also that some people who are open to the influence of novels are more or less impervious to short stories. The number of readers who like or who are really moved by the best short stories is far smaller than the number of fiction readers as a whole. Even the mood of the moment may spoil the readers' response to a short story. Let us, however, look at some of the problems of writing a short story from the author's point of view. How can he establish his position with the reader?

Short stories arrive in writers' minds in various different ways. Somerset Maugham's notebooks show sometimes quite full synopses for the outline of a story, with a suggestion as to the position of the personal narrator. With some authors, on the other hand, a story begins in a kind of flash; a short story is suddenly put before them in a startlingly visual form. There is evidence of such flashes to be found in Katherine Mansfield's jottings. Her note to herself about 'The Doll's House' is, for instance, almost exactly the same as the closing words of the

[5] Charles Lamb, 'Estimate of Defoe's Secondary Novels', *Complete Works* (Chatto and Windus, 1901), p. 358.
[6] W. M. Thackeray, *Works*, vol. V, *SketchBooks, Caricatures, and Lithographs in Paris* (Smith Elder, 1902), p. 155.

story, as she wrote it: '"The little lamp. I seen it." Then they became silent.'[7] It shows that the whole situation that makes these words the end and climax of the story must have been present in an instant in Katherine Mansfield's vision.

As Katherine Mansfield knew only too well, it is one thing to see or, as it were, to foresee a short story in this way, and another to write it down adequately. She could at times make some extremely bad attempts. As she grew older, she moved more and more towards the method of using no narrator, of allowing no comment from any implied narrator, of making the scene and the events of the story reveal themselves. In this way she is in direct contrast to Somerset Maugham.

Any writer who has written fifty short stories, or even one, may pass in his mind through the whole historical development of the various methods of telling the story in written form. To narrate as 'I' seems natural and easy. Yet if he is to be the 'I' to whom it all happened, this of course confines the whole vision to one point. The other people can be seen only as 'I' sees them. 'I' himself cannot be set in the scene or characterized in the same objective way as the others. The author meets at once with the difficulties of an actor who is also a narrator.

If he decides that it would be better to be a narrator passing on to the reader a story which a friend has told him, a different set of problems arises. He finds he has had to confine himself not only to the viewpoint but also to the conversational limitations of one chosen character or else he has to keep turning aside from the 'I' of the story to another 'I' who is a kind of interviewer. Another method is to pretend that the complete manuscript of another 'I' has come into his hands; but he will soon grow dissatisfied with manuscripts left in bureaux or in bottles. The description of how the manuscript was found is only too apt to develop into another story. 'The Turn of the Screw' is an extreme example of this.

He may well begin to feel that the use of 'I' is involving himself in a kind of half-truth, half-lie; for 'I' exists already in the world of fact or history. He may wonder at this point if the 'I' is

[7] *Journal*, 27 October 1921 (Constable, 1927).

B

any help at all. It might be better to drop the personalized narrator and be a camera which sees but does not comment. He may think of Zorba the Greek, who could dance his stories to his friends. He may remember from Aristotle that 'mimesis' can be effected by flute playing and dancing without the use of words at all. He may find himself putting down one or two quite general observations to set his story in motion, drifting into a kind of essay, setting up his own pulpit; this, in fact, used to be a very usual way of telling a story. In the eighteenth century short stories began to emerge from essays in just this way. He may, for instance, recall Leigh Hunt's essay 'On Washerwomen', which chats agreeably for two or three pages, and then includes a germinal short story towards the end: the story gains acceptability from the general truth of Leigh Hunt's remarks. Is he to use his own personality or to try and abandon it; to be or not to be? Does a narrator help truth or hinder it? Throughout the historical changes these problems of story-telling are constantly recurring: whether it is Marie de France or Chaucer who is telling the story, an unknown medieval priest, Chekhov or Kipling.

There are other familiar problems. Does a short story need to contain a wonderful or remarkable happening? Does it need a dramatic drop of the curtain? To what extent should it be based on a single unified event? Ought it to contain some social or political message? These are points which have been considerably discussed.

A short story may take only a few minutes to read. It may be written in unobtrusive prose. Yet in those few minutes it may enter into the reader's mind, in a way which will never be forgotten. Plainly it must go deep to do this. It is not a trick. It is an encounter between two people—a passage of truth from one mind to another. This is the nature of the modest art.

II

Antiquities: the Parable, the Ballad, and the Mime

We referred to Chaucer as a 'gateway ancestor', and before we follow our theme of the English short story, let us look very briefly at the short stories of the ancient world that lie behind Chaucer.

If we retrace these antecedents through the centuries we discover an interesting point. There are two different sources, two different forms from which the modern short story might have descended: the ancient spoken story and the acted mime. However, its descent has been almost exclusively from the narrated story. The mime of Greek and Roman times disappears from view, though one or two survive, notably the fifteenth Idyll of Theocritus, which are much nearer in spirit and execution to many modern short stories than anything to be found in a medieval collection of tales such as *Gesta Romanorum*.

Many of these medieval stories have ancient origins. It is customary to trace the earliest history of the short story to the Jatakas, which came to Europe from the East, and can be described very briefly as a collection of stories emanating from the teachings of the Buddha. From this source came such famous stories as 'The Goose that laid the Golden Eggs' and many others that descended to medieval times as fables, parables, and moralizing incidents. The Hindu Panchatantra was another collection, somewhat later, but also migrating far and wide for centuries. These ancient prototypes, in fact, came into existence as vehicles of religious and moral instruction. The whole practice of teaching by fables and parables descends from them, and the parables of

Christ are the supreme examples. It is sometimes said both by priests and literary historians that the parables of Christ are the most wonderful of all short stories; but this judgement almost invariably refers to the acceptance of the parables as divine revelation, and it is extremely hard to think of them merely as ancient literature, emanating from a human source.

However, the very fact of their historical existence emphasizes that the short story is from the outset deeply involved with a religious mode of thinking. Thus the idea that short stories ought to be nuggets of moral teaching, that they ought to have a moral motive, and that this is their true *raison d'être* is very deeply rooted. For many generations the teacher, the preacher, the essayist, and the lecturer have used the short story to point a moral. Medieval homilists had books full of anecdotes arranged alphabetically, so that they could look up any vice or virtue from accidie to zeal, and tell a story about it. Eighteenth-century essayists were for ever insisting on the moral purpose of their anecdotes. Short stories still arise today because they illustrate some generalized social or political argument in the author's mind, rather than any vision of individual being. A number of stories, in fact, still have their element of teaching intention.

This, however, is to anticipate. Returning to a view of stories from the ancient world, we find that the Old Testament books of Esther and Ruth are sometimes referred to as early examples of the long short story; a more truly unified short story is 'Susanna and the Elders' in the Apocrypha. This, with its man-of-the-world approach, its complete lack of miracles, its account of the surprising and deplorable behaviour of two old lechers, and its last-minute legal climax, does indeed appear to be that very rare thing, an antique example of the modern art. One might in fact say it is a story suited to Somerset Maugham or Maupassant.

There are other striking short stories in the Old Testament: David and Goliath, for instance, which is an archetype of an ever popular story; or Naaman the Syrian. This, however, with its many queer side issues and its miraculous climax, has the typically archaic ring, while 'Susanna and the Elders' is remarkably modern. But these stories are not put forward as fiction. They are all said to be history, including the minor incident of Susanna, which is the kind of smaller, more personal historical happening that was very seldom written down as an event complete in itself.

Other traditional short stories came from Greek myth, undergoing much alteration as they passed through the dark ages; others came from *The Arabian Nights*, from the giants and trolls and elves of many centuries and countries. In late Greek and Latin literature we begin to see the origins of the novel in the longer Greek Romances, which had a considerable influence on the Elizabethans, but there are very few short stories of realistic contemporary life from the ancient world. One well-known one is 'The Widow of Ephesus', from *The Satyricon* of Petronius Arbiter, a gay little *farce noir*, which is told very briefly but which is surprisingly modern in spirit, and provided Christopher Fry with the basis of his play *A Phoenix too Frequent*.

Throughout the Middle Ages short stories that were preserved in writing were dominated by the idea of moral teaching: and they also, were usually put forward as true histories. Between the efforts to make history moral and the attempts to give made-up stories a historical respectability, truth, fiction, and preaching became inextricably mixed. Even as late as Elizabethan times, it was the exception for an author to say, as Barnabe Rich does, that some of his stories were 'forged only for delight'. At that time an original story had a slight air of counterfeit: while today it is the over-obvious assertion that 'this really happened' that strikes a false note. The art thus grows up in the form of a known narrator telling the story in his own person, vouching for its factual truth, and usually pointing a moral.

In contrast to the whole conception of the moral and sermonizing stories are the best of the medieval ballads. They are anonymous; they tell their stories without comment, without moralizing, and they use the minimum of narration. Often they put the whole stress on a single scene. They can be astonishingly impressive in their concentration, and their dramatic form has been described as 'beginning with the fifth act'.[1] The stories they tell are astonishing, often tragic, and sometimes magical. They were

[1] M. J. C. Hodgart, *The Ballads* (Hutchinson, 1950), p. 10.

designed, however, to be sung or chanted by a professional performer, and many were never written down till they were collected centuries later as antiquities. It is strange how little effect they had on the slow development of the written short story, as they are often wonderful examples of the short-story art.

There were yet other stories not important enough to be written down, not suitable for the more formal occasions, and often impossible for the preachers to assimilate. What were they like? The answer is to be found in the folk collections of the brothers Grimm, and other philologists whose studies came just in time to catch these spoken stories before they were overwhelmed in the world of print. The first volume of Grimms' *Household Tales* (*Kinder- und Hausmärchen*) came out in 1812, the result, the brothers tell us, of thirteen years' work. Translations and adaptations have been appearing in many languages ever since.

Grimms' *Tales* are not merely a few quaint fairy stories, which have at times haunting poetic overtones, but which by their nature are stories for children. They are in truth the survivors of an immense range of folk-tales. Once the brothers Grimm had published their *Household Tales*, an enormous impetus was given to the collection of the folk-tales of many countries, and people rapidly became impressed by two aspects of these stories: first was the magical and extraordinary world in which they took place, a world, says Andrew Lang, 'in which queens are accused of giving birth to puppies and the accusation is believed'. 'The tales', he writes, in his Introduction to the full translation of 1884, 'are of a monstrous irrational and unnatural character. . . .'[2]

Secondly, the stories collected by the Grimms were not confined to the Germanic or Scandinavian scene. The Italians had long been famous for collecting homely as well as literary stories, and Straparola's *Tredici Piacevoli Notte* of 1550 has resemblances to Grimm; while in French, Perrault's *Histoires et Contes du Temps Passé*, 1697 (the original *Contes de Ma Mère l'Oye*), which contained Bluebeard, Cinderella, The Sleeping Beauty, and other famous stories, also drew on the common fund of folk-tales.

[2] Grimms' *Household Tales*, ed. Margaret Hunt, with an Introduction by Andrew Lang (Bell and Son, 1884), p. xii.

Perrault rather charmingly tells us that his little boy was the author.

This, however, is only a first glimpse of the researches and comparisons that soon revealed that Grimms' *Tales* not only were spread through many countries but were of great antiquity; simple people like Red Riding Hood turned out to have an immense ancestry. Some stories could be traced back through the Middle Ages to *The Arabian Nights*, to corrupted forms of classical myths, and beyond these past the imaginary story-teller Aesop and the old Eastern collections.

In fact, the substance of a number of Grimms' *Tales* goes even beyond the Indo-Aryan culture, and can be found among North American Indians, among Swahili and Zulu speakers, among Maoris and Samoans. Some even have an ancestry in papyri enclosed in ancient Egyptian tombs. It seems as if some of the stories come by spontaneous generation.

The anthropologists and folklorists of the nineteenth century had a field-day with all this material, some of them began to draw up immense charts and categories, showing different themes and their changes from culture to culture. They noted, for instance, the ill-treatment of the youngest child, and his or her eventual triumph; the abduction of the bride and her pursuit by a supernatural father; the forbidden chambers and the awful results of looking into them; the good effects of kindly treatment of animals who turn out to have magic powers. They pondered over mutations, cannibalism, incest, the birth of animals from human wombs and of human babies from animals. In fact, the stories are full of sphinx-like riddles which are a happy-hunting-ground for the modern psychologist as they were formerly for magicians and interpreters of dreams.

It is strange that these should be the 'household tales' that have reached us, the stories that have been kept alive during centuries by speech. Where there is no magic, comedy is usually pushed to the point of violence or extreme farce. Hans takes away his front door and carries it on his back, so that thieves cannot break it open and enter the house. Clever Else sits weeping with her jug in the cellar and persuades all the family to join in her lamentations.

She is afraid that if she marries the young man who has come to court her and they have a child she may send him down to the cellar to draw beer, and the pickaxe hanging on the wall may one day fall down and kill him. So the suitor decides to wed her with various fantastic results. Natural short stories, as Andrew Lang pointed out, seem to be the 'fruits of civilised thought and literary experience'.

There is, however, at least one short natural story in Grimms' *Tales*, a story which takes place within an ordinary family circle, and the point of which is a study of character and the movement of a human emotion to a climax. This is the story, number seventy-eight in Grimms' numbering, of 'The Old Man and his Grandson'.

A small boy lives with his mother and father, who is a wood-cutter. His father goes out to work all day, and his mother is a bustling energetic woman, often made cross by the housework. With them there lives also the husband's father, an old feeble man who, like the little boy, is often scolded by the busy housewife. One day the old man, whose hands shake, drops his earthenware plate at dinnertime and breaks it. The wife pushes him angrily from the table and from that day he has to sit apart from the family at meal times, and eat out of a wooden bowl. The little grandson sees his grandfather's eyes fill with tears.

Some time later the two parents see the boy playing with some pieces of wood on the floor, and they ask him what he is doing.

'I am making a little trough', answered the child, 'for father and mother to eat out of when I am big.' The man and his wife looked at each other for a while, and presently began to cry. Then they took the old grandfather to the table, and henceforth always let him eat with them, and likewise said nothing, if he did spill a little of anything.

When I began to be able to read to myself, this soon became my favourite story in Grimm. It seemed that I understood and became all the people in the story, and in some way I also became the scene itself. It was not that I wanted the other stories altered. Rapunzel would be a poor affair if the heroine let down a rope instead of her hair: and Rumpelstiltskin would not have been

Rumpelstiltskin if he had not stamped so hard that he became rooted to the spot. These were fairy stories: but 'The Old Man and his Grandson' was true. It could not be denied, and it could not be removed.

'The Old Man and his Grandson', like most of Grimms' stories, is found in many versions. Something like it can be traced in Arabic as well as in European languages. However, it is striking that the version given in Grimm is put into a normal modern home; and the revealing rebuke comes from the matter-of-fact clarity of a child. It has a touch of genius. In fact, the contrast between the earthenware plate and the wooden bowl must have represented in Grimms' day an almost contemporary re-casting.

Before we leave Grimms' *Tales* it is worth noticing that the narrator usually occupies a very unobtrusive position; and the brothers Grimm were careful to write down the stories just as they heard them. 'Once upon a time' is a very simple device for lifting a curtain upon a scene, while keeping the narrator out of the way.

Let us return to that other completely different prototype of the short story—the mime of ancient Greece. In evolving over centuries out of spoken apologues and personal narration, the written short story had a very long way to come. Yet curiously enough, if it had developed directly from Theocritus it would have had a very short way to come. The origin of that wide group of short dramatic displays known as mime seems to have been in dance and gesture as much as in speech. They were brief spectacles; sometimes farcical, sometimes obscene, sometimes purely knockabout. Some had, however, an approach to small plays, to naturalistic representation of life. The best known mime-writer appears to have been Sophron, but only fragments of his work have survived. The mimes of Herodas were not discovered till 1890, so they also were lost to the medieval world. These do not stand very high as literature, and one or two of them are rather unpleasant, but they are remarkably interesting as small pieces of realistic fiction, told in dramatic form.[3]

[3] *Mimes and Fragments of Herodas*, eds. W. Headlam and A. D. Knox (Cambridge University Press, 1922).

Theocritus, on the other hand, was a poet of genius: a poet who had the ancient Greek gift of combining depth with apparent simplicity. In the Idylls[4] we can see the figures on the Grecian urn of Keats in living movement and hear what they are saying. In Idyll XV especially, the human characters seem to be close at hand, breathing, and laughing. This poem tells simply of two young married women who leave their household chores to visit the crowded Adonis festival. Praxinoa calls on Gorgo at her house; they discuss their husbands with wonderfully modern gossip. They set off through the streets talking volubly about everything they see. They are foolish, yet endearing, and they are put before us in all their human frailty with loving care.

Then the mood changes. They arrive at the performance and fall silent as they listen to the incantation of a richly beautiful and allusive poem about the risen Adonis. They are deeply moved, but when it is over, their comments are hopelessly inadequate. 'The woman's a marvel,' they say of the singer, 'happy to know so much. Still its time for home.' Then the stream of their chatter is renewed and they go off home talking of their husbands' dinners.

This mime, written in the third century before Christ, comes as near to a modern short story as anything in the ancient world. At one stroke the mime form gets rid of the need to prove the authority of the narrator. It gets rid of comment, explanation, and moralizing. It moves at one stroke, because it must, into dialogue and development of character. Scenes from everyday life are obviously within its scope, while violent movement and amazing events are not. Here it is different from the chanted ballad. Finally, it does not and cannot claim to be factually true, and so rests on its own truth of mimesis.

Scholars, editors, and professors whose interests have been all to expound classical Greek literature rather than to appreciate the twentieth-century short story have frequently praised this Idyll of Theocritus in much the same language as critics have used of modern short stories. Professor Hadas calls it 'a masterpiece in a

[4] *The Idylls of Theocritus*, translated and edited by A. S. F. Gow (Cambridge University Press, 1950).

humble style'. 'So vivid a picture', he writes, 'is given not only of the characters of the ladies but of the gay turbulence of the streets, and the emotional excitement at the service, that one is amazed on turning back to the text to find that the whole thing is done in less than six pages.'[5]

The *Adoniazusae*, moreover, while it is written in the exacting mime form, has survived as literature. It has a quality that appeals to the imagination of a reader as much as a spectator. It is a poem, not just a 'script', waiting for actors to bring it to life on the stage.

The poetry exists not in the verse form alone but in the whole conception of the work. As Greek critics of the ancient world point out, poetry was not then, any more than now, a matter of writing correct hexameters. Mimesis, which roughly corresponds to our use of the word fiction, was in itself considered to be a true part of poetry. The short mime, like the short story, is deeply concerned with certain aspects of human nature, that cannot be expressed in a longer form, or in a form which wears too ostentatiously the outward assumptions of poetry. And this is the art form which Aristotle says is curiously anonymous.

There is further an art which imitates by language alone, without harmony, in prose or verse. . . . This form of imitation is to this day without a name. We have no name for a mime of Sophron or Xenarchus and a Socratic conversation; and we should still be without one even if the imitation in the two instances were in trimeters or elegiacs, or some other kind of verse. . . . [6]

It is, in fact, the modest art.

[5] Moses Hadas, *A History of Greek Literature* (Columbia University Press, 1950), p. 207.
[6] Aristotle, *On the Art of Poetry*, translated by I. Bywater (Clarendon Press, 1909), p. 5.

III

The Return of the Exile

I

It is often said that the literature of the Anglo-Saxons is impersonal. It tells us little of private states of mind or intimate feelings.
Ranging from Bede to *Beowulf*, it consists on the one hand of
Christian apologetics, the lives of saints, religious miracles, and
legends; and on the other hand of the public work of the scop and
minstrel, designed for performance in the great hall, when the
earls, the companions, the spear-warriors, had laid down their
bright helmets. Near the beginning of *Beowulf* [1] we learn:

Then was the sound of the harp, the clear song of the minstrel. He who
could tell of men's beginnings from olden times spoke of how the
Almighty wrought the earth, bright in its beauty. . . .

Yet already we have a reflective mood, a mood of wonder, of
probing into men's sorrows.

Thus the noble warriors lived in pleasure and plenty, until a fiend in
hell began to contrive malice. This grim spirit was called Grendel, a
famous marsh-stepper who held the moors, the fen and fastness. This
hapless creature sojourned for a space in the sea monster's home, after
the Creator had condemned him. The eternal Lord avenged the murder
on the race of Cain, because he slew Abel. He did not rejoice in that
feud. Then the Lord drove him from mankind for that crime. Thence
sprang all evil spawn, ogres, elves and sea monsters, giants too, who
struggled long time against God.

Here we may see the grafting of Christian hope on to an older
stem—the terrors of those dark spirits of the marsh, that have

[1] *Anglo-Saxon Poetry*, selected and translated by R. K. Gordon (Everyman
Dent, 1926); following quotations, ibid.

been pushed away from men's minds and dwellings and yet 'rise up again from the cold mists'. In a sense that is what *Beowulf* is all about rather than battles of men with men. Yet these dark spirits are foes not so much of human virtue as of human existence. They come by night and it is the daylight life of happiness that they want to destroy.

We hear also from these far-off times the reverberating sound of Old English, a language of solid splendour. It is hard to believe that men used it for trivialities, and yet it rings on under our own speech with an odd friendly familiarity. But it is not all solemn. Songs could also be heard in the great hall. King Alfred himself was a lover of English poetry, which would have been sure to include some stories, but he did not record what he knew. Yet at moments when the poets unlock their 'word-hoards' in between the battles and the lives of saints, an unexpectedly personal voice, with its intimate moods and feelings, reaches us. Sometimes it is the voice of the bard himself: 'I will say this of myself that once I was a minstrel of the Heodeningas dear to my king. Deor was my name', and Deor goes on to add his own personal experience of loss and sadness to the griefs of other men that he has been recounting. The voice in 'The Seafarer' is also a personal one. 'I can utter a true story about myself, tell of my travels, how in toilsome days I often suffered a time of hardship.'

This is a distinctive voice, the same mood echoing repeatedly. Often it is a voice of quiet sadness, telling us of exile, and of loss. It comes to us with images of frost and marshland, of icy seas, and great ruined buildings. Where have past glories gone? asks this voice in 'The Ruin' and in 'The Wanderer'.

Whither has gone the horse? Whither has gone the man? Whither has gone the giver of treasure? Alas the bright cup. Alas, the warrior in his corselet. Alas, the glory of Princes. Then comes the darkness, the night shadow casts gloom, sends forth from the north hailstones to the terror of men.

Once this voice is known it can be heard even in the more public poems; at the close of *Beowulf*, for instance, in the last lines of the whole poem:

Thus did the men of the Geats, his hearth companions, bewail the fall of their Lord: they said that among the kings of the world he was the mildest of men and the most kindly, most gentle to his people and most eager for praise.

It is unexpected to find an ancient warrior king praised for his gentleness; yet gentleness and restraint in sorrow are an essential part of this mood. 'One must check a violent mind and control it with firmness,' says the Seafarer, 'and be trustworthy to men. And Deor the bard who has been dispossessed of his own position bases his poem on the repeated refrain, 'þœs ofereode, þisses swa mæg' ('that passed over, and so may this').

This is a frame of mind that is stoical but not harsh: it is the voice of one who can survive sorrow: an acceptance of bleak and wintry thoughts, with a firm but gentle heart.

Within this range of feeling it is often the particular thought of an exile and of a longed-for return that dominates the mood. Yet curiously enough this state of exile is often self-imposed. It is a wandering from one kind of searching to another. Summer brings to the Seafarer not peace but strange foreboding.

The fields are fair; the world revives; all these urge the heart of the eager-minded man to a journey. . . . The man knows not, the prosperous being, what some of those endure, who most widely take the paths of exile. And yet my heart is now restless in my breast, my mind is with the sea flood over the face of the earth, and comes again to me, searching, unsatisfied.

Again, this is personal. 'The Seafarer' is not merely a poem that deals with snow falling over the sea waves, rather than bright helmets and warrior friends: it is a spiritual as much as a physical wandering. It is a poem that is surely more suitable to be read and to be pondered alone than to be performed in the 'mighty mead dwelling'. 'The Wanderer' at times seems to be almost a voice speaking to itself.

Often I must bewail my sorrows in my loneliness, at the dawn of each day: there is no living man now to whom I dare speak my heart openly.

These again are unexpected moods to survive from an antique literature that is said to be impersonal. In some ways 'The Seafarer' and 'The Wife's Lament' can be thought of as the germ of short stories. They are in fact telling us the story of a particular human situation, and what it is like to be in that situation: and they are doing it in terms of imagery and personal speech. If, as some people think, 'The Seafarer' is really a conversation between two different people, a young man and an old, this dramatization of form brings it nearer to the idea of fiction. These glimpses of stories come from personal poetic insight; and they also convey a distinctive Anglo-Saxon feeling, one that we shall see surviving among modern English short-story writers centuries later. These Anglo-Saxon fragments, moreover, are quite unlike the fairy tales that we meet in Grimm. There is nothing among the *Hausmärchen* of which 'The Seafarer' or 'The Ruin' could be a progenitor.

H. S. Canby points out in *The Short Story in English* that the earliest written passage that can be called a short story in Anglo-Saxon can be found in the tenth-century Blickling Homilies. Once again it deals with the constantly recurring theme of exile. It tells of a rich man who owned 'treasures very splendid and manifold' and lived in happiness. Then in the midst of his worldly blessings he died.

Suddenly, there came to an end this loan of life. There was one of his kinsmen and worldly friends who loved him more than any other man: and for the grief and sorrow of his friend's death he could no longer stay at home, but with a sad heart he left his native land and his own dwelling, and stayed for many winters in another country; but the longing never wore away, but greatly beset and troubled him. Then he began after a long time to long for his own land, so that he could see again and gaze on the burying-place and know what he was like, whom he had often before seen in his fair fortune and his fruitful years. . . .

Then there called out to him those dead bones and said 'Why do you come to gaze on us? Now you may see a piece of the earth's share and the leaving of worms, even where you once saw fine cloth with gold embroidery. Gaze now on dust and dry bones where you once saw limbs that were fair to look on, after their fleshly kind.

'Alas, my friend and kinsman, think of this and understand thyself what I was formerly; and you shall be after a while what I am now. . . .' Then he, thus sad and thus mourning, went away from this showing of the dust, and turned from all this world's doings and began to learn and to teach the praise of God's love.[2]

This brings the story to its homilectic point: yet the story is complete without the moral. This experience of wandering, of turning away, is much the same as that of 'The Seafarer', but now the mood is taken yet a stage further. The journey is not only self-imposed, but it has no outcome in human life. The return is not after all a return, but only a new setting out. The preacher, or possibly the scribe, of the Blickling manuscript has headed the passage 'Saules ðearf'—'Soul's need'. He too has not been dealing with a physical exile.

II

As a short story, this is of course still germinal. It is only an acorn: but out of an acorn may come a forest of English oaks, and we can find the same experience and even the same story in English hands a thousand years later. One can find it, for instance, in Hardy. *The Return of the Native* is not only the title of one of Hardy's most famous novels: it is the linking theme of a whole group of his short stories, *A Few Crusted Characters*. We see at the beginning of these stories a country carrier's wagon trundling off from a market town to make its slow journey back to the village of Long Puddle. The passengers all know each other. To their surprise they are joined by a stranger. Then, as they talk, he turns out to be one John Lackland, a man who left the village thirty-five years before with his family. Lackland is now alone in the world, and has long 'nourished a thought' that he would like to return to the home of his childhood.

The plodding journey back to the village is occupied with talk, and soon the different passengers are telling stories of the lives of people whom John used to know years ago. The old device of linking a group of story-tellers together is used here with exceptional point because all the stories combine to build up to the

[2] *The Blickling Homilies of the Tenth Century*, Author's translation given here.

final outcome of the story of John Lackland: the other stories all become his story.

The returned traveller puts up at the inn: and then late at night goes out for a solitary moonlight stroll to revive his old memories. Like the Anglo-Saxon exile, he is impelled to look at the dead.

He walked on, looking at this chimney and that old wall, till he came to the churchyard, which he entered.

The headstones, whitened by the moon, were easily decipherable; and now for the first time Lackland began to feel himself amid the village community that he had left behind five and thirty years before. Here beside the Sallets, the Darths, the Pawles, the Privetts, the Sargents, and others of whom he had just heard, were names he remembered even better than those. . . . Doubtless, representatives of these families, or some of them, were yet among the living: but to him they would all be as strangers. . . . The figure of Mr. Lackland was seen at the inn, and in the village street, and in the fields and lanes about Upper Long Puddle, for a few days after his arrival, and then, ghost-like, it silently disappeared.

This is the story of the exile's return in its basic form, as we might call it; but the same theme appears in various guises. We could well say this is one of the most typical moods of Walter de la Mare's stories, with their constant images of a journey, whose end is lost in marsh fires. As Graham Greene has pointed out, in *The Lost Childhood*, an unfinished journey is not only a recurring theme in de la Mare's stories, but it approaches an obsession.

A more general mood of quietly seeing through the surface appearance is a marked characteristic of Somerset Maugham. And in more than one story of his we meet again this theme of the wanderer and his fruitless return. In 'Mirage', for instance, the seedy Grosely, who has made a fortune by swindling the Chinese customs, has looked forward for many years to returning to the bars and prostitutes of London. When he does so his dream all turns to ashes and he drifts back again to smoke opium in the Far East. 'Red' is another of Maugham's stories of a returning wanderer. After many years at sea Red finds again the lovely native girl he had once adored. All he can see in her is a fat, grey-haired, Kanaka woman, who does not even recognize him. Like

c

the Anglo-Saxon exile, he simply turns away from this 'dust-showing' and passes on.

Another modern short-story writer who evokes the same mood is Malachi Whitaker, whose quiet laconic stories of Yorkshire, often very short, have been compared to the grey stone walls and open moorland of their setting. 'Home to Wagon Houses,' one of her best-known stories, tells how a wife goes to bring home her husband, who deserted her years ago for another woman. She finds him lying in bed ill and alone. She helps him into a farm cart and the husband and wife, both white-headed now, set off home.

Ill and uncared for. Of course she would take him back. Wasn't that what she had really come for this morning? Not with fine brushed hair and high heeled shoes, but in her old working clothes she had hurried to fetch him. . . . No use wondering how long he'd be there. Life wasn't just a matter of years.

Proud and smiling, she looked down at the emaciated figure by her side. Her husband was whispering something, 'Sarah, Sarah, you won't leave me, will you?'

'No,' she answered, serene and sure, 'I'll never leave thee.'[3]

Yet both know he is coming home not to live but to die.

However, it would be pointless to pursue this theme too far among thousands of stories. Nevertheless, it is strangely re-current, and the Anglo-Saxon exile, and those other stories of return, all have their common element. The mood reached is not so much disillusion as a conscious willing away of illusion. Though it may mark the long decline of hope, it does not tear a passion to tatters. It is a matter-of-fact penetration beyond matters of fact. Because the Anglo-Saxon story was told by a Christian priest, it leads on to a new affirmation; but this is not inherent in the mood. With Grosely and with Red this bearing of the wound of life led to mere torpor. With the more sensitive spirits the 'saules ðearf' may be tempered and turned to many levels of self-knowledge that can include humour as well as irony.

This is an English mood, and one suited to the nature of the short story. Frank O'Connor calls his book on the short story 'The Lonely Voice', and he considers that the short story is a form

[3] *Best Short Stories of the Year*, ed. E. J. O'Brien (Cape, 1933).

in which we find 'an intense awareness of man's loneliness' in the very midst of gregarious life.

III

Yet with an accepted grief there may come also a far darker side of the picture. There can be despair and solitary madness. In another sermon in the same tenth-century collection which contains the story of the exile we are given a glimpse of that bleak horrifying landscape that haunted the Anglo-Saxon imagination— the marsh from which the slayers of mankind's happiness creep out.

He saw above the waters a hoary stone: and north of the stone had grown woods, very rimy. And there were dark mists; and under the stone was the dwelling place of monsters.

This, the black frost of the mind, is at times the very mood of 'Snarley Bob', the leading character in that strikingly original book of reflections and stories published in 1910—*Mad Shepherds*, by L. P. Jacks. Some thought that Snarley Bob, who was melancholy-proud and a master genius at breeding sheep, was a bit mad himself; but there was no doubt about the madness of his friend old Shepherd Toller, who gradually forsook all human dwellings, lived in a remote turfed hut, and armed himself with a sling and with a genuine stoneage axe stolen from a museum, with both of which weapons he was extremely dangerous.

Things from the abyss of time that float upwards into dreams . . . these had become the sober certainties of Toller's life. The superincumbent waters had parted asunder, and the children of the deep were astir. Toller had awakened into a past. . . .

These are the old enemies of Beowulf, the marsh-steppers, the fiends who are the slayers of all life.

Toller's strange mood of withdrawal can be matched in a far more famous story by D. H. Lawrence, 'The Man Who Loved Islands'. The title character also withdraws into a solitude of dark madness. Lawrence, curiously, never gives 'the man who loved islands' a name, which moves the story towards a poetic symbol, resembling 'The Seafarer' or 'The Wanderer'. On the first island he had pleasant notions about an ideal community; he dressed the part; he consciously savoured influences from men of the past who had come and gone. Then strife breaks into his small community and he goes to a smaller, more remote island; he then withdraws farther to an island that is little more than turf-clad rock with a small stone hut. Here, entirely alone, he fights his final battle amid wraiths of whirling snow and spray.

Hoarse waves rang in the shingle, rushing up at the snow. The wet rocks were brutally black. And all the time the myriad swooping crumbs of snow, demonish, touched the dark sea and disappeared.

This is almost the same language as 'The Seafarer'.

The hail flew in showers. There was naught there save the ice-cold billows, the sea booming; at times the song of the swan. The shadow of the night grew dark, frost-bound the earth: hail fell on the ground, coldest of grain. No protector could comfort the heart in its need.

And the man who loved islands also despairs:

Was it night again? In the silence, it seemed he could hear the panther-like dropping of infinite snow. Thunder rumbled nearer, crackled quick after the bleared reddened lightning. He lay in bed in a kind of stupor. The elements! The elements! His mind repeated the word dumbly. You can't win against the elements. . . .

'The Man Who Loved Islands' is a wonderful *tour de force*. It is a series of visions with a rising cadence, written with Lawrence's full powers of incantation, conjuring up again and again the sensation of loud rushing movements between the world of nature and the subconscious mind of man. Lawrence is not seeking any affirmation through disillusion. His story is a warning, a parable of the effects of rejecting a full-blooded life and attempting to escape into islands of the mind. Lawrence hopes rather for some new man, some more vital co-operation between man and the underlying forces of nature, a way different from both the Christian and the Stoic.

IV

These comparisons are merely intended to trace and rediscover one ancient Anglo-Saxon mood in later times; a kind of groundswell. Moreover, the Anglo-Saxons are not the British and the mixture of the British race has continued down the centuries, with the blood of the Celts, the Scandinavians, and the French Normans. Yet that Anglo-Saxon landscape in which years are often reckoned by their winters rather than their summers can still be distinguished from the Celtic mist, and if we compare the close of the 'The Man Who Loved Islands' with the snowstorm at the end of James Joyce's famous short story 'The Dead', we find a different experience.

In this story, after an evening at a New Year family party, Gabriel Conroy returns to sleep at a hotel with his wife. When Gabriel is alone with Gretta, he suddenly feels an urge of yearning and physical passion for her, but at this very moment she finds that one of the songs sung during the evening has reminded her of a boy who loved her many years ago, and has been long dead. This boy may even have hastened his death through waiting on a cold night underneath her window. Gretta weeps at this memory and then suddenly falls asleep.

His curious eyes rested long upon her face and her hair: and as he thought of what she must have been then, in that time of her first girlish beauty, a strange, friendly pity for her entered his soul. . . . One by one they were all becoming shades. Better pass boldly into that other world in the full glory of some passion than fade and wither dismally with age. . . . The tears gathered more thickly in his eyes, and in the partial darkness, he imagined he saw the form of a young man standing under a dripping tree. Other forms were near. His soul had approached that region where dwell the vast hosts of the dead.[4]

It is unfair to quote from the closing passages of this beautifully wrought story, but it will be seen, if it is read, that Gabriel Conroy is still very much the eager and social man: his mind is all the time passing from lights to shadows and back again. Though in the final words of the story he drifts into a cloudy vision of the snow falling upon many graveyards, this is a dream; and his mood is still one of overwhelming nostalgia for the world of colourful life; better to depart 'in the full glory of some passion'; and he

[4] James Joyce, *Dubliners* (Cape, 1944).

imagines that Gretta and he 'have escaped from home and friends and run away together with wild and radiant hearts for a new adventure'. That is the diaphanous mist shot through with gold, the illusion that the Anglo-Saxon exile had outgrown.

The Irish do not submit so calmly to hoar-frost, to hearing the sea beat on the iron rocks of the heart. The later poems of Yeats, which in some ways have a resemblance to those scattered private utterances of the Anglo-Saxon poets, are very different in temper. They too are stories of a heart full of years and full of disillusion: but they are also full of the anger of old men. Through Yeats's deepest gifts of imagery and association we hear his hoarse cries that he must nurse his *saeva indignatio*:

> I pray—for fashion's word is out
> And prayer comes round again—
> That I may seem, though I die old,
> A foolish, passionate man.[5]

In contrast, again, are the words of the Anglo-Saxon poet.

> Thought shall be the harder, heart the keener,
> courage the greater; as our might lessens.

[5] W. B. Yeats, 'A Prayer for Old Age', from *A Full Moon in March*, 1935, in *Collected Poems*, 2nd edn. (Macmillan, 1950).

IV

Chaucer:
A Touchstone of Truth

I

Secular literature developed and changed very slowly during the generations that came before and after the Norman Conquest. Throughout this period we must still guess at the existence of a folk literature or of popular stories. Even if more had survived in manuscript, modern readers would still be baffled by the language. Indeed, up to the time of Caxton it was difficult to know how to write down English in a form and spelling which most people could understand. While the Old English of Anglo-Saxon days was developing into the beginnings of modern English, three languages, each with its own uses, were current, Latin, Norman-French, and the changing hotch-potch of the spoken vernacular, with its strong regional variations. The material that was written in the vernacular consisted of sermons, a few songs, a few stories, and a rather haphazard supply of translations from the Latin. Often enough the songs or fragments of anecdote seem to have survived by chance, being copied on the back of more serious documents, turning up in backings and bindings, exactly as described in Kipling's story of a literary forgery, 'Dayspring Mishandled'. Chaucer himself was well aware of the limitations of the language and at the end of *Troilus and Criseyde* he points out:

> And for ther is so grete diversite
> In Englissh and in writyng of oure tonge,
> So prey I God that none myswrite the,
> Ne the mysmetre for defaute of tonge,

And red wherso thow be, or elles songe,
That thow be understonde. God I beseche.[1]

This passage is interesting for two reasons. It refers not only to the fluidity of the language but also to the fact that stories could be either read or sung. A plentiful demand for fiction was arising by the time Chaucer was alive. *The Canterbury Tales* is constructed as a book and a book implies readers. Surprisingly enough there is evidence that even before the days of printing, and quite apart from courtly entertainments and from the libraries of great castles, some medieval equivalents of circulating libraries were already coming into existence. John Shirley, who died in 1456, and was a copyist, included in some of his manuscripts an appeal to borrowers:

And of the other take yee none hede
Bysechyng youe of youre godely hede
Whanne yee this boke have over-redde and seyne
To Johann Shirley restore yee hit ageyne.[2]

It is for these reasons inevitable that if we look at the historical development of modern short stories in English, as apart from the early moods and far-off echoes of the Anglo-Saxons, we must begin with Chaucer. The achievement of Chaucer stands alone; and it will be helpful to consider the immense creative development brought about by Chaucer first, and to look at some of the lesser known collections of stories that were in circulation at the time in the next chapter, even though some of these precede him in date.

As soon as we pick up *The Canterbury Tales* we see that many generations have elapsed since Anglo-Saxon days. Chaucer may be ironical, coarse, gay, quizzical, by turns, but the prevailing weather of his mind is fair. The famous opening lines to *The Canterbury Tales* tell us that April is a happy month; the open air is hopeful, the cuckoo is no longer ominous. As for a Christian

[1] *Troilus and Criseyde* (*Complete works of Geoffrey Chaucer*, ed. F. N. Robinson (O.U.P., 1933)), ll. 1793–8.
[2] Quoted in H. S. Bennett, *Chaucer and the Fifteenth Century*, Oxford History of English Literature (O.U.P., 1947).

pilgrimage, it is a friendly affair, Christian in intention but undertaken in good company.

Although *The Canterbury Tales* is one of the most famous books of short stories ever written, it is in many ways extremely unlike the modern notion of the short-story art. A reader who knew and appreciated the general field of modern short stories and, in taking up Chaucer, dipped into medieval literature for the first time might be forgiven for saying, 'But these are not what I really mean by short stories.' We find tales of sorcerers, Christian miracles, talking animals and strange, unbelievable events; we find homilies and learned divagations. We seem partly to be in the world of Grimm, dressed up for a more learned and literary audience. Into these surroundings Chaucer puts some strikingly real contemporary characters.

In the story situations, however, contemporary reality is seen mainly in the coarse fabliaux, which involve a great deal of jollity about cuckolding, people getting into each other's beds in the dark, and other violent slapstick scenes. These are in their way natural enough, earthy enough certainly. Yet we feel that these, also, are scarcely to be believed as true scenes from life, and that their medieval hearers knew just about what they were in for, as soon as one of these 'churl's tales' began. In fact, Harry Bailey, the Host, tries to stop the Miller even before he does begin his story, but the Miller, who is rather drunk, refuses to be checked. We have already been told he is a great bull-necked ginger-haired man, his shoulders strengthened by carrying sacks of flour, who can butt a door down with his head if he feels like it. So nobody does stop him.

This brings us at once to the main point of *The Canterbury Tales*, in so far as we are searching in them for a resemblance to modern fiction. Though the tales themselves are medieval and antique, the tellers of the tales, the twenty-nine Canterbury pilgrims, are set down with vivid reality. The art with which they are depicted is startlingly modern. However, before we look into this interplay of realistic tellers and extraordinary tales, let us see how Chaucer handles the incident of the Miller.

The Knight, who is the most dignified and considerable member of the pilgrims' company, has just finished the first story, a tale of courtly love, jousting, of a sad death, and a final happy marriage. Everyone thought it a 'noble story', and it was especially pleasing to the 'gentils'. However, the Miller, who had been drinking heavily, felt jealous of all this praise for the Knight and broke in clumsily:

> Oure Hoost saugh wel how dronke he was of ale,
> And seyde, 'Robyn, abyde, my leve brother,
> Som bettre man schal telle us first another;
> Abyd, and let us worken thriftyly.'
> 'By Goddes soule!' quod he, 'that wol nat I,
> For I wol speke, or elles go my way.'
> Oure Host answerede 'Tel on, a devel way!'
> Thou art a fool; thy witt is overcome.'
>   'Now herkneth,' quod this Myller, 'al and some;
> But first I make a protestacioun,
> That I am dronke, I knowe wel by my soun;
> And therfore if that I mys-speke or seye,
> Wyte it the ale of Southwerk, I you preye . . .'[3]

Before he begins he says his tale is going to be about a carpenter and his wife. This annoys the Reeve, a carpenter by craft, who tells him to shut his trap or in the original, 'stynt thi clappe'. The Miller shouts the carpenter down and Chaucer interpolates somewhat ruefully:

> What schuld I seye, but that this proud Myllere
> He nolde his wordes for no man forbere,
> But told his cherlisch tale in his manere.
> Me athinketh, that I schal reherce it heere;

Chaucer, it seems, simply cannot help the way that these people behave. Who is he to mis-report the doings of knights or millers? Thus he turns us away from the unreality of the tales to the living reality of the people who tell them. While we are thinking of their stories, we hardly notice that Chaucer is himself the narrator, the prime mover who is inventing the tellers, and we come to discuss Chaucer's pilgrims and think of them as real people.

[3] Geoffrey Chaucer, *The Canterbury Tales*, edited by A. Burrell (Everyman, Dent, 1908).

It is frequently said that the Prologue to *The Canterbury Tales*, in which Chaucer introduces and describes the pilgrims, is the jewel of all medieval story-telling. If we look at it from the point of view of the history of fiction, it is an almost unbelievable step forward with its human interest, crispness, and visual effect. People are apt to forget, however, that the story of the pilgrims is not confined to these first static portraits. It continues in various incidents between the stories. However, once Chaucer has introduced his characters he uses very little narrative. He simply lets them speak and act for themselves, almost as if he had read his Flaubert. In fact he gave the notion of a narrating 'I' a deft twist by letting himself appear occasionally in an amiably foolish light. After the Prioress has told her miracle story, the Host begins to tease Chaucer because he keeps so quiet, and stares at the ground, as if he 'were looking for a hare'. He seems to be a dapper, neat little person. 'This were a popet in an arm to embrace for any woman,' says the Host; and asks him to tell a 'tale of mirth'.

Chaucer replies timidly, or so it seems, that he knows only one old story. The Host says, 'Now shul we heere som deyntee thing.' Chaucer then begins the Tale of Sir Topaz, which is in the very feeblest style of a picture-book knight adventuring in a cardboard fairyland. It soon becomes so silly that the Host cries out, 'No more of this, for Goddes dignitee!'

It is hardly possible to conceive anybody less likely to create the astonishing character of the Wife of Bath than the teller of the Tale of Topaz, yet this is the self-obliterating device that Chaucer uses. Dame Alison of Bath is interesting enough when we first meet her, with her great cartwheel hat and her scarlet stockings, and the fact that she is known to be a successful business woman, and to have had five husbands. Yet it is when she opens her own mouth and tells her own story that she springs to life as one of the most wonderful, harshly comic characters in the whole of drama or fiction. She is intimidating, yet fascinating; mad, yet full of worldly wisdom. She leaves Becky Sharp and Moll Flanders far behind; but if we look for the narrator, he has vanished off the scene.

II

Chaucer has not always been admired. Some critics have thought him buffoonish and hopelessly antiquated, Dr. Johnson among them. Samuel Johnson, in fact, pronounced it extremely stupid and ignorant to mix up ancient Greek heroes with medieval jousting, and he writes of 'The Knight's Tale' in his *Lives of the Poets*:

... the story of Palamon and Arcite containing an action unsuitable to the times in which it is placed, can hardly be suffered to pass without censure of the hyperbolical commendation which Dryden gives it in the general Preface.

Let us turn back to Chaucer's contemporaries, and then see how his reputation has fared down the generations. In the later part of his own life, and for two or three generations after his death, he was widely praised, and recognized by other authors as a beloved master. He was admired for his control of poetic form and his 'honeyed tongue', his verbal felicity in handling the changing English language. These are qualities that with the further development of language have been largely lost to us. He is also praised for his erudition; and these displays of learning lightly worn and worked into the stories are also more or less lost to the modern reader. It needs a medievalist to relish a great deal of what he is doing.

As the appreciation of the first novelty and brilliance of his language began to fade, comments on Chaucer as an interesting moralist appeared. The Elizabethans began to find him out of date, and before long obsolete. During the seventeenth century the understanding of his metrical system vanished. He was censured for failing to scan, and for writing in a barbaric language.

Sir Francis Kynaston, a medievalist and poet, published in 1635 a translation he had made of the first two books of Chaucer's *Troilus and Criseyde* into Latin rhyme royal. He accomplished this extraordinary feat in order to preserve the work for posterity, for, as he tells us in a Latin preface, Chaucer was becoming forgotten in his ancient tongue, and Latin was the language to preserve him.[4] We may remember that Pope in his day lamented the instability of English in the *Essay on Criticism*, and Dr. William King seriously regretted that Shakespeare had not been written in Latin.

Meanwhile Pepys rather unexpectedly buys a Chaucer and spends money on repairing it, and Dryden's praise of Chaucer in the preface to his *Fables* brings in a new mood of serious appreciation. Dryden calls him a fountain of good sense, tells us he brings the pilgrims to life so clearly that he feels he might have supped with them at the Tabard, and his well-known 'here is God's plenty' is the most quoted phrase in all Chaucerian criticism. Perhaps Dryden took it from the Miller's own remarks when he says it is best not to inquire too closely into God's purposes or into the behaviour of wives.

> So that he fynde Goddes foysoun there
> Of the remenaunt needeth nought enquere.

Pope is reported by Spence to have said, 'I read Chaucer still with as much pleasure as almost any of our poets. He is a master of manners and description, and the first tale-teller in the true and enlivened natural way.'[5] A few follow Dr. Johnson in his censure, but from now on, eighteenth-century readers begin to admire Chaucer for two distinct reasons. Some find in him simply a coarse, jolly fun-maker: others more discriminatingly admire his 'natural art'. Various writers follow the lead of Dryden and dress Chaucer up in smart heroic couplets for eighteenth-century taste. The Chauceriana of the eighteenth century in fact have an inimitable flavour of their own. The 'honey-tongued' poet vanishes into a lusty portrayer of the human scene, whose honest frankness has to be rescued from the Gothic obscurity of his language.

By the nineteenth century, however, medievalism was becoming picturesque and desirable. It is the conception of the poetic Chaucer that fills the imagination of the Romantic revival. Scholars and poets began to recover the understanding of his

[4] See C. F. E. Spurgeon, Introduction, *Five Hundred Years of Chaucer Criticism and Allusion* (Chaucer Society, O.U.P., 1924).

[5] Joseph Spence, *Observations, Anecdotes and Characters of Books and Men*, arranged with notes by Edmund Malone (John Murray, 1820), pp. 84–5.

rhymes and stresses. Leigh Hunt was enthusiastic and wanted him to be adapted and modernized as little as possible. Keats shared his friend Hunt's enthusiasm and acquired a black letter edition of *The Canterbury Tales*. *St. Agnes Eve* and more especially *The Eve of St. Mark* are thought to owe a good deal to Chaucer, although the changing and melting images are far more typical of Keats's own vision than of the clear heraldic tinctures of Chaucer. One may detect a slight feeling of Biedermeier as Bertha pores over her ancient books by firelight on the Eve of St. Mark, and the comparison with Chaucer brings it out. In fact, the difference between Keats and Chaucer as tellers of tales in poetry is more interesting than their resemblances.

Now the admiration for Chaucer swings in the very opposite direction from that taken by the eighteenth century. There is always a stream of sound understanding, but during the nineteenth century and up to the time of William Morris and Burne Jones, Chaucer is apt to become part of a medieval dream: he is seen in the soft colours of stained glass falling on ancient stone-flagged floors, and the more aesthetic-minded neglect his boisterous coarse-grained element.

Caroline Spurgeon wrote in 1927 that she had spent twenty-one years in assembling a guide to the huge quantity of writing about Chaucer. In fact, every generation seems likely to refresh and to renew its own understanding of Chaucer. Such excellent new versions as Nevill Coghill's, with their contemporary presentation, yet with their clear comments on the medieval background based on deep scholarship, could not have been produced by other generations. Nor could anyone in the nineteenth century have looked at Chaucer as a story-writer, with knowledge of Kipling, Maupassant, and Katherine Mansfield in his mind.

It is striking, however, that the most enthusiastic of all praises of Chaucer in English come from the visionary writers and from poets who were apt to engage their whole personalities in their judgements: Blake, Wordsworth, and Ruskin, for instance. Ruskin, who might easily have attacked Chaucer, not so much for his masculine coarseness as for his surface appearance of pococurantism, tells us that he is one of the men who taught 'the purest theological truth' and he makes a list of seven authors for a proposed edition of standard theological writings—St. John, Moses, David, Hesiod, Virgil, Dante, and Chaucer—a remarkable tribute to the supposedly anti-clerical Chaucer.[6] Blake saw also a prophet in Chaucer and says his pilgrims bear the 'lineaments of universal human life'.

Chaucer himself is the great poetic observer of men, who in every age is born to record and eternise its acts. This he does as a father and superior, who looks down on their little follies from the Emperor to the Miller, sometimes with severity, oftener with joke and spirit.[7]

III

Whether we share Blake's visionary view of Chaucer or not there is something extremely compelling in this quiet man and gifted poet, who can amuse, talk easily, describe vividly, see into other people's characters, and tell stories in twenty different moods. In what way is this many-sided genius to be compared to a modern writer of short stories? How does he add to the history of short-story writing? In the first place, simply because his best-known book, and one of the most famous books in all literature, is a book of stories: by this alone he has given a lustre to the idea of 'tales'. In the second place, as we have already seen, he brings suddenly to the art of fiction a surprisingly modern equipment, an intense vision for people and places, together with the detachment of the great artist.

The pilgrims are steeped in their medieval thought, telling stories that are cast in an antique mould. Yet with them all rides Chaucer, creating the tellers of the tales: and it is in the presentation of their characters and the immediate present that surrounds them, that Chaucer takes his remarkable step into the future of fiction, and achieves something which even Boccaccio did not attempt.

Not only in their individual prefaces and conversational exchanges, but in the tales they choose and the way they tell them, Chaucer is continually revealing the characters of the pilgrims. The outstanding instance is the Wife of Bath. She is interesting

[6] John Ruskin, *Fors Clavigera*, letter 61, January 1876.
[7] Alexander Gilchrist, *Life of Blake* (Macmillan, 1863), vol. II, p. 124.

enough merely as an apparition when we first meet her, but it is when she speaks for herself that she becomes overwhelming, and all her various traits of dress and behaviour begin to mean more and more. Her ruthless self-revelation of her own personality, lustful, businesslike, set on mundane enjoyment, powerful in the world's ways, yet aflame with a daemonic lightning, is an invention of comic horror. One feels she could have swallowed Falstaff for breakfast. Blake thought she was a devil, yet one that ate and drank and rode to Canterbury.

The story she tells takes our knowledge of her further. She does not tell an obviously coarse story like the Miller or the Reeve, but a tale about an enchanted lady and a bewitched knight. It is a fairy story in the style of the Breton *Lai*, but shot through with sexuality.

As she talks, we begin to see a changing image beneath the carapace. She is utterly restless. She has been on pilgrimages throughout Europe. She has visited the Holy Land three times, no small labour in the fourteenth century. Moreover, she is far better read in theology, far more self-questioning, than her outward show betrays. Her remarks are full of self-justification that could only arise from inward doubt. She has married five times, and she speaks violently against marriage, yet she cannot refer to her five husbands without quoting the story of the Woman of Samaria at the well, and Christ's teaching. If she herself did not know the medieval mystical interpretations of the story, that the five husbands are the five senses, and that none of them can be the true husband of the soul on its journey, one feels that Chaucer is giving us a strong hint that he did, and is applying it to her. No husbands, and no pilgrimages, can satisfy her soul's yearning; nor can her crude biological urges nor her aggression.

> Venus me yaf my lust and licorousnesse.
> And Mars yaf me my sturdi hardynesse.
> My ascent was Taur, and Mars therinne;
> Allas, allas, that ever love was synne.

How are the company affected by the Wife of Bath's exhibitionism? When she has finished her personal story she says she will go on to tell them her tale if they want to listen. The remark seems challenging, and one wonders if the others, even the Host himself, were not avoiding her eye. Then, notably, the answer comes from the sophisticated Friar, that festive and friendly fellow, who was in all four Orders, and was an expert in hearing ladies' confessions, with a special licence that went beyond the ordinary priestly limits. The Friar remarks suavely to Dame Alison that she has made a long preamble. This immediately arouses the Summoner, who dislikes the Friar, and proceeds to rebuke him for interrupting. They both start bickering. The Host calls them both to order and says, 'Do dame tel forth your tale.' Dame Alison replies that she is ready 'if I have licence of this worthy Frere'. She has not liked his cool attitude and she begins her tale with this wonderful comment on the habits of friars.

> In olde dayes of the kyng Arthoúr,
> Of which that Britouns speken gret honoúr,
> This lond was al fulfilled of fäerie;
> The elf-queen, with hir joly companye,
> Dauncède ful oft in many a grene mede.
> This was the old opynyoun, as I rede;
> I speke of many hundrid yer ago;
> But now can no man see noon elves mo.
> For now the grete charitee and prayeres
> Of prechours and of other holy freres,
> That sechen every lond and every streem,
> As thik as motes in the sonne-beam,
> And bless the halles, chambres, kichenes, boures,
> Citees and burghes, castels hihe and toures,
> The thorpes, barnes, stables, dayeries,
> That makith that ther be no fayeries.
> For where was wont to walken many an elf,
> There walkith non but the prechour by himself,
> In evening tymes and in morwenynges,
> And saith his matyns and his holy thinges
> As he goth prechyng through villáge and toun.
> Women may now go safely up and doun,
> In every bush, or under every tre,
> There is no other incubus but he,
> And he wil do women no dishonoúr.

D

Dame Alison may have thought she was snubbing the Friar heavily or she may have meant it in good part. When she finishes her story with a conclusion that once again rubs in her determination always to be the master of her husband, the Friar turns politely, blesses her, and with an affable yet patronizing air suggests that she should leave the various points of doctrine that she has raised to the clergy. For, he reminds her, the object of the stories is only for amusement; and so just for amusement he will now tell a good story about a Summoner. There follows the contest in which the Friar tells an anti-Summoner story and the Summoner an anti-Friar story. Views may differ about the victor. My own vote goes unquestionably to the Friar, who shows a light touch in leg-pulling which rouses the Summoner to anger.

Some people have seen in Chaucer a marked anti-clerical point of view. It is true that he pokes fun at various members of the clergy: but he also pokes fun at husbands and wives. On the whole it is not embittered fun, and he has a humorous eye for the whole human scene. This again is a surprisingly modern attitude for his day.

In his country parson he draws, and even idealizes, a sincere country priest, placing him high in the esteem of the pilgrims, even above the Knight. The Priest is brother to the hard-working ploughman, who also gives generous service to the community and is a tower of strength to his fellows 'for Christ's sake'. Chaucer may have thought the church was over-organized and contained some ridiculous and unpleasant individuals, but he is not for that reason anti-clerical. He is a humanist of the early Renaissance and an observer of the human scene; but humanists of the early Renaissance did not have to live professedly outside the church.

I have ventured to go over some well-known ground in order to illustrate Chaucer's technique as a modern rather than an antique story-teller. The narrative device of creating the characters while appearing to concentrate on the stories they are telling is extremely effective. Yet it all happens so naturally as almost to defy the word 'technique'. There are many other touches with which Chaucer builds up the personality of the pilgrims in the brief interludes and in the way they tell their stories; the way, for instance, in which the Monk establishes his dignity after the Host's banter had become almost insulting; the professional skill with which the somewhat foolish-looking Prioress carries off her miracle story; the unexpected incident in which the Canon and his Yeoman gallop up 'to ryden in this merry company', and the Canon soon dashes off again in a huff. In these and other scenes Chaucer is making a contrast between the whole conception of the set telling of a tale and life as it really is. He is gently rejecting the idea of the absurd and the exaggerated in fiction, and showing that unforced realism can be the essence of poetic story-telling.

It is likely that Chaucer, who was praised for his learning, would have been familiar with Aristotle's *Art of Poetry*. Perhaps he would have known Aristotle's views on the relation of mimesis to poetry and the 'anonymous art'. He knew by nature, although Aristotle would have reinforced his feeling, that the best story-tellers do not butt in themselves; for the simple reason, as Aristotle puts it, 'The poet should say very little, because he is no imitator when he is doing that.'

Nearly all Chaucer's story-tellers do comment and speak of themselves, thus relating everything they tell us to the orbit of their own personalities. Practically the only comment that Chaucer makes direct to the reader comes in the few quietly ironical verses at the end of the Oxford Scholar's story of the patient Griselda.

Yet in spite of his modesty, Chaucer is revealed through his creations as a man of heroic breadth. He has a sophisticated knowledge of court life, combined with a surprising simplicity. He can be serious without being pompous. He has the quiet cheerfulness of courage, unlike the loud-voiced heartiness of the Host. He understands hypocrites, but he does not display anger; he laughs at foolishness without being a biting satirist. He depicts people in bright clear colours, that have remarkable depths when one looks into them.

Although Chaucer became so much more a man of the world than Blake, he kept that purity of insight that Blake recognized and praised. Who would have appreciated more than Chaucer that scene in which Blake and his wife were found sitting naked in their back garden in the middle of London.

At the end of the little garden in Hercules Buildings there was a summer-house. Mr. Butts calling one day found Mr. and Mrs. Blake sitting in this summer-house, freed from 'those troublesome disguises' which have prevailed since the Fall. *'Come in!'* cried Blake, *'it's only Adam and Eve, you know.'*

Husband and wife had been reciting passages from *Paradise Lost*, in character, and the garden of Hercules Buildings had to represent the Garden of Eden.[8]

That is perfect Chaucer.

[8] Gilchrist, *Life of Blake*, vol. I, p. 115.

V

Some Other Medieval Story-tellers: A Moral in Everything

I

In *The Canterbury Tales* Chaucer sums up and represents the art of the English short story in the Middle Ages. He looks back over the previous centuries collecting together the various kinds of story well known in his day; and he does this with a difference, bringing a new wealth of character drawing, a new vision in portraying the living presence of his own story-tellers.

The names of Gower, Lydgate, and Occleve are often associated with Chaucer. They all wrote collections of stories, but unlike Chaucer they have not been kept alive by twenty generations of readers and critics. Their interest nowadays is relative, and their creative gifts are confined within the conventions of their day. Gower, who was Chaucer's contemporary and knew him personally, is usually considered the best of the three and is often quoted affectionately by other poets as 'honest Gower'.

In one version of his *Confessio Amantis* Gower tells an attractive anecdote of his meeting King Richard II while rowing on the Thames. Gower was invited into the king's boat and Richard asked him personally to write 'some newe thing'. However, he followed the medieval notion of writing stories to illustrate ideas. His language, his people, are less alive than those of Chaucer. He is also very long-winded, and one feels he would have agreed with Lydgate's view of story-telling as stated in his Prologue to *Falls of Princes*:

> These ookes grete be not down ihewe
> Ffirst at a strok, but bi long processe;
> Nor longe stories a word may not expresse.

The conception of fiction, however, was developing and, in due course, various apocryphal Canterbury Tales and continuations of the story of the pilgrims began to appear. It is of interest to look briefly at the period both before and after Chaucer and to see something of the material which Chaucer transmuted.

II

If we study the slow changes of thought during the centuries that follow the Norman Conquest we realize that to expect a modern point of view in short-story writing would be absurd. Stories are intended for moral advice or mystical interpretation. The *Ancrene Riwle*, a book written as early as the twelfth century, is often mentioned for its intimate understanding of human foibles, and especially of self-deception. We cannot call it story-writing, yet if the author had lived today he might well have been a writer of fiction: and those same accounts of virtues and vices that he gives as a priest might have taken shape as characters in stories.

The *Ancrene Riwle* was written for three ladies who were well-born, we gather, and who wanted to undertake the life of anchoresses. The work consists of guidance in prayer, confession, control of the thoughts and feelings, and it finishes with a chapter of sound practical advice such as this.

Unless need compels you, my dear sisters, and your director advises it, you must not keep any animal except a cat. An anchoress who keeps animals looks more like a housewife, as Martha was, and cannot easily have peace of heart, and be Mary, Martha's sister; for in such a case she has to think of the cow's fodder and the herdsman's wages, say nice things to the hayward, call him names when he impounds the cow and yet pay damages nonetheless. It is odious, Christ knows, when there are complaints in a village about the anchoresses's animals.[1]

One can certainly see a short story hovering round this passage. It could be called 'The Anchoress and the Cow', and one can imagine it in the hands of Frank O'Connor or Liam O'Flaherty, who would understand both the religious and village aspects of the situation; or of T. F. Powys, who would perhaps enter into

[1] *The Ancrene Riwle*, ed. M. B. Salu (Burns and Oates, 1955) p. 185.

the Cow's point of view, and would compare her meditations with those of the Anchoress. It would suit several Italian authors, ancient and modern.

Another anecdote is related under the head of 'hidden temptations', in which a woman through tenderness of heart begins to make charitable collections but gradually drifts into ownership of a fund, helps her own friends, and finally gives a notable feast— 'transformed from an anchoress into the lady of a great house'. This is a broader form of social satire than 'The Anchoress and the Cow'. Thackeray would have relished the theme and would have spun it out to a long short story after the style of *A little Dinner at Timmins's*. Dickens would have caricatured it in his own way; and among the short-story writers of the 1950s and 1960s Muriel Spark could use it and give it an imprint of her own.

Here again is the *Ancrene Riwle* with a shrewd eye for a backbiter, who introduces his own evil-speaking like this:

It's very unfortunate, and I'm very sorry that so-and-so has got such a bad name. I tried hard enough but couldn't do anything about it. I've known about it for a long time, and although it would never have gone further, as far as I'm concerned, now that other people have spread it about so much I can't say that it's not true. They say that it's bad, but it's worse than they say. . . .

This form of character drawing looks forward not only to the 'characters' of the seventeenth century but straight on to Mrs. Candour and Sir Benjamin Backbite. Evidently short stories in the form of scandal-mongering were already well established in the thirteenth century.

However, the *Ancrene Riwle* is first and last a book of devotional guidance, and on page after page one can see at work the serious medieval mind, which cannot mention any biblical or legendary story without giving it a symbolic meaning. For instance, when Christ left his tomb early in the morning, one of the minor aspects of the Resurrection was that He rose early as a rebuke to people who lie in bed. Here is that depth and simplicity combined, with which we have lost touch. Why should not Everyman, arising from the little death of sleep every morning, think first of the Resurrection? The medieval preacher is for ever peeling away outer layers of the world to reveal meanings within. This metaphorical habit of thought has its counterpart in modern writers. When D. H. Lawrence sees and describes people in terms of animals, which he does with great force, he is often curiously close to some striking passages in the *Ancrene Riwle* which do the same. Lions, foxes, and doves lurk within us.

Fiction was beginning to gain ground by the fourteenth century. By Chaucer's time there was a large supply of gestes, of romances, of collections of stories often woven into tapestries of dreams and allegory. These fall into a number of themes and groups. There were the Arthurian stories; the Charlemagne stories; stories of Alexander the Great, of Godfrey de Bouillon, of Troy, Thebes, and Byzantium; a whole series which might be called the Griselda and Constance groups; and coming to more native and homely themes, Havelok the Dane, Hereward the Wake, and Guy of Warwick.

All of these, however, tend to be voluminous. Their literary interest, moreover, is bound up with their sources, their verse forms, and with sidelights on the sociology and thought of the times. We are confronted, for instance, with the fascinating subject of the mysterious and rapid spread of the Arthurian stories, and their connection with the vanishing rituals of a hidden religion.

The more foolish of the romantic stories are satirized in Chaucer's Sir Topaz, or in another way by the jolly account of *The Tournament of Tottenham*—an anonymous poem in which the jousting of knights is transposed into a mock battle between Hawkyn and Henry and Tomkyn and Terry, who clank about on cart-horses breaking each other's heads, not only to win the hand of Tibbe, the fair daughter of Randall the Reeve, but also to gain a spotted pig into the bargain.

Among all these a very few short stories have been preserved. One of the most usually quoted is *Dame Siriz̧*. This is a story of Eastern origin in which the old Dame Siriz, who is a procuress, undertakes to persuade a young wife to sleep with another man while her husband is away at the wars. Among other inducements she exhibits a 'weeping' bitch whose eyes have been irritated with pepper; she tells the girl that the bitch was once a young woman like herself, who has been transformed into this shape because she refused to listen to a lover. The story is, like *The Miller's Tale*, a coarse and fantastic fabliau. It is, however, interesting in technique as it is told mainly in a clear-cut dramatic form with little comment or narration and thus without prolixity.

Dame Siriz is supplied, in the traditional manner, with a moral, surprising even among medieval morals. The chaste wife is the soul purified by baptism. The soldier-husband is Christ. The lover is worldly vanity. The go-between is the devil. The bitch represents the hope of a long life, and too great a dependence on the mercy of God, because just as the bitch weeps because of the pepper, so hope frequently afflicts the soul.

The story of *Sir Cleges* is another comparatively short verse-tale. Sir Cleges is a knight who has given so much away that he is in dire need himself. One day he finds that he has a cherry tree which is full of ripe cherries, although it is Christmas time and snow is on the ground. He goes to the court of King Uther to make a gift of the cherries, but finds that various doorkeepers and stewards will not allow him to see the king unless he promises to share his reward among them. In due course the king asks Sir Cleges what reward he would like. He asks for a beating, as he had to promise to give his reward away; so the blows are shared out among the culprits. It is curious that both cuckoldry and the violent physical punishment of wrongdoers are constantly presented merely as objects of crude mirth that people are simply bound to find funny.

Such stories have no pretensions to originality. Minstrels added them to their stock-in-trade and adapted them to time and place. For instance, G. M. McKnight, in *Middle English Humorous Tales*, says that the story of *The Blows Shared* can be traced in Arabic countries and in Italy (where both Sachetti and Straparola use it), in Spain, in Sweden, and in Germany. It turns up yet again in Elizabethan days in *The Pleasing Conceits of Old Hobson—the Merry Londoner*, and it was included in Grimms' *Tales*.

A far more graceful short verse form of story was developed by the French rather than the English. Those tales known as the

Breton *lais* were usually based on Arthurian and other Celtic legends. They are not only short, but they have a light touch and they are told for entertainment rather than pious instruction. Some of these were translated or adapted in English, and the best known is *Sir Orfeo*, which illustrates delightfully how Greek and Celtic myth could intermingle and flourish together. One of the best-known authors of the Breton *lai* was Marie de France. Her stories may have been written in England, but she wrote in the Norman French spoken at the English and French courts, using occasional English phrases. As there were no direct contemporary translations of her work into English, she cannot truly be given a place in the development of the English short story. One would certainly like to claim her as a literary ancestor, for her lays are short and graceful; they build up visual images and have an artistic brevity and unity of form.

Although knights sometimes meet fays in these stories, they are by no means all founded on magical or strange adventures. One at least, *The Lay of the Honeysuckle*, might be the substance of a short story in which a lyrically presented mood is more important than the event. It tells simply how Tristan sent a lover's message to Isoude by peeling and carving a hazel wand and planting it near a honeysuckle.

The Lay of the Nightingale, in which a grim reality suddenly breaks through the dream-like atmosphere, is also free from medieval magic and moves suddenly much closer to modern ideas of a short story. A certain lady married to a knight used to leave her bed on moonlit summer nights to talk to her lover through an open window. When her husband becomes suspicious she tells him in very poetic language that she loves to sit and hear the song of the nightingale. 'When the husband heard these words he laughed within himself for wrath and malice.' He limes and nets all the trees and bushes in the neighbourhood, and captures a nightingale. He then takes the bird to his wife and says, 'He will never disturb you more.' Then he wrings the nightingale's neck so violently that he tears the head from the body and 'right foully he flung the bird upon the knees of the dame, in such fashion that her breast was sprinkled with the blood'. The lady understands his sinister meaning, wraps the body in 'white samite, broidered with gold', and sends it to her lover. As Marie de France says, 'This adventure could not long be hid. Very swiftly it was noised about the country, and the Breton folk made a lay thereon, which they called *The Lay of the Laustic* in their own tongue.'

This brings us suddenly close to the idea of modern short-story writing. Marie also had an unusually modern awareness of the problems of the narrator and the need to establish authenticity. More than once we find her insisting on her personal reputation as an author, and building up the veracity of her stories. 'Hearken now, gentles, to the words of Marie,' she will say. Sometimes she gives a local habitation and a name to build up veracity, as in *The Lay of The Dolorous Knight*:

Hearken now to the lay that once I heard a minstrel chanting to his harp. In surety of its truth I will name The City where this story passed. . . . The Lay of the Dolorous Knight my harper called his song, but of those who listened some named it rather, The Lay of the Four Sorrows. In Nantes of Brittany there dwelt a dame . . .

Marie had trouble with critics. After her death Denis Pyramus, who tells us that 'she is much praised', also says her stories 'are not in the least true'. 'But this is the way of the world,' says Marie at the beginning of *The Lay of Gugemar*. 'The craft is hard . . . when a man or woman sings more tuneably than his fellows, those about him fall upon him pell mell by reason of envy.'

One is reminded of Somerset Maugham arguing back with his critics: or Conrad assuring us in a Preface that parts of his stories are factually true.

III

Various collections of short stories were from time to time brought together, mainly for moral purposes. The two best known are probably the *Gesta Romanorum* and the *Book of the Knight of La Tour Landry*.

The *Gesta Romanorum*, first written in Latin, and possibly in

England, belongs to the thirteenth century. It became famous in a number of different European countries, but was not translated into English until about 1420, with the title *Deeds of the Romans*. The *Gesta* is to modern eyes an extraordinary medley of over a hundred and fifty anecdotes taken from Oriental sources, from Christian legends, from classical myth, from popular tradition, all lumped together as a supposed Roman heritage.

It was the best-known and most long lasting collection of anecdotal short stories of medieval times. Wynkyn de Worde produced the first printed English edition between 1510 and 1515, and new editions went on well into the eighteenth century. It is certainly a strange book to find still current at a time when the Royal Society and the Bank of England were already in existence. Yet we find in it the germ of many famous stories, for instance, several of Shakespeare's themes. There is a story resembling Shylock's bond, and also the story of the three caskets. We find a story of hands that are bloodstained and unwashable after a murder. We find a story resembling that of King Lear, although in one version of the *Gesta* this story is told of the Roman Emperor Theodosius.

'Vergil the felosofere' makes a somewhat apocryphal appearance and a surprising story is told of Socrates. A Roman Emperor gives his wife to Socrates, on the condition that if she dies Socrates must also die. In time the wife falls very ill and Socrates is in great danger, but he meets a mysterious old man in a forest who helps to cure her; this is a Socrates who seems to have affinities with Merlin rather than Plato. The moral follows, as usual. The Emperor is Christ, who gives to mankind (Socrates) a soul, which is the wife: the old man in the forest who helps to cure the wife is a wise confessor, who helps the sinner to contrition and self-realization. Thus the soul and the man are saved together. 'We teach the people by apologies,' says Wycliffe, yet by the sixteenth century we find Tyndale complaining in *The Obedience of a Christian Man* that the discovery of allegorical and anagogical meanings had been carried to unreasonable lengths.

The *Gesta* was collected within the cloister, and in spite of its wide popularity was intended partly as a handbook for preachers.

Other collections were frankly reference books for sermons. In the *Alphabet of Tales*, for instance, the anecdotes were given in alphabetical order, so that the preacher could go into what modern comedians refer to as a 'routine'. This is in fact exactly what the Monk in *The Canterbury Tales* did when he decided to impress a little solemnity upon the party, and reeled off twenty stories under the heading 'Tragedy'.

A far more homely collection of episodes and anecdotes is found in *The Book of the Knight of La Tour Landry*. This was written in French in 1371. It was translated into English and printed by Caxton, and had a great popularity for several generations. Geoffrey de la Tour Landry, the author, was a knight and landowner in Anjou: he had three daughters and two sons, one of whom was killed at the battle of Agincourt.

At the beginning of the book he describes how one day, in his garden, he saw his three fair daughters coming towards him, and recalled how he had known young men make false vows to young women—'for there is many of them deceived by the foul and great false oaths that the false men use to swear to women'. He decided then and there to make a book of stories and examples to guide his daughters. He gives us a typical collection of medieval stories, but he gives them with a light touch of his own. They are strung together with a running commentary by himself with much advice and a good many incidents drawn from his own experience of life.

The knight is greatly concerned with sex and courtship. We notice a curious ambivalence between the 'foul and horrible sin of lechery', of which examples with horrific results are given and the 'gracious and courteous' pursuit of fair and virtuous dames by noble puissant knights and squires. The end attained often seems to be the same.

It is the knight's anecdotes and episodes about the world of his own time that are the most attractive. Yet one is astonished at the roughness, even brutality, with which men of good position treat their wives. In one story a man who has a nagging wife hits her so hard that she falls down. Then he kicks her in the face and breaks her nose. She is so blemished that it is 'a mark of shame' to her ever afterwards—a mark of shame to the wife but apparently not to the husband. It is with the example of such stories that good, wifely behaviour is recommended to the knight's three young daughters.[2]

Punishments in purgatory and even in hell are, according to visionary insights, given to women for faults no more serious than 'painting and popping'. However, a lady who spent too much time in front of her mirror was rebuked in a milder though highly startling way. God allowed the devil to take charge of her case, and because she kept the priest and the people waiting in church while she arrayed herself, some of them said:

The devil array her once, and be her mirror. . . . And as God would shew for example, at the same time and hour as she looked in a mirror, instead of a mirror, the devil turned to her his arse, the which was so foul and horrible that for fear she was wode and out of her mind, and was so sick long; and at the last God sent her her wit.

When he is dealing with the human scene the Knight of the Tower begins to remind us of the eighteenth-century essayists. In the following story the setting is completely medieval, yet the way in which anecdotal example is woven into the moral is not unlike the *Tatler* or the *Spectator*. Here common sense is the point rather than anything else.

How love will be kept warm

Sir Foucques de Laval was a fair knight, clean and well beseen among other, and was of good manner, and of fair maintaining. It happed to him, as he told me, that once he was gone for to see his paramour, in the winter season, that the frost was great, and the weather passing cold. He then had in the morning coynted himself of a scarlet gown well broidered, and of a hood of scarlet single and without furring, and nought else he had on him save only his fine shirt; For he had no mantle, neither gloves in his hands. The wind and the cold were great, wherefore he had so great cold, that he became of colour black and pale, for the pearls nor the precious stones which were on the broidering of his single gown, could give him no heat, nor keep him from the cold. Then came another knight, which also was amorous of that lady, but he was not so gay adorned, nor so single of clothes, but he had on

2 *The Book of the Knight of La Tour Landry*, ed. G. S. Taylor (John Hamilton, 1930).

him good and warm gowns, and had a mantle, and a double hood, and was red as a cock and had a good living colour. The lady then welcomed this knight, and made to him better cheer than she did to Sir Foucques, and held with him better company. And said to Sir Foucques, 'Sir, hold you near the fire, for I doubt that ye be not all whole, for your colour is dead and pale.' And he answered that his heart was joyous and well at ease.

This other knight was fairer to the lady's sight than Foucques. But within a while after, Sir Foucques espied the knight, which was going toward the place of his paramours. He arrayed him otherwise than he was wont to do, And so much hied him, that he came hither as soon as the other knight did, for to prove how the matter and his fate should end. But certainly he was then taken of his lady for the fairest and best coloured. Wherefore he told me how love will be kept hot and warm. And how that he had proved it.

IV

Geoffrey, the Knight of the Tower, has the appeal of an amateur of letters who can chat on paper. A far more powerful and professional collection of stories is the older book, *The Handlyng of Synne*, by Robert Mannyng of Brunne. This book, which precedes both Chaucer and the Knight of the Tower by about two generations, was begun as the author tells us in 1303, although it is not known when it was completed. It is taken, here, out of its historical sequence because it represents the virtues and the disadvantages of the priestly story-telling that continued for centuries.

Robert Mannyng of Brunne was a monk of the Gilbertine order; he was not merely a priest who was a man of letters, but unquestionably a writer who rejoiced in stories, could describe daily life among the village people, and was not over-impressed by worldly rank. He tells sixty-five stories in verse, and if he had written a century later in more modern English he might have been much better known today.

This work began by being a translation of the *Manuel de Pechiez* written by an Englishman, William of Waddington, in French. Robert Mannyng of Brunne not only translates but livens up the original. He cuts down the moralizing, tells more everyday stories, and helps his readers by explaining the algebraic language of symbolic references. He puts in conversations. In fact, he writes for simple people, and like a good many other preachers of the day he puts his stories in simple terms.

All this is good story-telling, but *The Handlyng of Synne* is nevertheless a thoroughly schematic preacher's book. The stories are there only because they illustrate the Ten Commandments, or the seven deadly sins. There are plenty of miraculous punishments. He condemns a great deal of pleasure and frivolity that seem to us harmless. He is apt, for instance, to describe hunting, dancing, and singing as if they belonged only to lives of sin, and makes generalized attacks on women in the dreariest vein of medieval priestliness, even holding them responsible for men's lust. He is, however, equally ready to attack knights, and as for tournaments, finds they are the occasion of every one of the seven deadly sins.

One of his best-known stories is the legendary *Dancers of Colbek*. This is a miraculous story telling of the fate of the young men and women who persist in dancing in the village churchyard on Christmas night, during a service. The priest curses them, his own daughter being among them, and they are condemned to dance on for ever. It is a strange story which seems to move in terms of some mythology other than Christian sin and punishment, but it gives some good scenes from village life. Another more realistic story tells of a priest who was a miser and so adored his gold that he tried to eat it and killed himself. Mannyng regularly builds up his stories with realistic conversation and lively pictures of the English scene.

Such a valuable study as G. R. Owst's *Literature and the Pulpit in Medieval England*[3] shows how scenes of everyday life similarly throng the sermons. We see the passage of noble families with their retainers from one house to another. We see a pageant of minstrels, jugglers, heralds, dancing women. We see especially the life of the poor and simple. The deep roots of short-story creation are seen in the need for the moralists to draw their

[3] G. R. Owst, *Literature and the Pulpit in Medieval England* (Cambridge University Press, 1933). See especially ch. I.

examples from familiar daily life of which we are given only
tantalizing glimpses.

We see the housewife and her servant sweeping the dust and
rubbish into the yard, only to find the hens scattering it again.
We watch the great black pot suspended over the fire, with the
smoke and sparks flying up all round it. We hear the weeping of
an infant through an open cottage door; the squeal of a cartwheel
outside; the roar of flames as the smith works his bellows; a peal
of bells. We see workmen plodding along with 'great dyne' and
with 'uncurteys woordys'. In the fields we see the birds flying
after the sower, the geese pecking at the children's legs; or a child
who gives his food away to the 'dogs and cattys'.

We meet pedlars crying out 'old pots to mend', whose own
clothes need mending worst of all; we find ingratiating fellows
who invite one to drink with them, but vanish when the bill is
presented. We see the horrible appearance of disease, the crippled,
the one-eyed, the ulcerated, the ragged. We learn of the bad
knights who never go into battle but live by plundering.

Through these scenes we begin to know the sorrows and the
joys of the people, to recognize the kindly toughness of the
English, their acceptance of good and bad fortune; we hear the
sigh of the overburdened and often saddened peasants, with their
mottoes which can be both beautiful and homely. 'Yf hope were
not, herte shulde breke'.

There is certainly the stuff of stories in these glimpses and as
Owst says, it was not really the poet or novelist who first saw
their significance:

Before ever the day of such literary realism and humanism had dawned,
it was the homilist who first stooped to raise them from the level of the
dusty commonplace and set them on high amid the wider concerns of
the human mind, thus 'making their dust fat with fatness'.

Here are the true ingredients of stories, scenes from everyday
life, that strangely enough had to wait centuries for the art of
Hardy, Coppard, and H. E. Bates. As Andrew Lang points out, it
is with great difficulty that mankind learns to write natural stories.

E

VI

The Elizabethans:
Through Pleasures and Palaces

I

People who tell stories to small children may have noticed that their listeners are of two kinds, those who keep still and listen with close attention, and those who want to act the story out even while it is being told. It is the spirit and ardour of this second kind of child that seems to be instinctive in Elizabethan literature. It goes without saying that the writers of the age poured their immense creative gifts into plays and into poetry, yet behind the great tragedies and comedies lies a very large field of story-writing. In fact, the numerous Elizabethan books of stories are nowadays encountered chiefly as the 'sources' of plays. A good many people must in their time have been able to include in examination answers the fact that *The Duchess of Malfi* was based on a story of Bandello, which appeared in William Painter's *The Palace of Pleasure* as the twenty-third story of his second volume. They might know also that the twenty-fifth story was *Romeo and Juliet*. They might well forget, however, that Painter was so carefully ransacked that the twenty-first story provided Beaumont and Fletcher with the material for *The Maid of the Mill*, the twenty-fourth and twenty-sixth supplied plot and counterplot for Marston's *Insatiable Countess*, and the twenty-eighth was the basis of Massinger's *The Picture*. Where, in fact, would the Elizabethan dramatists have been without stories drawn from the Italian novelle? What would Shakespeare's comedies have been like without Venice, Verona, Navarre, and Illyria?

All this has perhaps led people to think of the Elizabethan

story collections simply as plot books into which the dramatists delved; but *The Palace of Pleasure* was first published in 1566, thirty years before *Romeo and Juliet* was produced, and forty years before *The Duchess of Malfi*. The story-books of the sixteenth century were a great deal more than 'compost', as C. S. Lewis aptly called them, for the dramatists, and were read eagerly for a generation or so before they were turned into plays. Indeed, Beatrice was teased by Benedick for having 'had her good wit' out of *The Hundred Merry Tales*, which was published in 1526, seventy-two years before Beatrice took the stage.

It is a paradox of the history of the short story that there is in English no written collection of short stories in prose before Tudor days, except the homiletic compilations. Boccaccio did not invent a naturalistic framework of modern surroundings as Chaucer did; but he did provide a fluent easy-going style of narration in prose. So did Straparola, who was a kind of early Grimm of the Italian scene; in France Queen Margaret of Navarre and La Sale also told their stories in prose.

The Hundred Merry Tales contains much that is still medieval and in its pages we can still see the tide of the old age running out while the tide of the new is pouring in. The time of the two Henrys is a strange transitional period in thought, and in its fiction we continually meet the curious figure of the jester, whose cap and bells turn up in many a woodcut, the anti-hero, the man who goes round playing 'mad and merry pranks' on society at large. Even so solemn and at times tedious a writer as Sir Henry More is often ready to break off his arguments and indulge himself in comic anecdotes or abuse. Social satire is extended in *The Ship of Fools*, adapted rather than translated from the German by Alexander Barclay. It was published in 1509, a huge poem with a good deal of laborious rebuking of follies and vices, and some scene-setting which, by stretching a very long point, may be said to have some place in the development of naturalistic fiction.

However, the protagonist of jesters was Till Eulenspiegel or, in English, Tyll Owlglass. He was not merely the hero of a book

but existed in real life, in the fourteenth century. A printed
account of his doings first appeared in Platt-Deutsch, the dialect
of his region, and was translated into High German, probably
by Thomas Murner. These jests are all of a piece with the
incidents and the mock morals that make up *The Hundred Merry
Tales*. Rastell the printer, who was a brother-in-law of More,
was also the editor of *The Hundred Merry Tales*; their authorship is unknown, but it has been suggested that More might have
had a hand in it. The book is not a mere chance compilation of
old and new anecdotes, and it has a satirical edge that cuts deeper
than might appear at first sight. A single example may give some
notion of the great variety of unexpected and human anecdotes
which form *The Hundred Merry Tales*.

A gentylman there was dwellynge nygh Kyngston uppon Temys.
rydynge in the contrey wyth hys servaunte which was not the most
quyckest felow. But rode alway sadly by his mayster and hade very
few wordys. Hys mayster sayde to hym John quod he why rydyst so
sadly. I wolde have the tell me som mery talyes to passe the tyme with.
by my trouth master quod he I can tell no talys. Why quod the
master canst not syng. no by my trouth quod hys servaunte I cowd
never syng in all my lyfe.
    Why quod the master canst thou ryme than.
    By my trouth master quod he I can not tell but yf ye wyll begynne
to ryme I wyll folow as well as I can. by my trouthe quod the master
that is well sayd that I wyll begyn to make a ryme let me se howe well
thou canst folowe.
    So the mayster musyd a whyle and than began to ryme thus. Many
mennys swannes swymmys in temmys and so do myne.
    Then quod the servaunt. And menny men lye by other mennys
wyves and so do I by thyne.
    What dost horson quod the master.
    By my trouth master nothynge quod he but make up the ryme. But
quod the master I charge the tell me why thou sayst so.
    Forsothe master quod he for nothynge in the worlde but to make up
your ryme. Then quod the master yf thou do it for nothing ellys I am
content.
    So the master forgave hym his saynge all though he had sayd the
trewth.

We can hardly trace in *The Hundred Merry Tales* much movement towards the modern conception of short stories. They
were, however, short and pithy in form, and compared with the
Gesta Romanorum, which was still current in printed editions,
they were brilliantly modern, although a good many of *The
Hundred Merry Tales* are less like naturalistic conception of
fiction than Chaucer's *Canterbury Tales*. The collection is, in
fact, a new wine poured into the old bottles of the homiletic
story, bursting the bottles yet taking no new form of its own,
and there is something very English in its gentle debunking of
heroics and moral preaching.

There is now a long pause in story-writing and it is not until
the brief reigns of Queen Mary and Edward VI are over, Lady
Jane Grey beheaded, and Queen Elizabeth safely on the throne
that stories begin to flow again from the printers.

These may be divided very roughly into three kinds. First, the
novelle of the Italian type: in these there is a great deal of event,
often of a startling and bloodthirsty kind. There is little portrayal
of character in the modern sense; people's feelings are usually
touched on only at the most extreme moments of grief or joy.
There is little attempt at scene-painting and on the whole only a
perfunctory attempt at moralizing. It is the strangeness, the sadness, the horror, and sometimes the clever cozenage of the story
that is the point.

Next are the ragamuffin, knockabout stories, which can be
divided into two groups: the stories of jokes and merry pranks;
and the stories of low life—the whole series of books about
'coney-catching', or tricking the young and innocent. Again
there is little attempt at characterization and often an astonishing
absence of sensitivity, with an assumption that the reader has no
interest in the story save curiosity about the action and unfeeling
mirth at the trickery.

A third kind of short prose writing is found in the 'character'
books. These have their own interest, although they belong to
the history of the essay as much as to the story. Their object is to
make a close examination of different kinds of people; and they
do, in fact, when mingled with the full essay-writing technique

of the eighteenth century, come very close to true short-story creation, leading on to such well-known pieces as Lamb's 'The Retired Man' or Leigh Hunt's 'On Washerwomen'. Their development towards the essay will be dealt with in the next chapter.

II

The most famous storehouse of stories of the whole Elizabethan period is William Painter's *The Palace of Pleasure*, which was published in 1566. It was such a success that Painter followed it with a second volume in 1567. The two volumes contained between them over one hundred stories.

Judging by the particular kind of interest that the Elizabethans took in *The Palace of Pleasure*, one might think that Painter was taking the great bulk of his stories from authors of the Italian Renaissance, especially Boccaccio and Bandello. It is unquestionably the more modern stories of life in the Italian cities that fascinated Elizabethan readers, but Painter drew on over thirty different authors, Herodotus, Livy, Tacitus, and Apuleius being among his diverse classical sources.

Painter is often spoken of as nothing more than a translator, basing himself largely on Belleforest's *Les Discourses Tragiques*. However, original short stories were not sought for, hardly dreamt of, in fact. To the Elizabethan author it was more important that a story came out of Seneca; or that Bandello had taken it from a tragical history, well known to the citizens of Verona. Translator or not, Painter does give to his rich variety of stories a certain unity of style and presentation, and that style is very different from the plain, brief pungency of *The Hundred Merry Tales*. It is polite, courtly, and literary; to our feeling it is long-winded, but not yet fully developed into the floweriness of euphuism.

Undoubtedly the main point of the stories in *The Palace of Pleasure* is the narrative movement. If we read *Romeo and Juliet* in Painter's version we may at first feel that it is a drab, heartless affair. The poetry as we know it is not there; and the devices, the contrivances, the moves and countermoves are told in great detail.

Yet in this very way the story achieves a certain sort of prose intensity. The sheer interest aroused in the event, the determination of the young lovers, the assistance given to them, the quarrels of those that hold them apart, soon begin to take hold; and one reads with growing interest, and an emotion that is created by sheer factual authenticity. The story seems to expand in the mind when the book is laid down and this is undoubtedly how it must have affected Elizabethan readers. Through its matter-of-factness it has a story quality of its own that *The Tragedy of Romeo and Juliet* lacks.

It is interesting to compare a few details in the two versions. People have often commented on the extreme youth of Juliet. This was Shakespeare's idea. Painter, following the French of Boiastuau (1559), who took the story from Luigi da Porto (1535), who took it in turn from Masuccio (1476), says that Juliet was nearly eighteen, a far more mature age for the times. Another point on which they differ is in the treatment of the love scene in the garden. According to Shakespeare's version, Romeo, in perhaps the most famous love scene in any play in any language, pours out his ecstasies to Juliet from the moonlit garden, while Juliet leans down from the balcony. In Painter there is only a brief conversation in the garden, where it is obviously too dangerous for Romeo to delay. The more mature Romeo and Juliet arrange to be married as quickly as possible, which they do with the aid of the expert and worldly intriguer Friar Laurence. Shakespeare's Romeo and Juliet also get married, but the scene takes place off stage. Painter's story gives a very full explanation of how the marriage is arranged and how in fact they are made husband and wife.

After the marriage Romeo takes into his confidence his servant called Pietro,

... and commaunded hym wyth expedition to provide a Ladder of Cordes wyth 2 strong Hookes of Iron fastned to both endes, which he easily did, because they were mutch used in Italy.

When Juliet's husband next returns to the Capulets' garden, all is made ready in the most practical way.

The apoynted houre come, Rhomeo put on the most sumptuous apparell hee had, and conducted by good fortune neere to the place where his heart tooke lyfe, was so fully determined of hys purpose, as easily hee clymed up the Garden wall. Beinge arrived hard to the wyndow, he percyved Julietta, who had already so well fastned the Ladder to draw him up, as without any daunger at all, he entred hir chambre, which was so clere as the day, by reason of the Tapers of Virgin Wax, which Julietta had caused to be lighted, that she might the better beholde her Rhomeo. Julietta for hir part, was but in her night kerchief: who so soon as she perceyved him colled him about the Neck.

There is another important difference to be seen in the status of the old nurse. Shakespeare created a famous bawdy acting part which may grate on some tastes; and in a way the better it is played, the more it grates. Shakespeare's old nurse teases Juliet in a familiar, often ribald, manner. In Painter's story, however, the nurse is 'an olde Gentlewoman of honor which had nursed her and brought her up'. At first she resists Juliet, but afterwards assists her in the idea of a secret marriage, as she judges this to be the best solution of the problem.

The part played by Friar Laurence is also far more elaborate in Painter's version. Friar Laurence is no pious simpleton, but 'through his vertue and piety, had so well won the citizens hearts of Verona, as he was almost the Confessor to them all, and of all men generally reverenced and beloved: and many tymes for his great prudence was called in by the lords of the Citty, to the hearing of their weighty causes'; in other words, a man very experienced in intrigues and well used to court life. In fact, we feel that Painter's Friar Laurence might well have brought his elaborate plan to a successful conclusion, while with Shakespeare's version the outcome is far from certain.

Painter pays his readers the compliment of assuming that printed stories need coherent explanations. His method follows the advice of Somerset Maugham that in telling a short story the author must not leave the 'whys' and the 'hows' up in the air. It would not be convincing story-telling to say that 'the noble Lord Romeo made all haste to ascend into the very chamber of the Lady Juliet'. We need to be told, as Painter tells us, how he did it.

In the novella kind of story we have in fact completely left the medieval world of miracle and unexplained event. Knights do not wander through forests without visible means of support. They tend to be 'a faire young man of noble birth in the employ of the Duke, and much valued for his courtly discretion' or 'a studious scholar of the university, whose father had amassed great wealth in the Damascus trade'. The main appeal of the stories still is the extraordinary and often bloodthirsty happenings. Sometimes the tricks and 'witty conceits' seem incredible, but they are given a corroborative setting, and are no more fantastic than the broad farces of Kipling.

The stories in *The Palace of Pleasure* are told as if they were authentic fact. The narrator is Painter, and if he cannot say the story comes from Livy or Cicero, then he tells us he 'had it out of' Cinthio or Straparola. This means that the stories are 'narrator stories', and partake of all the advantages and limitations of this method of telling a story. It is a method more suitable for dealing with action, and providing information about the characters, than for entering into their minds and feeling.

There is also little conversation. When people talk they are apt to converse in polished speeches, which aim at setting out all that might be passing in two people's minds during a whole conversation. This again is the historian's method. The rapid naturalistic exchange that we see in the quarrel scene between Brutus and Cassius has creative truth, but it does not claim to be historical fact. Such conversations are hard to fit into a narrating style.

This technique of authenticity frequently leads to the beginning of the story with a *sententia*—a general expression of opinion which lends verisimilitude. Thus the story of *The Duchess of Malfi* begins laboriously: 'The great Honour and authority men have in thys World, and the greater their estimation is, the more sensible and notorious are the faultes by theim committed, . . .' This vein of thought goes on for a whole page. This may seem far removed from the technique of the modern short story, yet it is remarkable how many nineteenth- and twentieth-century stories that follow the narrator technique do begin with a general statement.

In the opening paragraphs of Painter's *Romeo and Juliet* we have two authenticating devices, neither of which is essential to the movement of the story. One tells us that the story that follows seems almost incredible, but that it is true. The other tells us something quite factual about the topography of Verona.

Both these devices can be found in Somerset Maugham; an opening which confesses that the story seems incredible is used in 'The Kite', and an opening that gives topographical detail is used in 'Footprints in the Jungle'.

There is no place in Malaya that has more charm than Tanah Merah. It lies on the sea and the sandy shore is fringed with casuarinas. The government offices are still in the old Raad Huis that the Dutch built when they owned the land, and on the hill stand the grey ruins of the fort by aid of which the Portuguese maintained their hold over the unruly natives. Tanah Merah has a history and in the vast labyrinthine houses of the Chinese merchants, backing on the sea so that in the cool of the evening they may sit in the loggias and enjoy the salt breeze, families dwell that have been settled in the country for three centuries.

Is this mere rambling? The author being Somerset Maugham, we may be certain it is not. Compare it with Painter doing exactly the same sort of thing for the benefit of readers who have never before heard of Romeo and Juliet.

If then perticular affection which of good right every man ought to beare to the place where he was borne, doe not deceive those that travayle, I think that they will confesse wyth me, that few Citties in Italy, can surpasse the sayd Citty of Verona, as well for the Navigable river called Adissa, which passeth almost through the midst of the same, and thereby a great trafique into Almayne, as also for the prospect towards the Fertile Mountaynes, and pleasant valeys whych do environ the same, with a great number of very clere and lyvely fountaynes, that serve for the ease and commodity of the place. . . .

Painter and Somerset Maugham have exactly the same end in view: the factual tone of voice, the air of professional certainty, the ability to tell a story that men and women of the world will believe. One can imagine some solid country squire or merchant of Elizabethan times preferring Painter's *Romeo and Juliet* to Shakespeare's, and many Elizabethans may have learnt about Romeo and Juliet from Painter rather than Shakespeare.

In time a number of other Elizabethan story books appeared, but Painter's was by far the largest, and perhaps also the most read. Indeed, it played an important part in the development of authentic story-telling. The whole tendency of Elizabethan taste moved away from the telling of stories briefly. The authors wanted to embellish. They wanted to give models of courtly letter-writing, of set speeches, and 'discourses'. In a sense they wanted everything to contain everything; for instance, in Fenton's *Tragicall Discourses* (1567), the author takes some stories from Belleforest, who had embroidered on Bandello and embroiders them yet again.

In 1576 came a book of stories by George Pettie, called, in frank imitation of Painter, *A Petite Palace of Pettie his Pleasure*. With this book we are in the full flower of euphuistic prose, swept along in a foam of alliteration, antithesis, consonance, proverbs, rhetorical questions, abstruse knowledge, mixed with sudden turns of homely speech.

But what perpetuitie is to bee looked for in mortall pretences? What constancy is to bee hoped for in kytes of Cressids kinde? may one gather Grapes of thornes, Sugar of Thistels or constancy of women?

Or, one might ask, may one gather short stories from this kind of prose style, because the emphasis is constantly on the manner rather than anything else.

Elizabethan taste in prose stories continued to run to immense length, and whether we feel we are in the presence of mere euphuistic excess or the true creation of a poetic world as in Sidney's *Arcadia*, the idea of short natural stories recedes farther and farther from view. Lyly and Robert Greene not only let off all the fireworks of fantastic prose; they also take us into fantastic countries with magical happenings and they employ every kind of interpolation and delay in the movement of the stories.

A book somewhat nearer to the modern idea of short stories appeared in 1581: this was *Farewell to Militarie Profession*, by

Barnabe Rich. Rich was a soldier, but he was also a professional author and had already published a diversity of works. Like Pettie, he writes a preface, addressing himself to ladies who he thinks will be his chief readers. His eight stories are shorter and far more compendious than most of Pettie's and Painter's. His style is lighter; he evidently enjoys taking a bantering tone with his readers and in this way he seems to be putting all far-fetched and over-romantic stories firmly into their place as amusing trifles.

At moments his approach is almost reminiscent of Thackeray, and surprisingly he reverses the usual Elizabethan method of claiming support and authority for the factual truth of his stories. He tells us that five of his stories are 'forged only for delight, neither credible to be believed nor hurtful to be perused'. His book, like others, was of great use to playwrights. The main love situation of *Twelfth Night* comes from *Apolonius and Silla*, and T. N. Cranfill, whose edition of *Rich's Farewell* was published in 1959, suggests that at least ten plays between 1598 and 1633 are indebted to Rich. Rich's own borrowings are no less extensive, and even if he does not claim a particular authority for his stories, he is much under the influence of the Italian novelle, and of their French and English adaptations. Cranfill says of his last story, *Philotus*, 'This rollicking, richly comic narrative is a smooth blend of such widely diverse ingredients as two histoires by Belleforest, novelle by Cinthio and Straparola, a story from Golding's Ovid, five stories by Pettie, and a play by Gascoigne.' This, in fact, is how he produced stories of 'his own forging'. He provides an interesting comment on the Elizabethan view of fiction in his Preface when he says of his stories that they are 'fitter to be presented on the stage as some of them have been'.

As I have mentioned, Rich's story of *Apolonius and Silla* is thought to be one of the sources of Shakespeare's *Twelfth Night*. The Olivia–Viola situation is similar, but Rich never dreamed of putting into his story such vividly created characters as Sir Toby Belch and Sir Andrew Aguecheek; there is no Feste, no Maria, and no Malvolio. Yet there is one interesting scene in *Apolonius and Silla* which perhaps gives a truer and more biting point to the main love story. Juliana, who is the Olivia of Rich's story, has been made pregnant by Silvio, and is under the impression that he and his sister Silla are one and the same person. Silla is accused and is liable to be arrested, and she has to undress to the waist before she can convince Juliana that she is not the prospective father. Here the story-teller has the advantage of the stage presentation.

It is, however, in Rich's personality and in the slightly mocking style of narration that he shows his originality. Only one of his eight stories, 'The Two Brethren and their Wives', is pitched in contemporary England. This again is a striking departure, but though we are told that one of the wives in the story is called Dorotie, there is not much that is distinctively English in the plot or scene-setting; but the style of narration is Rich's own.

. . . but for your better confirmation, I have set forthe this historie of twoo brethren, the one of them married to a wenche, that could so cunninglie behave hereself towardes hym, that he had thought she had beloved there had been no other God but himself, and yet by your leave, she would take reason when it was proffered her, but what of that: the harte never greeves, what the eyes see not. The other was married to a dame, that from her navill downeward was more chast and continent, but otherwise of her tong such a devill of helle, that the poore man her housebande could never enjoye merrie daie nor houre, although he devised many a pretie remedie, . . .

Unless we are to think of this story purely as a broad farce, Rich's view of marriage and human nature seems far from happy. 'The Two Brethren' tells of two disastrous marriages. One brother marries for beauty; his wife takes three successive lovers. There is some crude play with a hamper, which may have given Shakespeare an idea for *The Merry Wives*. The husband is left foolishly doting and the wife coldly triumphant. The other brother marries, for the sake of her money, a 'scold' whom he eventually exposes in public in a brutal, mocking way, which drives her mad. This may have given Shakespeare a hint for the mocking of Malvolio.

There are other minor collections, and one called *Westward for Smelts*, which appeared in 1620, introduces us to a number of fishwives who have had a good market day and tell stories as they are rowed home up the river. This sounds as if it might deal with good everyday stories, and it has a fascinating sub-title, 'The Water-man's Fare of mad merry Western wenches whose tongues, albeit like Bell-clappers, they never leave ringing, yet their tales are sweet, and will much content you. Written by Kinde Kit of Kingstone.' The tales they tell, however, are in the old-fashioned style, still copying plots from numerous sources, although they may be given an English setting.

III

The 'cozening' element of Barnabe Rich, seen in his plots and in his personal style, makes a link between the novella type of story and books which stand at the other extreme of Elizabethan taste. That is the ragamuffin books: the books that are both about ragamuffins and are written in a ragamuffin style, which relishes words from low life and runs at times into a voluble knockabout language which might be called guttersnipe euphuism. Books and pamphlets about 'coney-catching' became, in the last twenty or thirty years of the century, a world in themselves. Coney-catching was a phrase used among thieves, referring to various methods of robbing people by tricks and violence. These tend to merge into the group of Jest Books, and the idea of 'mad and merry pranks' is apt to infect and drag down material that might have developed into a powerful and indeed terrifying literature.

A certain current had been setting ever since medieval times towards stories of the anti-hero. A poem called *The Hye Way to the Spytel Hous* (published after 1531) began to set the tone of this tramp literature, but fashion for 'coney-catching' books seems to spring from John Awdeley's *The Fraternitye of Vacabones* (1575) and Harman's *Caveat for Commen Cursetors* (1567). Awdeley introduces us to the tramps' slang which was far too picturesque for Elizabethan taste to overlook—'The lewd lowsey language of these loitering luskes and lazy lovels.' Awdeley sets the vocabulary going and other writers soon add to it. We learn that 'the Abraham man' feigns madness; 'the ruffeler' pretends to be a broken-down soldier; and the 'whippiacke' a shipwrecked sailor. The 'prygman' steals horses. The 'upright man' is the boss and rules a crew of thieves; 'a swygman' carries a pack on his back (as an Australian swagman does). 'Barnard's Law' is a confidence trick which needs five different people. A 'mort' is a woman; a 'glimmering mort' is a married woman who pretends her house has been burnt down. A 'kitchen cove' is a little boy trained to creep through narrow windows just as Oliver Twist did. A good deal of this slang was current up to the eighteenth century and even later.

Awdeley's book is mainly a dictionary of thieves' slang, but Harman's is a rich store of anecdotes that verge on short stories. A typical anecdote from Harman tells of an old countryman who came up to London to sell farm produce. On the way home a ruffeler begins a friendly conversation with him, but when they reach a lonely place demands all his money. The old countryman admits that he had some loose change, but conceals an angel piece; whereupon the ruffeler searches him and then abuses him for his great dishonesty in trying to hide the gold coin.

'good lorde, what a worlde is this! howe maye' (quoth hee) 'a man beleve or truste in the same? se you not' (quoth he) 'this old knave tolde me that he had but seven shyllings, and here is more by an angell: what an old knave and a false knave have we here!' quoth this rufflar 'oure lorde have mercy on us. wyll this worlde never be better?'

Strangely enough, Conrad uses a very similar incident in a short story, 'Il Conde'. In this also there is the concealment of a gold coin by an old gentleman who is being robbed, and its later discovery when the victim walks into the same café as the young robber, and feels that he has now been put in the wrong, and that revenge will be taken. Conrad tells us in the Preface to *A Set of Six* that this had in fact happened to 'a very charming old gentleman whom I met in Italy'.

Soon there was a wealth of books about ruffelers and morts, written by a variety of authors, among whom are some well-known names, such as Thomas Dekker, Samuel Rowlands, and Robert Greene. Robert Greene, especially, identified himself with coney-catching books, abandoning his euphuistic and marvellous romances for this rather exaggerated realism. We move towards stories, but for the most part find ourselves in a welter of mere anecdotes, and we soon weary of the heartless and sometimes brutal tricks played on the innocent 'coneys'.

Greene's *Notable Discovery of Cozenage* was published in 1591 and was rapidly followed by *The Second and Last Part of Coney-Catching*. In 1592 came *The Thirde and Last Part of Coney-Catching*, and other books followed.

In 1602 the vein was still being kept alive by Rowlands with *Greene's Ghost Haunting Conny Catchers*. In 1608 Dekker wrote *The Bel-man of London*, which was pillaged largely from Harman, Greene, and Rowlands. Greene, if anybody, develops the incidents towards stories, and his *The Thirde and Last Part of Coney-Catching* consists of ten complete stories; but there is only a glimmer of a more artistic and interesting form, and the stories are little more than bald incidents.

IV

The old Jest Books which proliferated in the second half of the century had links with the coney-catching pamphlets. They share the taste for low life, the accounts of simple people duped, and they shade off into half-true picaresque accounts of real people, such as Long Meg of Westminster. She was a noted character who was a fierce virago, lived partly as a man, might well have been hanged or killed in some tramps' quarrel, but as it happened ended up safely, and achieved some celebrity as an alewife, a natural sister, one might say, to Skelton's *Elynour Rummyng*. She became the heroine of Dekker's *Roaring Girl*.

The Jest Books proper are on the whole kindlier than the fierce world of the coney-catchers, and they are the descendants, or rather the poor relations, of *The Hundred Merry Tales*. They consist of similar short anecdotes of varying amusement and point. There is a proliferation of titles and editions which are in themselves a subject for specialized study, for example, such titles as *Merry Tales*, *Witty Questions and Answers very pleasant to rede*, *The Mad Men of Gotham*, *Mother Bunche's Merriments*, and so on.

Others are built round real people but report jests and adventures which are almost certainly imaginary. Of these Tyll Owlglass is the prototype and once again we find stories pilfered from one collection to another. *The Jests of Scoggin* (1655–6), for instance, contains several anecdotes from Tyll Owlglass. Scoggin was a real person who apparently was a man of some learning and a university graduate, yet he came to lead the grotesque and precarious life of a court jester. On one occasion it is said that the hounds were set on him by the king's orders; however, he solved this problem easily enough by having a live hare hidden in a sack and letting it go just as the hounds were coming up to him. At times his jests seem almost incredibly coarse and insensitive. One story, for instance, tells how he drove a young woman in tears from the court because of his jesting about her face which 'was full of pimples'.

Other Jest Books were produced about popular fictional characters, such as Bottom the Weaver; or sometimes about real people who by a long stretch of the imagination could be connected with some of the stories. There is, for instance, a collection of *Merie Tales of Skelton*, the poet laureate. He was, it is true, fairly brash and even violent in some of his activities, but plainly many of the stories are simply tacked on to him from other Jest Books. Tarlton, the well-known comedian, was also the subject of many jest-stories, and a fair example of incidents from the Jest Books is this story of *Tarlton's greeting to Banks his Horse*:

There was one, Banks, in the time of Tarlton, who served the Earle of Essex, and had a horse of strange qualities. . . . Tarlton then, with his fellowes, playing at the Bel by, came into the Cross-keyes, amongst many people, to see fashions, which Banks perceiving, to make people laugh, saies Signor, (to his horse) Go fetch me the veryest foole in the company. The jade comes immediately and with his mouth drawes Tarlton forth. Tarlton, with merry words, said nothing, but 'God a mercy, horse'. In the end, Tarlton, seeing the people laugh so, was angry inwardly, and said: Sir, had I power of your horse, as you have, I would do more than that. What ere it be, said Banks, to please him, I will charge him to do it. Then, saies Tarlton; charge him to bring me the veriest whoremaster in the company. The horse leades his master to him. Then 'God a mercy horse, indeed,' saies Tarlton. The people had

F

much ado to keep peace; but Bankes and Tarlton had like to have squar'd, and the horse by to give aime. But ever after it was a by word thorow London, God a mercy horse! and is to this day.[1]

Can we call them short stories? Hardly. But they are brief and they have a lively movement. They give a variety of pictures of real life. Even when they are too farcical for belief, the settings are often real enough, and the conversations are colloquial. They are a welcome antidote to the euphuistic pomposity and the cardboard emptiness that often besets the more serious tales.

V

Thomas Deloney is one of the very few authors of the time who can tell pleasant and realistic stories of people in the course of ordinary life, and this, as we have seen, is a rare achievement. E. J. O'Brien edited in 1937 a volume of twenty-five *Elizabethan Tales*. He finds in Deloney 'a neglected genius scorned by his contemporaries'.

We may not rank Deloney quite as highly as O'Brien, who sees in his work 'the spirit of Chaucer's *Canterbury Tales* embodied again in English flesh and blood. . . . Life triumphs overwhelmingly at last over bloodless romance.' 'Bloodless' certainly seems an inappropriate adjective to apply to Painter. It is true, nevertheless, that Deloney's achievement in regularly writing natural stories of his own period and country is at this time unique. He belongs, however, to the history of the novel or documentary rather than the short story. His best-known story, *The Gentle Craft*, is based on the life of a man who rose from being a cobbler's apprentice to becoming Lord Mayor of London. It is made up of several linked incidents, skilfully compressed and selected, the whole life being well within the compass of a long short story. It shows yet once again how valuable the story-writers were to the dramatists, for it gave Dekker the whole scaffolding for *The Shoemaker's Holiday*. There is a tendency to pile up round the famous personality good strokes of business that we have met in other stories, but Deloney's style is clear, straightforward, with a

[1] From *Tarlton's Sound City Jests* (1844 edn.).

pleasing homely rhythm, and he gives a good sprinkling of conversations and pictures of ordinary life. Here is an incident when
Simon has just been made a sheriff, and has come home with an
alderman and a couple of wealthy commoners:

Nay, I pray you come in and drink with me before you go. Then said
he, Wife, bring me forth the pasty of Venison, and set me here my little
Table, that these Gentlemen may eat a bit with me before they go.

His wife which had been oft used to this terme, excused the matter,
saying; The little table! Good Lord, husband, I do wonder what you
will do with the little Table now, knowing that it is used already? I
pray you good Husband, content yourselfe, and sit at this great Table
this once. Then she whispered him in the eare saying; What, man, shall
we shame ourselves?

. . . Trust me, we are troublesome guests (said the Alderman), but
yet we would fain see your little table, because it is said to be of such
prize.

Yea, and it is my mind you shall (quoth Master *Eyre*) therefore he
called his wife again, saying good wife dispatch and prepare the little
table for these gentlemen would fain have a view of it.

Whereupon his wife, seeing him so earnest, according to her
wonted manner, came in: and setting her selfe down on a low stool,
laid a fair Napkin ouver her knees, and set the platter with the pasty of
Venison thereupon, and presently a chear was brought for Master
Alderman, and a couple of stools for the two commoners, which they
beholding, with a sudden and hearty laughter, said: Why, Master
Sheriffe, is this the table you held so deare?

Yes truly (quoth he).[2]

It is curious that Deloney stands almost alone in telling simple
everyday stories of individuals without blood and thunder or
crude farce; yet the century added the homely irony of *The
Hundred Merry Tales*, the authentic 'narrator technique' of
Painter, and a great deal of realistic material from the back-streets.

[2] Thomas Deloney, *Works*, edited by F. O. Mann (Clarendon Press, 1912).

VII

The Character Books, and the
Story Emerging from the Essay

I

As we have seen, the innovations of short-story writers in the sixteenth century were varied and remarkable. A view of the period from Painter onwards might well lead to the conjecture that something far more like the modern short story was just round the corner. However, this is not so. The modest art, the whole notion of the single but significant incident, vanishes into the distance; and the story-telling urge takes many other turns. Taste in the seventeenth century runs rather surprisingly to the reprinting of the discursive novels of Greene and Lodge, and then to translating the immense heroical romances of Scudéry and Calprenède. It would be hard to imagine anything farther removed from a short story than *Le Grand Cyrus*.

The poetic genius of the century for saying something short yet poetically significant, a characteristic that we see in Donne, Herbert, or Marvell, has no counterpart in prose fiction. That Traherne, who saw men as angels and the countryside in the light of eternity, should have cast his vision into the form of everyday stories was at this time impossible.

However, after the Restoration a less voluminous form of fiction began to appear, at first mainly translated from the French. This was the story of gallantry and intrigue, often pretending to be a revelation of scandalous goings-on among the gentry and nobility—and sometimes really being so, with thinly disguised references to real people. These stories, abounding in cuckoldry and heiress-stealing, developed into the novel rather than the short story, and their influence can be seen in the work of Aphra Behn, Mrs. Marley, and Mrs. Haywood, who was editor of the short-lived *Female Spectator*, 1744–6. One may find echoes of them in the fifty years' run of *The Ladies Magazine* from 1760 to 1811, and they play their part in the situations of *Tom Jones* and *Clarissa*.

In 1692 Congreve began his career with *Incognita*, a polished and brilliant skit or modernized example of the well-worn novella story. It is very well done, but Dr. Johnson, writing on Dryden in his *Lives of the Poets*, said of it, 'I would rather praise it than read it.' Cleophil, who can be assumed to be Congreve, gives some interesting views about the development of fiction in the Preface to *Incognita*:

Romances are generally composed of the constant loves and invincible courages of hero's, heroins, kings and queens, mortals of the first rank, and so forth; where lofty language, miraculous contingencies and impossible performances, elevate and surprise the Reader into a giddy delight, which leaves him flat upon the ground. . . . Novels are of a more familiar nature; come near us, and represent to us intrigues in practice, delight us with accidents and odd events, but not such as are wholly unusual or unpresidented, such which not being so distant from our belief bring also the pleasure nearer us.[1]

Congreve, in fact, while seeking for the artistic truth of events which can be believed, places the general theory of what a story ought to be very much where Painter had left it; although strange, its details should be well authenticated. Congreve himself echoes the views of Rich when he says, 'There is no possibility of giving that life to Writing or Repetition of a story, which it has in Action.'

II

The kind of story for which Congreve aimed, like the stories of scandal, moved towards the development of the novel rather than the short story. To find an influence on fiction which was to

[1] In *Shorter novels; Jacobean and Restoration*, ed. Philip Henderson (Everyman, Dent, 1949).

keep a story short and to concentrate it on a unified and single idea, we have to turn to a genre that was not fiction at all, that is, the books of 'character' writings which became popular at the beginning of the seventeenth century, and continued with many variations for the next thirty or forty years. Indeed, Butler's *Characters* were not published till 1759, sixty-seven years after his death, and one may still trace the 'character' writings in such essays as Leigh Hunt's 'The Old Lady' or Lamb's 'The Poor Relation' or best of all, perhaps, Lamb's 'The Superannuated Man'—a 'character' developed to a high degree of human perception. It contains almost exactly the qualities that stories such as those of Barnabe Rich lack, while never itself developing into a story.

We can find signs of the movement towards character writing during the sixteenth century. Harman, for instance, in *A Caveat for Commen Cursetors* (1567) had given ten 'characters' of rogues and vagabonds, and Jonson's *Everyman in his Humour* and *Everyman out of His Humour*, which were printed in 1600, provide 'a character of each Individual' with the dramatis personae.

It was, however, the characters of Theophrastus, which were translated into English in 1593, which supplied the model. Theophrastus followed Aristotle in the presidency of the Lyceum, and his object in writing characters was analytical rather than literary. He wanted to make a kind of botanical collection of human nature and tried to pin down the characteristics of 'the coward', 'the brave man', and so on. For condensed observation he often surpasses the English authors of the seventeenth century, who tend to be more interested in showing off fireworks of style than in trying to describe human character. Sometimes they deal purely in abstractions; for instance, Bishop Hall's book published in 1608 is called *Characters of Vertues and Vices*, and others follow him in describing broad types. One of the most unusual and intriguing of these 'character' books, slight though it may be, is *The Man in the Moon telling strange stories*, by M.W., published in 1609.

It is possible that the whole fashion for 'character' writing was given a chance impetus by the startling death of Sir Thomas Overbury, one of the best known of the character authors. The unfortunate Sir Thomas was the victim of a slow poisoning plot in which the Earl and Countess of Somerset were involved, and it was an extraordinary *cause célèbre* of the day. The 'characters' of Sir Thomas Overbury were first incorporated in the second edition (1614) of his poem 'A Wife', and the full title reads '*A Wife, now the Widdow of Sir Thomas Overburye, Being a most exquisite and singular Poem of the choice of a Wife. Whereunto are added many witty Characters, and conceited Newes written by himselfe, and other learned Gentlemen his friends.*'

The characters that follow are less concerned with abstract moralizing than those of Bishop Hall; they contain promising ideas: a French cook, an ostler, a country gentleman, and so on. Overbury's 'Milkmaid' became one of the most famous of characters. He has an eye for visual peculiarities; sometimes he expresses ideals of human behaviour, or attacks whole classes of people, but like others he is as much interested in showing off his style as anything else. In due course more character books followed. They range farther afield, moving on from human subjects to scenes such as 'An Inn', 'A Horse Race', 'A Country Fair'. The best are fresh and amusing, but one grows weary of the crackle of wit and the way in which almost the same character is bandied about from book to book.

One of the best of the character books was *Micro-cosmographie: or, a Peece of the World Discovered in Essayes and Characters*, 1628, by John Earle. Earle was chaplain to Charles I, went into exile during the Commonwealth, and after the Restoration became Bishop of Worcester and Salisbury. He, also, is a practical moralist, but his characters have more human solidity than the abstractions of Bishop Hall, or the characters in such pieces as Overbury's idealized 'Milkmaid'. Here is part of his picture of 'A Meere Young Gentleman of the Universitie':

His father sent him thither, because hee heard there were the best Fencing and Dancing Schooles, from there he has his Education; from his Tutor the oversight. The first element of his knowledge is to be shewne the Colledges, and initiated in a Taverne by the way, which

hereafter hee will learn of himselfe. . . . His Studie has commonly hand-
some Shelves, his Bookes neat Silk strings, which he shewes to his
Father's man, and is loth to untie or take downe for fear of misplacing.
Upon foul days for recreation he retyres thither, and looks over the
prety booke his Tutor Reads to him, which is commonly some short
Historie or piece of Euphormio.

Upstarts who went to the university or who sought places at
court make a recurrent theme among the character writers,
illustrating the strange yet perpetual surprise of the English at the
fact that people can and do by their own efforts rise to wealth
and social position. Every age seems to think such achievement
is something quite new.

Clearly the translation of Theophrastus had a marked effect on
character writing, and such that one regrets that no one had
translated the fifteenth idyll of Theocritus with its sympathetic
characterization and 'subtle psychological understanding'. The
characters at this time remain entirely static, like so many wax-
works. Yet they are distant cousins of the short story and they
convey a great many pictures of contemporary life.

III

Character writings were not always clearly marked off from
essays; a typical title is *Essays and Characters of a Prison and
Prisoners*, a book by Geoffrey Mynshal, published in 1618. The
well-known essay-writers of the end of the seventeenth century,
such as Sir William Temple, at times verged towards character
writing, just as the character essay in its turn was to move towards fiction. H. S. Canby points out that *The Gentleman's
Journal*, a monthly magazine which appeared from 1691 to 1694,
carried regularly 'novels' of a few pages in length, which were in
effect short stories of contemporary life. Some were told partly in
verse or were joined on to a poem or small disquisition; one was
sent with some verses and 'with two goldfinches to a Lady that
played finely upon the Guitar'.

A fairly full quotation from one story in the first number,
January 1691, 'The Vain-glorious Citt; or The Stock Jobber'
will illustrate their nature more effectively than analysis: it has

very slight claims to be literature, but it shows most interestingly a 'character' turning into a story.

About Thirty Miles from Augusta are some Wells where the presence of a Princess, no less eminent by a Thousand Accomplishments, than by her Birth, draws most of the Court and Gentry every Summer. The goodness of the Air, and the agreeable ways of living there, contribute not a little to the Recovery of those who seek their health in the mineral Waters. . . .

Every day ushered in some Comical Adventure: And indeed where the Flower of both Sexes is, it is morally impossible there should be no Action; as between two Armies that seek each other. . . . To this place the Ambition of a certain Citizen brought him: Fortune had lately met him on the way, and her blindness hindring her from knowing him, whom but lately before she had used very scurvily, she fell into his hands, tho' to say the truth, this was but a just return to one who uses to sacrifice all to her, and who, High Gamester-like, running at all, will venture you his all at the modern Trade, or rather Game, called Stoc-Jobbing; which being something new among us, I hope it will not be improper to describe to you. Some Trades are managed by Companies; that is to say, by a Joynt-Stock. Now supposing that a Man hath put an hundred pounds into this Stock at the first Establishment, and find that his profit is greater, than if he had put out his money to use, this may occasion another to offer him two hundred pounds for his hundred, in hopes to sell it for more. But often the price suddenly falls very low, and thus prodigious Sums are won and lost in a very short time. Considerable Wagers are laid about the Stock's Rise or Fall, and hedged in by the craftier sort. False News are spread, Letters and Expresses feigned, and Agents employed to buy at a low price.

The story comes to an end, almost before it begins, with the failure of the Citt (another upstart), and the loss of his money, together with his hopes of a place in the world of fashion. Yet this brief form is a departure; so is the working of a story round new documentary information in place of the stale paraphernalia of amorous intrigue.

As character writing died out, it was the essayists who took the next clear step towards modern fiction. In the first place,

Addison and Steele followed the lead given by Dryden in develop-
ing a graceful prose that was suited to accounts of everyday life.
Defoe had his own equally clear though more homely style.
Addison and Steele in the *Spectator* and *Tatler*, and Defoe in his
Journal, are for ever on the verge of stories. Yet their declared
object is not to create fiction but to discuss moral ideas.

Very early in the *Tatler* series, in no. 23 (2 June 1709), for
example, Steele approaches the short-story form. We see a
husband dealing with a difficult wife, this time a petulant *malade
imaginaire*. This story makes an interesting contrast with the
coarse-natured and even brutal husband-and-wife stories of
Barnabe Rich. The lady completely dominates her first husband
by her pretended convulsions. Her husband dies and she re-
marries. One can hardly believe that the new husband's quiet
method of calling his wife's bluff really worked, but we are not
asked to laugh at brutality or cuckolding. The mood is altogether
more affectionate, though there is still an air of polite amusement.
We are given, in fact, a compressed version of the kind of scenes
and situations that Goldsmith was to work into social comedy.

As soon as the essayists began to invent individual people
rather than characters, and give them ordinary modern names,
they at once gave them a more vivid human life. In the course of
writing the *Spectator* essays the authors invented not just 'a
country Knight' but that very particular and special old gentleman Sir Roger de Coverley, with his group of sharply depicted
country friends. We meet Sir Roger at home; we go riding off to
the court where he sits as a magistrate; we make a trip to see an old
woman reputed to be a witch, whom Sir Roger treats with en-
lightenment. Here, then, is a living contemporary character, unforced, undramatized, and moving through a number of simple,
self-contained incidents that could well form short stories. Essay
no. 116, for instance, takes us for a day's hunting with Sir Roger's
harriers. The country scene is delightfully set, with a gentle
narrative movement, and a humorous unexpected ending, when
Sir Roger steps in, rescues the cornered hare, and has the hounds
called off: a most mellow picture of the English countryside and
of Sir Roger's nature. (Incidentally, this number of the *Spectator*

was not written by Steele or Addison, but by Budgell.) As a story it is a great advance on 'The Vainglorious Citt'. It is short by nature, rather than by compression, for it is contained in a single scene, and it has almost broken away from the essay and the moral.

The *Spectator* and *Tatler* essays also include a good many short stories that were more deliberately presented as stories, and as a rule they are told simply to illustrate moral ideas, as in *Spectator*, no. 123, dealing with lack of education:

This makes me often think of a story I have heard of two Friends, which I shall give my reader at large, under feigned Names. The Moral of it may, I hope, be useful though there are some circumstances which make it appear rather like a Novel than a true Story.

This is still the old art of the apologue, the narrator personally vouching for the truth of the story even if it seems like fiction and then assuring us it has a moral purpose. Nevertheless, stories were pushing their way up for their own sake and Hawkesworth writes in the fourth number of *The Adventurer* (14 November 1752):

. . . although formed upon a single incident, if that incident be sufficiently uncommon to gratify curiosity, and sufficiently interesting to engage the passions, may afford an entertainment, which, if it is not lasting, is yet of the highest kind . . . but it should be remembered, that it is much more difficult and laborious, to invent a story, however simple and however short, than to recollect topics of instruction, or to remark the scenes of life as they are shifted before us.

It certainly is; and the creative difference between the pure story and the story that is forcing a moral was never pinned down more clearly than in this somewhat unexpected eighteenth-century tribute to story-writers.

Other magazines followed, such as the *Ladies Spectator*, and presently a graceful invention came out of the urge to moralize in story form—the 'oriental' tale. This is really the form given by the age of reason to the medieval beast fable. Stories are set in imaginary lands called China, Persia, or Abyssinia, and we have short-story versions of the longer oriental tales such as 'Rasselas' or 'Vathek'. Often the richness of the setting, the inventions, and descriptions are delightful pieces of chinoiserie, but the various grand viziers, princes, and philosophers who people the stories are little more than abstract notions.

Goldsmith remarked that an oriental tale should be 'sonorous, lofty, musical and unmeaning'—and he himself wrote some letters from an imaginary Chinaman in London. These were afterwards reprinted as *The Citizen of the World*, and they are in their way a reversal of Goldsmith's own recipe for the oriental story. Instead of the story having an oriental setting, the Chinaman describes the English scene with an air of fresh surprise. The best known is probably the very human tale of the old one-legged soldier, who has had many misfortunes, and very little recompense, but is, in spite of all his troubles, a true-blue Englishman. 'I will for ever,' he says, 'love liberty and old England.'

The oriental tale of the richly ornamented kind survives in Meredith's 'Shaving of Shagpat', written in the nineteenth century, and in Ernest Bramah's books about 'Kai Lung', written in the twentieth century.

IV

Meanwhile the author who really could practise fiction in short form for its own sake was Defoe. Defoe's great contribution was his gift for building complete verisimilitude with quiet authentic touches. He absorbs the factual information into the story, in a way that the author of 'The Vain-glorious Citt' did not know how to do. His object was to make Robinson Crusoe, or Mrs. Veal, tangible. He takes you through their actions minute by minute with the authenticity of a 'log-book' as Lamb points out. Defoe employs his apparently guileless craft with the cunning of a serpent and at times one does not know whether he is writing fiction or reporting fact. There is a link between Defoe and some of the Kipling or Maugham techniques.

Early among his voluminous works are, unexpectedly enough, several short ghost stories. If Defoe had been alive today I think he would use the word 'para-sensory' rather than ghostly; but whatever one calls it, 'A True relation of the apparition of one

Mrs. Veal . . . to one Mrs. Bargrave' (1706) is a remarkable story
and attained considerable fame. It tells how Mrs. Veal came to see
her friend Mrs. Bargrave. They talked of family affairs; they
exchanged normal pieces of information; dress was noted. All
this is done with utter conviction, indeed at times with the
assumption of a slightly clumsy air. 'I forgot to mention . . .' and
so on. The point is that Mrs. Veal was dead at the time of the
interview. Mrs. Bargrave did not know this and the visit seemed
to her to be absolutely natural, and unfrightening.

Mrs. Bargrave asked her, whether she would not drink some tea. Says
Mrs. Veal, 'I do not care if I do; but I'll warrant this mad fellow
(meaning Mrs. Bargrave's husband,) has broke all your trinkets.'
'But,' says Mrs. Bargrave, 'I'll get something to drink in for all that.'
But Mrs. Veal waived it, and said 'It is no matter; let it alone'; and so it
passed.
    All the time I sat with Mrs. Bargrave, which was some hours, she
recollected fresh sayings of Mrs. Veal. And one material thing more she
told Mrs. Bargrave, that old Mr. Breton allowed Mrs. Veal ten pounds
a year, which was a secret, and unknown to Mrs. Bargrave till Mrs.
Veal told her.

Now such a common-sense housewife of a ghost is extremely
rare, and the story had a curious sequel. It was often praised by
nineteenth-century critics as an early example of Defoe's art of
verisimilitude. It was supposed that he had invented the story to
make a kind of advertisement for another man's book. However,
it was later discovered that the story of Mrs. Veal was, in fact, a
report, and a very careful account based on current evidence. The
point about the modest style, however, remains. Gone for ever,
one might feel, is the need to indulge in rhodomantade in the face
of queer happenings; and gone it was until the writers of the
'horrid' and 'Gothick' school arrived a hundred years or so
later.

V

Defoe's contributions to the short story were not followed up
in succeeding years. When the fictional element in the essay-
writers broke away from the essay, it developed into the novel

rather than the short story: Sir Roger de Coverley and his circle of friends, for example, are always given a place of importance in the emergence of the novel. It still seemed that the short story could not stand on its own.

By the end of the eighteenth century, however, the essay was at length drifting away from its painstakingly expository purpose. Charles Lamb and Leigh Hunt were both more interested in depicting scenes and people than in telling how they ought to have behaved, and Lamb at times brings single essays very near to short stories. 'Dream Children', which appears among the *Essays of Elia*, has often been anthologized in books of stories. In this famous essay an elderly bachelor designated as 'I' is sitting in his armchair, and in a half-waking, half-dreaming reverie, he conceives that he married a girl whom he had loved years ago but who had in fact refused him. In his dream the lady is dead, as she is in fact dead in real life, but two children, a boy and a girl, remain with him. Now these dream children are in the room with him, and they are just beginning to be old enough to understand some of his memories of their dead mother. The children are a dream, but the memories are real.

This, surely, is a story rather than an essay, and though it all takes place within a dozing hour, it has narrative movement, and the entries and re-entries, between the present moment and changing points in the past, are most subtly managed. Katherine Mansfield's 'The Daughters of the late Colonel' is not at all similar in situation, but both stories deal with the fancied presence and influence of a dead person, and the technique of the time movement is worth comparing. To call them 'flashbacks' in either story seems too crude a term; that Charles Lamb has caught the most delicate method of moving on different planes of time is unquestionable. As Katherine Mansfield herself once noted, 'It is all a matter of time levels'.

It might be objected that 'Dream Children' is sentimental, and the modern taste for the bitter joke might prefer an indigestion dream of a disastrous marriage, unpleasant children, and an awakening into a happy release. But to celebrate being an old bachelor is not to celebrate very much, and one of the best points about 'Dream Children' is that the awakening is an astringent. The dream children vanish: the dreamer faces reality with an abrupt laconic self-knowledge. We remember the mood of the Anglo-Saxon returning from exile; Sir Roger turning away from the slaughter of a hare; and other kindred spirits, whom we now see can be gentle and humorous in their stoicism.

Mario Praz in *The Decline of the Hero* calls 'Dream Children' Lamb's masterpiece, and for an extremely interesting reason. He is thinking not so much of the movement of the essay towards the short story but rather of the evocation by 'Dream Children' of a still moment of time, a tranquil vision seen amidst the cataract of confused passing moments: the clear drop of water, in which one begins to perceive the ocean. Mario Praz is concerned at this point in his work with genre painting, and he draws a distinction between the art of Vermeer exemplified in the pellucid quality of 'The Lady at the Virginals' and the crowded incidents of some of the later genre painters. Vermeer, and in a rather different way, Chardin, have in their apparent simplicity an insight that is free from any kind of 'committed content'. The pre-Raphaelites, on the other hand, Praz maintains, tend to load the moment that they select, as in the 'Awakened Conscience', with too much deliberate intention.

If the comparison holds good, and Charles Lamb's reverie can be likened to the clear light of 'The Lady at the Virginals', then 'Dream Children' resembles Katherine Mansfield's art more closely than might be thought and must be one of the first pieces in the language to convey the significant depths of many years of life in a few quiet pages of prose fiction. In fact, Mario Praz notes a resemblance between the subtle harmonies of Chardin and the work of Virginia Woolf or Proust.[2]

Once again we see the essay turning into the short story almost by chance. Charles Lamb said in 'Mackerye End' that narrative 'teased him' and the essay was his chosen form, and it is interesting that when he tried his hand at the art of story-telling, he gives us not a short story but a rather undistinguished condensed

[2] Mario Praz, *La Crisi Dell'Eroe Nel Romanzo Vittoriano* (Sansoni, Florence, 1952), Introduction and p. 70.

novel with far too many digressions and twists, as in 'Rosamund Gray' or 'Old Blind Margaret'.

Both Charles Lamb, however, and his sister Mary wrote some short stories, and *Mrs. Leicester's School* is, for the date, an interesting little book in which girls tell stories about themselves. The stories are intended for young people, but to put oneself sincerely and not whimsically into the world of a child is often a good approach to a short story. These stories have a welcome lightness of touch. In 'The Witch Aunt', for example, we hear of a small girl who simply could not resist the notion that her kindly old aunt turned into a witch by night—a genuine short-story situation.

So we approach the modern short story which, during the mid-nineteenth century, was to develop more rapidly in some other countries than in England. By this time some of the greatest classics of the English novel had already been written. If, however, we ask ourselves where are the short stories that correspond to a single incident, to a chapter of, say, Jane Austen, the answer is that they do not exist; Mary Russell Mitford probably comes as near as anyone to achieving this result, but much development is yet needed. It would be fascinating to take one unified incident out of Jane Austen, and to consider it as a short story written with modern technique. That famous picnic, for instance, in which Emma, by indulging her own wit, insults defenceless Miss Bates, and is then rebuked by the man she is eventually to marry. This one scene could well be the basis of a short story: and the creative spirit could safely have handed it over to Elizabeth Bowen, who would have given it colour, speed, and acute social observation; and would have left in our mind brilliantly hinted suggestions of Emma's final yet distant yielding to Mr. Knightly. This, however, and others that it would be a delight to imagine, are only dream stories. The various streams that had been drawing together during centuries to make the modern art of the short story had by no means completed their course.

VIII

Frank Moralizing
and Gothic Emotion

As an appetite for reading had from various causes been increasing among the inferior ranks, it was judged expedient at this critical period to supply such wholesome aliment as might give a new direction to the public taste, and abate the relish for those corrupt and impious publications which the consequences of the French Revolution have been fatally pouring upon us. . . . And as these stories, though *principally*, are not adapted *exclusively* to the inferior classes they are here presented to the public in an enlarged and improved form.[1]

So writes the redoubtable Hannah More, frankly stating that her stories are written for moral purposes. They owe their existence to their intention to reform and instruct, and they were originally printed over the signature 'z' among the immensely popular *Repository Tracts*. Millions of these were sold. Hannah More, somewhat forgotten now, was in her lifetime a blazing portent of international fame. Coming more or less unknown and unintroduced from Bristol to London, she rapidly became the friend, and probably mistress, of Garrick, friend of Dr. Johnson and Sir Joshua Reynolds, author of famous tragedies and poems, and a star of the first magnitude at blue-stocking parties. It would be attractive to examine at greater length than is possible here the many gifts that she brought to the stories written in her middle age.

Nobody ever wrote moral tales with a greater zest or with a message made more plain than Hannah More; but the interesting point for the date is that they are stories, not essays. They are

[1] Hannah More, *Works* (T. Cadell, 1830), vol. III, Advertisement.

stories with a moral, not morals with a story. Also, they deal in a simple, straightforward way with working-class lives: post-boys, orange girls, footmen, farmers, and well-to-do tradesmen. As H. S. Canby says, she 'harks back to Defoe and forward to Dickens'. For all her pre-eminence with the intellectuals, Hannah More seems to understand and sympathize with the working people about whom she writes. Here are the opening paragraphs of *Betty Brown, the Orange Girl*:

Betty Brown, the Orange Girl, was born nobody knows where, and bred nobody knows how. No girl in all the streets of London could drive a barrow more nimbly, avoid pushing passengers more dexterously, or cry her 'Fine China Oranges' in a shriller voice. But then she could neither sew, nor spin, nor knit, nor wash, nor iron, nor read, nor spell . . .

The longest thing Betty can remember is, that she used to crawl up out of a night cellar, stroll about the streets, and pick cinders from the scavengers' carts. Among the ashes she sometimes found some ragged gauze and dirty ribands: with these she used to dizzen herself out, and join the merry bands on the first of May.[2]

The story tells how Betty, a cheerful, good-natured, healthy, but utterly ignorant girl, contrives to rise to the height of her own juvenile ambition, by becoming an orange girl with a barrow; but in so doing she falls entirely into the hands of Mrs. Sponge, who is a money lender and a fence. Mrs. Sponge takes all her profits from her in the form of exorbitant interest, and supplies her with a hot supper and a bedroom, shared with other girls. She also encourages her to drink gin, and pass bad sixpences.

Betty's natural bounce and good spirits keep her going, and she even looks on Mrs. Sponge as a benefactress. Hannah More guides us through these Hogarthian scenes with a cheerful bustle, for Betty is not really having too bad a time.

One day Betty talks to a lady who wants a special order of oranges, and this lady explains to Betty how she is being robbed by Mrs. Sponge, which she can at first hardly understand. Gradually, however, she manages to break away from Mrs. Sponge, and takes to porter instead of gin, buys herself some

[2] More, *Works*, vol. IV.

better clothes, and manages to save a little money. Further help, including a regular Sunday dinner, are given to Betty on the condition that she should go to church. She begins to receive religious instruction.

The Christian story, the Commandments of God, the sacrifice of Christ, are absolutely new to Betty. As she learns, she is extremely moved. She responds on the deepest level, and takes up her life as a convinced Christian. Betty has now learnt among other things that there is not merely civil wrongdoing, there is also sin; and her profound acceptance of this may be compared with Somerset Maugham's ironical reference to the missionary's wife in 'Rain' who complained that it was 'so hard to give the natives a sense of sin'.

To say that Hannah More's stories are old-fashioned in their outspoken religious teaching is to put it mildly: but they avoid the odious sanctimony of many later stories. The people who move through her pages are saved not merely from sin but from the real horrors of Gin Lane, and are sent to the tangible welfare of Beer Street. Of course, everything works out far too completely. Betty Brown ends up comfortably, keeping a sausage shop and married to a hackney coachman. The good are rewarded materially, the really bad pass through the hell of eighteenth-century squalor and punishment. Well-to-do benefactors pop up in the nick of time.

Hard on the heels of Hannah More, in time and in purpose, comes Maria Edgeworth, and what Hannah More began to do, Maria Edgeworth carries out with greater artistry. Though she is still apt to conceive that the main purpose of a short story is to illustrate a moral, she gives us far more story and far less moral. She shows us a far greater variety of life and people, and her situations, scene-setting, and dialogue are all in advance of the work of Hannah More. The *Moral Tales* (1801), the *Popular Tales* (1804), and others have qualities of natural characterization that are remarkable among short stories of this date. Remarkable too is the amount of documentary knowledge of trades and crafts that is absorbed without fuss into her narrative. Furthermore, the stories are often truly short and unified incidents.

To return after many years to the straightforward simplicities of Maria Edgeworth's stories is to find them better than one had expected. This is what Thackeray's daughter, Lady Ritchie, once wrote of them:

The stories are interesting and suggestive: they take one out of morbid preoccupations into the fresh air—into the fields and cottage gardens. One can almost see the apple trees growing, the flowers in bloom, the crops waving in plenty, the sleek cattle grazing or driven by the farmer. . . . It has been a real surprise to the writer of this essay, on re-reading some of those scenes of scenery and adventure, which she had not looked at for years, to find that details she had imagined spread over much space and print are all contained in a few sentences.[3]

It is true that many things in Maria Edgeworth's stories happen far too neatly. If a little leather purse is unobtrusively lost, as in 'The Limerick Gloves', it is not lost because of the confusion of its owner. It will turn up later as part of the plot. Everything is tied in bows. The style abounds in wise saws: 'Waste not, want not', 'Out of debt, out of danger', which are both titles of stories; or more homely and amusing sayings such as 'The smith that will meddle with all things may go shoe the goslings.'

At times the comic traits of the characters are overplayed; at times the morals are too relentlessly rubbed in as in 'Out of Debt, out of Danger'. This is the story of a foolish and showy young couple, who live beyond their means and are altogether too fear-somely punished. The husband is tempted by his debts into passing bad notes, and the wife brings about his arrest and execution by breaking into his desk because she cannot wait for money; and having lost her husband, she also loses her looks, because a beauty preparation injures her skin. It is not often, however, that Maria Edgeworth carries affairs to these extremes, and for the most part her stories move in a world of common-sense reality.

At the time she wrote, people were often apt to suppose, as some still do, that short stories which were on the face of them simple could not really be of interest to the learned or the clever. Maria Edgeworth's rather trying father, who apparently used to

[3] Introduction to Maria Edgeworth's *Popular Tales* (Macmillan, 1895).

'hot up' the preaching side of his daughter's stories, explains in his Preface to the 1856 edition of *Popular Tales* 'The title of *Popular Tales* has been chosen, not as a presumptuous and premature claim to popularity, but from the wish that they may be current beyond circles, which are sometimes exclusively considered as polite.'

Some of her stories—the *Moral Tales* and *The Parent's Assistant*, for instance—are intended for children, and I am glad that I was born at a time when they were still to be found on the shelves of great aunts and grandmothers in spite of their alarming titles. It needed no experience to see the difference between those stories that allowed the moral point to browbeat the characters, and those which had sufficient life and truth as stories to make the moral innocuous. If the story lives, one can from a very early age draw one's own moral, and neglect the author's. There is, however, a certain modesty about the moralizing of Maria Edgeworth. She is referring only to the accepted moral teaching of the day; and she includes the moral as a necessary part of the craftsman's art in story-telling. She nowhere sets up as an amateur prophet with notions of her own.

There is a good deal to be said for the better children's writers of this time, though the worst are appalling in their self-righteous absurdity and even cruelty. If we turn to the short story as it was being written for more fashionable tastes, we find vapourings and absurdity—Gothic and the Romantic—the heroine of unworldly beauty and of amazing sufferings. Here is a sample.

Thus passed away her early youth in sorrow: she grew up in tears, a stranger to the amusements of youth and its more delightful schemes and imaginations. She was not however unhappy: she attributed indeed no merit to herself for her virtues, but for that reason the more were they her reward.

The peace which passeth all understanding disclosed itself in all her looks and movements. It lay in her countenance, like a steady unshadowed moonlight: and her voice, which was at once naturally sweet and subtle, came from her like the flute tones of a masterly performer, which still floating at some uncertain distance, seem to be created by the player rather than to proceed from the instrument.

This curious passage comes from Coleridge. The heroine of his story is Maria Schöning, and he insists, as so many narrators do, that the story is a true one, although it may seem incredible.

I can scarce summon the courage to tell what I scarce know whether I ought to tell. Were I composing a tale of fiction the reader might justly suspect the purity of my own heart, and most certainly would have abundant right to resent such an incident, as an outrage wantonly offered to his imagination.

Maria Schöning has spent the years of her youth looking after her diseased father. As soon as he dies, the tax officials descend on his house and seize it and all his property for arrears of taxes. Utterly destitute and friendless, Maria wanders about, and sits on her father's grave in the evening light, where, as far as one can gather from Coleridge's vague remarks about churchyards at night, she is raped. This is only a beginning. Maria and Harlin, an equally ill-used friend, go from misery to misery. Maria, now half crazy, confesses to destroying a baby, which she never had. Harlin is condemned as an accomplice. The double execution is delayed by an agonizing wait for a reprieve which never comes. Harlin is executed. The crowd shrieks. The executioner faints; and Maria dies before the sword can be wielded again.

One must believe that Coleridge wrote this in all sincerity. He was not a man to churn out penny-dreadful pot-boilers, and he breaks in on the narrative once or twice to tell the reader how very much it is moving him. Yet to convey all this wild suffering, with its half-demented idiot saint of a heroine, its numerous turns and twists of event, and its final horrific scene, in a few pages of overblown narration is just transcendental bathos. There is practically no visual scene-setting, no direct conversation; all that Coleridge's poetic genius told him to do in *Christabel*, helped by the old ballad models, deserted him in the presence of a short prose story.

Where Coleridge failed, a great many lesser writers were to fail also. The pages of the magazines and annuals of this period have endless examples of stories of an almost incredible degree of silliness, the lost snippings of the romantic imagination. Even such a distinguished name as Mary Shelley cannot raise them very high. These stories run riot with brigands who have noble minds, and noblemen who have brigands' minds; with lovers united in 'lambent' moonlight or parted in thunderstorms 'as wild and pitiless as ever pelted on a human head'; and with heroines who are falsely imprisoned, wrongfully accused, captured by bandits, clapped into convents, and 'almost cease to respire' when they are shown 'horrid instruments of torture'. All this can be had either with or without ghosts.

These stories, however, foolish as they are, have certain points to their credit. In the first place they are not concerned with moralizing. Though the heroines are often full of pious exclamations and the villains have 'turned their backs on God', religion is not the concern of the writer. Tales of terror are not usually connected with any moral teaching. Such as they are, they exist simply for the sake of being stories. Moreover, they aim, however feebly, at a poetic intensity and concentration. Thus they play their small part in the 'Romantic Agony' and they lead directly towards the art of Edgar Allan Poe. In fact, by an astonishing feat of imagination, the burning glass of Poe's mind produced its haunting witch flames from a heap of this mouldering Gothic rubbish.

If any author succeeded in uniting the aesthetic leanings of the Romantic period with a short narrative that dealt with the ordinary scenes and events of human life, it was Mary Russell Mitford. She is very much alive to the delights or rigours of the country scene and she is a descriptive writer of poetic charm, even if the style of her country-side descriptions has been staled by custom. As far as her characters are concerned, Mary Russell Mitford keeps her feet firmly on the ground. She shows us the people she saw, and she shows the kind of incidents in their lives that make stories. Though her great ambition was to write tragedies, and she achieved more than a little success in doing so, she kept her ranging romantic themes, such as *Rienzi*, for Drury Lane, and she did not write bombastic or soulful short stories.

Her own life story is interesting. Although she had been brought up to be a well-to-do and fashionable young woman of her time, her spendthrift father threw away all the money that ever came near him; he was not even satisfied by winning a £20,000 lottery prize, with a ticket taken in Mary's name. That money went with the rest, and in the long run her parents were reduced to living in a very small house in the country, and Mary's earnings became the family's income. She tells us she was in a constant state of anxiety over money.

Out of these matter-of-fact difficulties came the long series on which her fame chiefly rests, *Our Village*. This began in *The Lady's Magazine* in 1819 and continued until five volumes were published in 1832. A freshness of atmosphere combined with an underlying sober reality form the general mood of these mixed essays, stories, and observations. Victorian taste was too apt to produce selections from *Our Village* that consisted entirely of embroidered country descriptions, with such titles as 'Nutting', 'The First Primrose', accompanied by refined or gently humorous wood-engravings. Yet *Our Village* also includes a number of genuine short stories, which have a sharp eye for character and unexpected situations; and although they may be discursive in the telling, they are free from moralizing. One, for instance, 'The Fresh Water Fisherman', leads in from a general description of Berkshire waterways to tell of the utterly surprising yet happy marriage of a very rough and unkempt water bailiff, to Laurette, the dainty, immaculate French lady's maid at The Park. Another story tells of Hannah Bint, who, when she was little more than a child, had had to face the difficulties of supporting a crippled father who had been forced to give up his work as a drover, and was apt to tipple away such money as came to him. Hannah very sensibly asked to be given, not money, but one cow, and by good management contrived over the course of years to build up a happy life and make a modest success out of this small beginning. Like 'The Fresh Water Fisherman', the story may not be of soul-shaking importance, but it has the ring of sincerity and truth. Simple as they seem, Mrs. Mitford's stories have their element of poetic insight, and they are on the verge of the modern short-story form. Elizabeth Barrett Browning coined a telling phrase when she called Mary Russell Mitford 'a prose Crabbe in the sun'.

All three of the remarkably gifted women whose work we have looked at in this chapter share certain qualities—secondary qualities, they might be called—that contribute to the effect and the form of what they are doing. The first is common sense, which kept them all three away from the excesses of Pecksniffian religiosity or Gothic horridness: there is plain common sense, which I think they all possessed, and also an artistic common sense, which is an ingredient of Jane Austen's work also.

It may also be said that they were in the best sense hard-bitten professional authors, who knew what they were about when they tackled short stories. Hannah More, a famous playwright moving in Dr. Johnson's circle, succeeded in using her talents in a form of simple yet effective narrative; Maria Edgeworth, almost a major novelist, has a sure and understanding touch for the simple limits of a few thousand words; and Mary Russell Mitford, whose gifts had run to successful romantic tragedies, saw the essential possibilities of the short story.

IX

Stories of Poets and Novelists

For generations, as we have seen in the last two chapters, various elements contributed in their turn to the development of story-writing; yet none approached very closely to the modern idea of the short story.

The character writings turn the attention from far-fetched romances to ordinary people. They remain static, yet even their static nature contributes something to the idea of a unity of purpose, and a centre of human interest rather than a chain of events. In due course they develop into the essay rather than the short story. The essayists make use of embryonic short stories to illustrate their moral points, but while the fictional element in the essays escapes into the wider scope of the novel, the essay keeps a firm grip on the short story, seen simply as part of an essay.

The genius of Lamb brings the essay itself to the verge of the short story. Yet this is done almost by chance. The authors discussed in the last chapter show a more conscious attempt to conceive a short story for its own sake, and in Mary Russell Mitford's 'The Fresh Water Fisherman' we can see how different elements have been brought together. The discursive essay on the byways of rivers, with which the author begins, is followed by the 'character' descriptions of 'A Water-Bailiff' and 'A French Lady's Maid'. Together they generate a narrative movement and turn into a story. The result is something completely different from the novelle of the Renaissance.

Another pervasive element has also entered into the story. That is a lyric freshness which is to be found not only in the country scenes but in the very conception of the story. Throughout the eighteenth century the short story had belonged very much to the world of prose. The essayists were in the best sense prose writers, and the novel was essentially a prose form—'a comic epic in prose', as Fielding said of *Tom Jones*. When a short story had a true concentration of theme, intensity of feeling, and a vivid eye for the living scene, it was usually conceived and regarded as a poem. People did not think of writing such things in prose. They had been seen for centuries in the form of ballads, with their close links with the story that is chanted and heard by an audience, rather than read.

As we have seen, the poetic emotions of the Romantic revival failed to combine themselves to any good effect with the short-story form in England, although they became the elements of Poe's transmuting art. In the next two or three decades of the nineteenth century in England, short stories were either the minor production of novelists, who did not as a rule think of the short story as a separate form needing its own kind of concentration, or else they were seen as poems. In this way the short story in prose form continued to remain fully and completely prosaic, while the poetic element in the short story became fully poetic, and was expressed in verse.

It was pointed out in chapter VII that it was unthinkable that some of the poetic insights of the seventeenth century, the heightened vision of Traherne or Marvell, should have been conceived in the form of short stories. Yet there could be a short-story vision—a vision of people—latent in such poetry, as well as the kind of reflective nature mysticism that was later developed by Wordsworth.

Meanwhile, as the short story emerged it was anything but a butterfly. 'The Vain-glorious Citt' is a grub of Grub Street. Nothing could be farther from Marvell's 'What wondrous life is this I lead' than this bankrupt stock-jobber. Moralizing conceptions of the short story in the eighteenth century continued by way of prose. Some earlier poems of Wordsworth were short-story conceptions, and the trouble sometimes is that they were over-consciously poeticized. 'The Leech Gatherer', however, and some others are approaching short stories, and are nearer the conception of a modern short story than the poetic romances of

Byron, such as 'The Giaour' and 'The Corsair', or some of Wordsworth's own narrative poems.

The story which is a professed poem is a subject in itself. Tennyson and Browning, Coventry Patmore and T. E. Brown, John Masefield, and others were all to explore themes which make poetic novels rather than short stories. On the other hand, some of Browning's shorter poems, such as 'Dramatis Personae', and some of Hardy's short poems come far closer to the modern idea of the short story than do many prose short stories written at the same date. 'My Last Duchess' is a famous poem, but if Browning had been a generation younger it might just as well have become a famous short story. All the implications of the sinister character of the Duke and of the situation revealed in a single scene are conveyed by the organic conception of the story itself, not by the surface of poetic language, nor by a narrator's comments. Another short story perfectly expressed as a poem is Hardy's 'The Tramp Woman's Tragedy'. Here there is a narrative movement, a mounting tension towards a moment of violence and tragedy, and then a haunting memory that glances back through the planes of time.

A good deal of the emotional effect of this poem is conveyed by Hardy's modern use of the form of an old ballad. The repetition of the heavy-sounding refrain should ensure slow reading— chanting to oneself. This story-poem in fact belongs partly to the old sung or chanted form of the story. The ballad indeed has played its own vital and interesting part in the development of the short story, and during centuries in which prose stories were developing in their looser discursive ways, many famous ballads were providing perfect examples of rigorous dramatic form, and of a style of narration far too austere to sermonize or explain. The ballad form had, however, been declining during many generations as the printed book gradually supplanted the ballad singers.

A major novelist who wrote a small number of short stories was Scott. 'The Two Drovers' is a moving and unhappy story of Highland pride leading to a tragic and unnecessary killing. It is the kind of conception that Hardy was to use in short-story form some fifty years later. Yet with Scott it still illustrates the idea that a printed story ought to arise within the framework of an essay. Scott occupies about 2,000 words at the beginning with a discussion of the kind of lives led by the Scottish drovers; yet when the story comes, it dramatizes creatively all that Scott has to tell us in essay form. Scott also told one or two ghost stories. We noticed in chapter I how he tells us at the beginning of 'The Tapestried Chamber' that a ghost story really ought to be told round a winter fireside, rather than be 'committed' to print, and here he in fact hankers for the spoken rather than the written story. In 'Wandering Willie's Tale' in *Redgauntlet* he again gives us a splendid yarn, told in broad Scots. It tells of a visit to departed spirits or demons, who seem to have an ancestral relationship to the devils in Stevenson's 'Thrawn Janet' and John Buchan's 'Journey of Little Profit'.

For over a century the main strength of the writers of creative fiction had been given to the novel, and we are already approaching the world of Dickens, Thackeray, the Brontës, and George Eliot. The whole way of conceiving the classic English novels of the eighteenth and nineteenth centuries worked against brevity, and the natural gifts of the authors consisted partly in their sheer volubility. Thackeray, especially, carried the essay-writing style over into the novel. Neither Dickens nor Thackeray are usually thought of as contributing towards a modern conception of the short story, and at times they seem never to have noticed the development of technique that had already been accomplished across the Atlantic. Yet it is interesting to see what these two great novelists could do on occasion, in conveying the essence of their genius in brief.

When Thackeray is at his best there is plenty of good reading in his minor pieces. He carries on the art of social discussion, in rather a more personal style than that of the eighteenth-century essayist, and he is frequently on the verge of stories; he is for ever, as it were, throwing off sketches for stories. Here and there, yet very seldom, one finds a narrative sufficiently unified and concentrated to be thought of as a short story, such as 'Dennis Haggerty's Wife'. This is a story of considerable power, and when we reach the end, even of passion. It is a remarkable example of Thackeray in miniature, and also a typical novelist's short story. It covers many years in narrative form, but it selects with great skill those few scenes that cover a single theme in a man's life. It is a narrator's story, told by Fitzboodle; the tone gradually grows more grave, more disillusioned as it draws to its final tragedy, and the half-comic style of Fitzboodle with which the story begins, ends with the passionate seriousness of Thackeray himself. The skill with which Thackeray tells us this story through a coarse-grained and worldly narrator is a typical example of his intricate yet easy-looking art.

Another typical Thackeray story in a purely light-hearted vein is 'A Little Dinner in Bittlestone Street' from the *Book of Snobs*. Here we see the customary free-flowing chat passing into a short narrative, in which a briefless young barrister entertains a rich and pompous elderly friend to dinner, and wilfully overplays the poverty in which he and his wife are supposed to be living.

While Thackeray seems to happen upon short stories almost by chance, Dickens sets out more deliberately to produce them. He took his Christmas books very seriously, and gave them his full creative energy. He often links several stories together; in 'Somebody's Luggage', for instance, the various stories are found in the luggage of an aspiring writer who has left his bags at an hotel. The results of this kind of notion with its various divagations are often pure Dickens, though they are seldom examples of the consciously controlled short story. In 'The Holly Tree', however, which has a magnificent description of a stage-coach battling its way through a snowstorm, there is a gem both of Dicken's art and of short-story writing. This is the story told by the Boots at the Holly Tree Inn—the story of a small boy and girl aged eight and nine who arrived at the inn by coach, and stayed the night, with the full intention of going on to Gretna Green to be married. The Boots is a kindly though sharp-edged character, a little like Sam Weller, and the result is a comically sentimental story, in which the sentimentality is kept in check by the Boots's sense of reality. 'On the whole,' Boots said, it had a tendency to make him feel he was in love himself, only he 'didn't exactly know who with'.

Occasionally Dickens's Christmas stories are complete and single long short stories. In 'Dr. Marigold's Prescriptions' Dickens tells us of a travelling tinker, who loses his own wife and child, and then adopts an ill-used deaf-and-dumb girl. He teaches her with infinite patience to read and write, and lives to see her married and the mother of a child who can speak normally. The story wanders, it is rampant with Dickens's melodrama and grotesquerie, yet the steps by which the child is taught are revealed with great insight, and the professional patter of Marigold, the tinker, is a *tour de force*. However, the main point is the sanity and patience of Marigold himself, who after terrible experiences and a hard lonely life still keeps his unwavering charity. This is the true popular heart of Dickens.

This certainly is not a genuinely short story, though it has a central unity of theme. There is a far shorter modern form of story embedded inside it, which A. E. Coppard or H. E. Bates might have written. Coppard at times has the power of combining the incongruities and even terrors of Dickens's stories with a simplicity characteristic of John Clare. Among writers of the present moment John Wain's story 'Death of the Hind Legs' shows a strong sympathy for the vivid human emotions that flower suddenly on stony ground. Dr. Marigold might well have walked into that crumbling small town theatre in Wain's story, and could certainly have entered into the wake party for the elderly actor who died on stage.

By the middle of the nineteenth century there is still no famous English author whom we can think of as a specialist in short stories. Mrs. Gaskell was another novelist of considerable stature who contributed short stories to the many magazines and annuals. However, in telling a short story she is apt to leave the quietly realistic vein of *Cranford* for rather melodramatic situations, such as that of a highwayman and murderer who leads the life of a country gentleman ('The Squire's Story') or the ghostly 'Old Nurse's Story' which has the spirit of a wounded child crying and trying to enter the house; a vision which seems to have links with *Wuthering Heights* and M. R. James's 'Lost Hearts'.

Trollope was another famous novelist who also wrote some

short stories, but 'Malachi's Cove' comes as a surprise from the author of the 'Barchester' novels. This story sets a rugged coastal scene near Tintagel, which is described with sharp clarity, and deals also with an unusual form of livelihood, that of collecting seaweed from the rocks, which is spread on the land for manure. The story moves among simple people struggling with natural forces, and the main character, Molly Trengloss, a small, tough young woman, seems very far away from a cathedral close. Trollope shows that he understood that such a scene and such people are likely to be better material for a short story than the more complicated and diffused social problems of the well-to-do. This is precisely the point emphasized to American writers by Sherwood Anderson.

Another remarkable phenomenon is a single short story, 'Rab and His Friends', by Dr. John Brown, author mainly of essays and scientific observations. This story tells of the illness and death of an elderly Scottish peasant woman, and the loving care of her dour husband, and Rab, her occasionally ferocious mastiff. Once again it is a story that seems almost to have been stumbled upon by an essay-writer, but it has the life of an intense yet simple feeling, and it is Rab himself, the mastiff, that gives a unity to its apparently rambling form.

Both 'Malachi's Cove' and 'Rab and His Friends' are unusual for their date in giving a short story a visual entity of its own, by picturing clearly one scene or small group of scenes. It is this unity of image and construction that strikes us when we turn to the work of Robert Louis Stevenson. In fact, in his first published short story, 'A Lodging for the Night', we feel that a new, clearer conception of the short-story form has arrived.

Meanwhile the short story had been steadily growing shorter.

X

Stevenson and Hardy: Two
on a Tower

Robert Louis Stevenson and Thomas Hardy are the leading short-story writers of the later nineteenth century. Stevenson could be called a specialist in the modern short story. He was highly conscious of the short-story form, and his work cannot be assessed without reference to his short stories, while Hardy's short stories are often overlooked. Stevenson, moreover, precedes Hardy as a short-story writer. Although he was born twenty years later than Hardy, his first book of short stories, *The New Arabian Nights* (1882), was published before Hardy's first collection, *Wessex Tales* (1888); and Hardy continued to write short stories after Stevenson was dead. Hardy's stories are a remarkable contrast to those of Stevenson, but both made an outstanding contribution to the English short story.

If our minds are fixed on contemporary themes and on the short story of the last thirty years, Stevenson now has an old-fashioned air. If, however, we think of the longer history of the short story we can see that he produced a brilliant, forward-looking version of the short-story form, the outcome of an original and flamboyant personality.

Stevenson in his day was a young writer with modern manners and mannerisms, and he aroused enthusiasm and even hero-worship. He had a brilliant gift for creating the reality of the moment, often a long-drawn and breathless moment. He is a fascinating word-spinner, often too much so. He has an intensity of vision which is usually more moral than aesthetic. There existed and in fact often raged within him the tensions of a man of action

H

frustrated by ill-health; a dissipated youth, checked by his own force of character as much as his family background; and the heightened feelings of the consumptive that he shared with Chekhov and Katherine Mansfield. He had a strange gift for dwelling on inner sleaziness and decay, which makes it surprising that sixty years ago he was often held up as an exemplar of manly attitudes.

As soon as we look at the best of his short stories in detail we find that we are no longer considering the antecedents of the short story, the eighteenth-century anecdote or the Elizabethan novella. Stevenson is a practitioner of the modern art of the short story. His early story, 'A Lodging for the Night', was almost a by-product of his research work on Villon, yet it shows him a born short-story writer, and in it his art is already at its best.

As the story opens, we see a bitterly cold winter night closing in on Paris in 1456. There is no personalized narrator; indeed, narration is almost completely absent. The necessary facts are slipped in and the scene is put before us with visual clarity. Stevenson weaves the story against the background of the darkened houses of the city, the mantle of snow, the bitter cold. We are introduced in the first paragraph to the poet Villon, who makes a joke about the angels moulting. He goes into a tavern with a splendid fire but dangerous company, some men gambling and a fat, disreputable monk.

A great pile of living embers diffused a strong and ruddy glow from the arched chimney. Before this straddled Dom Nicolas, the Picardy monk, with his skirts picked up and his fat legs bared to the comfortable warmth. His dilated shadow cut the room in half; and the firelight only escaped on either side of his broad person. . . . His face had the beery, bruised appearance of the continual drinker's; it was covered with a network of congested veins, purple in ordinary circumstances, but now pale violet, for even with his back to the fire the cold pinched him on the other side. . . . So he straddled, grumbling, and cut the room in half with the shadow of his portly frame.[1]

Villon is writing a ballade, helped by an admiring companion Tabary; a pity, perhaps, that Stevenson flourished this rather obvious decoration, but it is well done.

[1] In *New Arabian Nights* (Heinemann, 1923–4).

Then the story flares into violent action. A gambler knifes his opponent and kills him instantly. There develops one of those scenes of cold-blooded evil of which Stevenson has a wonderful understanding—the behaviour of thieves and murderers under their own self-generated tension. The murderer now goes through the dead man's possessions, and shares out the loot. Villon makes some forced jokes, then suddenly breaks down hysterically. While he sits with his face in his hands, the monk picks his pockets.

Villon now wanders about the deserted snowbound city. He dodges the watch and discovers that he has been robbed. He thinks of the wolves who have invaded the city and killed people on such nights as this. At last when he is beginning to fear he will not survive the dark hours he sees a light and is taken in by a courtly old white-bearded soldier, who happens to be alone in his house. He tells Villon he is the Sire de Brisetout, gives him food and wine, and puts him in front of a fire.

At first Villon is obsequious, but he soon perks up. He examines the gold plate with notions of theft. Then, growing bolder, he begins to criticize, to make sarcastic remarks about worldly success and honour. He compares soldiers to thieves, does some obvious and cheap debunking, and behaves like a very unpleasant and snarling angry young intellectual, slightly reminiscent of Jimmy Porter talking to his father-in-law. The old knight, without losing his temper, defends his position in simple terms; but finally he calls Villon a black-hearted rogue, and says his hospitality is now at an end.

The old man preceded him from a point of self-respect; Villon followed, whistling, with his thumbs in his girdle.

'God pity you,' said the lord of Brisetout at the door.

'Good-bye, papa,' returned Villon with a yawn. 'Many thanks for the cold mutton.'

The door closed behind him. The dawn was breaking over the white roofs. A chill, uncomfortable morning ushered in the day. Villon stood and heartily stretched himself in the middle of the road.

'A very dull old gentleman,' he thought. 'I wonder what his goblets may be worth.'

'A Lodging for the Night' takes place in one continuous scene. It has the striking visual unity of the snow-covered city of Paris at night, through which runs a certain coloured image that keeps recurring to Villon's mind; the murdered man's red hair. This impression of orange-red against the snow is heightened by the two firelight scenes, first in the tavern and then in the knight's house. Finally, the story is short in essence; though it conveys a great deal about the people and the night concerned, it has no feeling of compression.

'A Lodging for the Night' is frequently referred to as a master-piece of short-story writing. Judged on the most exacting level, the story is slow off the mark: there is a suggestion in the first two pages that we are listening to a mellifluous essay-writer, but this persona of Stevenson rapidly disappears: he tells us a few facts to set the story going. It is also a disadvantage that this is a historical short story set in a picturesque past, in a place and period already overworked in Stevenson's day, and taking for its main character a famous thief-poet, about whom readers are bound to have various preconceived ideas.

There is no question that the historical setting is beautifully handled. It is true that Villon was arrested for killing a monk in a brawl in 1426, and we may like to guess that this was the fat drunkard who robbed him in the story. It is true that Tabary was a friend of Villon and was associated with him in a robbery some years later. This is, however, simply the good craftsmanship of a historical fiction writer. It does not add to the poetical truth of the story. In fact, it conflicts with it. It moves it towards documentary interest, towards the story built round a clever idea, such as Anatole France's well-known picture of Pontius Pilate in retire-ment. The two levels of truth, fact and fiction, interfere with each other.

The overspill from Stevenson's historical studies gave him the material for another of his finest short stories—'The Sire de Malétroit's Door'. In this story the leading character is imaginary: or, if the young Monsieur Denis de Beaulieu aged two-and-twenty, and already an experienced campaigner, has any historical fact in him, it is too remote to matter. He appears before the reader simply as the hero of a newly created story.

In this story Denis de Beaulieu is spending the night in the town of Chateau Landon. The town is full of troops. Though Denis has a safe conduct, he feels it will be little use at night with a patrol of tipsy soldiers. He has the ill-luck to lose his way in almost pitch-darkness and hearing a patrol approaching, he shelters in a porch and presses himself against a door which swings open behind him. A moment later it swings back, shutting him inside.

He has in fact been caught in a strange trap: a trap which was meant for another man altogether—the man who had a secret assignment with Blanche, the niece and ward of the Sire de Malé-troit. The Sire has made this plan to capture the man who has been visiting his niece and then force him to marry her at once. In the presence of the old man the two young people are brought to-gether, and Blanche assures her uncle that de Beaulieu is the wrong man. The Sire regards this as a mere subterfuge, but says even if de Beaulieu is not the man he was seeking, Blanche has compromised her honour; they must marry before sunrise or de Beaulieu will be hung out of the window.

The main point of the story now unfolds. It consists of the moving scene in which these two young people of honour and dignity settle the matter, each preserving the finest scruples of care and courtesy for each other. Each refuses to accept a sacrifice, and they are both determined to sustain their ideals. Without this aristocracy of the spirit, the happy ending to the story would be quite meaningless. Perhaps it is far too romantic for the taste of the moment, but I agree with Sean O'Faolain, who finds it deeply moving and in his book *The Short Story* gives 'The Sire de Malétroit's Door' high praise.

If the story does not respond perfectly to the vital test 'Is it true?', the difficulty is not so much the plane of feeling but the improbable behaviour of the Sire de Malétroit. Yet the novelle stories, in Belleforest, in Cinthio, in Painter, are full of tricks and turns of this kind.

Stevenson has in fact investigated the inner truth of a situation that one might easily have found in *The Palace of Pleasure*: he may perhaps have found it in one of the Renaissance collections, for he refers to it as 'a true novel, in the old sense' in a letter to Sidney Colvin, August 1877. Instead of the long narrative in general terms and the 'amatory discourses' cast into formal oratory, he has imbued the scene with a life and a brevity that the Elizabethans handled only on the stage and with living actors. In fact we have only to think of what Pettie or Rich would have done with the story to realize the nature of Stevenson's achievement.

These two stories deal with the real world, but Stevenson is famous also for one or two ghost stories, the best known of which is 'Thrawn Janet'. This is confessedly a traditional goblin story from beginning to end. Mr. Soulis, the Minister, has been a strange character for many years, and the preacher of horrifying sermons. Why? After a page or two of discussion of Mr. Soulis, we are told that occasionally one of the older folk of the village 'would warm into courage over his third tumbler and recount the cause of the minister's strange looks and solitary life'. This double start introduces a narrator who tells the story in broad lowland Scots, but it at once puts it into the realm of a tall story that we are hardly asked to believe. It is legendary goblin stuff. Yet it need not be. Because there is, running parallel with the spook story, a very interesting true story of village malevolence and superstition from which Stevenson turns aside.

Years ago, Thrawn Janet, the middle-aged and saturnine servant of the Minister, had been suspected of being in league with dark forces. The women of the village attack her. Mr. Soulis rescues her, but makes her swear in front of her tormentors that she has no dealings with the devil. The next day she appears in the village with her head askew, her neck 'thrawn' as if she had been hung. She has also lost her power of speech.

This seems to me a wonderfully arresting theme. Janet is 'thrawn' (she has had a minor stroke presumably). There is a lingering belief in witchcraft among the neighbours. A steam of daemonic forces might well have arisen from the subconscious and invaded the homely village life with hate and violence. It is merely childish to turn away from this theme of tangible evil to a spook story in which a black demon appears amid strange portents and Janet's body 'lowed up like a brunstane spunk and fell in ashes to the grund'; and poor Mr. Soulis 'lang lang he lay ravin' in his bed.

'The Body Snatchers' is another story in which a contrived bogey destroys the effect of a true insight into evil character and unpleasant doings. One wonders again why the Stevenson who wrote 'A Lodging for the Night', wasted pages in this story on the building up of double-banked conventional narrators. In fact, Stevenson the *raconteur* takes over from Stevenson the writer, and the introduction of this kind of narrator is often a sign that the author does not wholly believe in his own invention. He in fact turns a tragic story into a mere yarn, with a trick ending.

Stevenson's output of short stories is not large, and those who have a special interest in either Stevenson or the short story may well enjoy deciding whether they would include 'The Treasure of Franchard', 'The Beach at Falesá', or others among his best work. Some, such as 'The Suicide Club', have no pretensions to be more than yarn-spinning.

In some ways Stevenson was not completely suited to short-story writing. He tended to work away from it, for he had a natural gift for elaborating. He also had little taste for quiet realism. He turns from Edinburgh, from the Scottish Lowlands, to the romantic and the supernatural. He wants to stress effects very different from the Scottish 'Rail-yard' school of the early years of the twentieth century, which came in for some mockery for being altogether too homespun. Stevenson also tends to make his moral arguments too explicit, as with the long argument with the *doppel-ganger* which occupies nearly half of 'Markheim'. Yet he must always stand high in the history of the short story. He combines a peculiar personal intensity with a creative perception of form. At his best it is his own genius and his alone that gives his stories their vitality.

Thomas Hardy is a remarkable contrast to Robert Louis Stevenson, and a dozen images will spring to mind to compare the graceful mountain ash, and the old oak; the man with the rapier,

and the figure with a targe and broadsword, who seems at times
to have stumbled out of an old country fair. Yet the man with the
broadsword is one of the greatest novelists and poets of the nineteenth century: one of its deepest spirits. The novels and poems
of Hardy have so overshadowed the short stories that these lesser
works are apt to be forgotten. But we find in them the essential
character of Hardy: the tragic vision; the irony that is at times too
relentless; the brooding poetry that comes from wonder and
sympathy.

While Hardy deals on the whole with contemporary themes
and people, he has the kind of imagination that looks back to his
own young days. He has a sense of the continuity of generations.
Although he lived till after the First World War, he was born
when Wordsworth and the Duke of Wellington were still living.
In his youth he could have talked to people who remembered the
Napoleonic wars; this historic sense he carries into his novels and
stories and in looking at human beings, he tends to see whole
lives. He sees the bride in the grandmother, and the grandmother
in the bride.

It is the age-old human scenes that are to him the contemporary
scenes: scenes of birth, love, and marriage. These are the fabric of
his shaping thought, rather than the latest events of his own day
or ideas from a colourful past. He says in the Preface to *Two on a
Tower*, that he felt

a wish to set the emotional history of two infinitesimal lives against the
stupendous background of the stellar universe, and to impart to readers
the sentiment that of these contrasting magnitudes the smaller might
be the greater to them as men.

In so far as he is able to do that, he enters the mainstream of
great literature, and his humanistic insight is allied to a serious
theology that is not confined to a particular creed. He has been
described as 'an atheist with a Christian vocabulary',[2] but this is
the only vocabulary of epistemology known to the characters of

---

[2] David Cecil, *Hardy the Novelist* (Constable, 1943), p. 22.

his books. How else could they have talked? It is left to *The Dynasts* to make Hardy's gnostic speculations explicit. He does not attempt to express them in his short stories.

These are the values, however, that caused Hardy from the very beginning to be admired for his charity, and yet attacked for his rank atheism. Lord David Cecil says of him, 'he must be honoured for that elevation of soul which enabled him to maintain the Christian temper without the Christian consolation'.[3] Edmund Blunden quotes with agreement a judgement of William Sharp given in the *New York Forum* as early as 1892:

Life, movement, humour, and the endless play of the forces of nature, afford him more than he reveals of his intimate sense of the insoluble mystery of existence, of our unguided way across a trackless plain of whose lost frontiers there is no resemblance, and whose horizons are seen of none. It is this steadfast austerity which has stood between him and so large a portion of the reading public. . . .[4]

This formidable point of view is allied to a strangely simple, homespun, and unequivocally English character. Hardy writes of country towns, of market-places, of country lawyers. His intimations seem at times to be half-articulate, as if we were listening to the weather wisdom of an old farmer. He watches the crops of humanity come up, to flourish, or be beaten down by storms.

All this is an awkward equipment to bring to the modest art of the short story; it is too large, too rambling, too brooding, and as a conscious artist Hardy is often a very uncertain performer. At times he spoils the truth of his stories by piling up malevolent turns of chance: too often the true lover arrives just after the second-best has been accepted. At other times his clumsy sentences defeat the interest of what he has to say. Let us look at the very worst of his style. It is almost unbelievable that any short-story writer could begin a story with this:

---

[3] Ibid., p. 156.
[4] Edmund Blunden quoting William Sharp, 1892, *English Men of Letters* (Macmillan, 1941).

Whether the utilitarian or the intuitive theory of the moral sense be upheld, it is beyond question that there are a few subtle-souled persons with whom the absolute gratuitousness of an act of reparation is an inducement to perform it . . .[5]

Here we are back with old medieval or Elizabethan *sententia*, in a singularly graceless form. It is small wonder that H. E. Bates points out that Hardy's personal style is directly opposed to the whole conception of short-story writing. However, Hardy is not always in this slow-moving vein, and there is not much wrong with such an opening as this:

To the eyes of a man viewing it from behind, the nut brown hair was a wonder and a mystery. Under the black beaver hat, surrounded by its tuft of black feathers, the long locks, braided and twisted and coiled like the rushes of a basket, composed a rare, if somewhat barbaric, example of ingenious art.

That is the opening of 'The Son's Veto', one of Hardy's best stories. 'The Son's Veto' tells us about Sophy, a very charming and kindly country girl, anxious to do her duty by other people, which she conceives largely in terms of helping to run a home comfortably. She is a little like Chekhov's 'Darling'—but more of a peasant and more strong-minded.

Sophy serves for many years in the house of an elderly rector, whose wife is ill. She regards this work almost as a calling, and rejects the proposal of Sam, a young gardener, whom she likes, but scarcely loves. In due course the rector's wife dies, and Sophy stays on to help him in his widowhood. One day she injures her leg badly, and learns that she will never be able to walk or even to stand much again. Almost her first thought is that she must leave the rector, and not be a nuisance, but he, in a burst of true but unexpected love, asks her to stay with him as his wife. So she becomes the lady of the house in which she was a servant.

The marriage is in its own quiet way happy, although Mr. Twycott knows perfectly well that he has 'committed social suicide'. He moves to a London suburb, and in due course he dies, leaving a son. The boy grows up to be a class-conscious

[5] 'For Conscience' Sake', in *Life's Little Ironies*.

snob. He too becomes a priest, but he is ashamed of his mother, and her lack of education. Gradually Sophy becomes saddened and more and more of an invalid.

Sam now enters her life again, her admirer of early years, who has become a modestly successful market gardener. He passes her house on his way to Covent Garden, and he takes her to see the market.

When she had opened the door she found Sam on the step, and he lifted her bodily on his strong arm across the little forecourt into his vehicle. Not a soul was visible or audible in the infinite length of the straight, flat highway, with its ever-waiting lamps converging to points in each direction. The air was fresh as country air at this hour, and the stars shone, except to the north-eastward, where there was a whitish light—the dawn.

Sam gives her a seat on the cabbages, then says, 'I forget, ma'am, that you've been a lady for so many years.' Sophy tells him, 'No, I am not a lady. I never shall be.' But the trouble is, as Sam finds out, that her son is a gentleman.

Sophy is happy with Sam, but the son, however, is horrified, and regards the whole affair as an impossible disgrace. Now a grown man and a priest into the bargain, he cajoles, then bullies his mother into a solemn vow that she will never marry Sam. Her invalidish ways become more marked as her health fails. In the final scene we see Sam waiting sadly at the roadside to watch her hearse go by '. . . While from the mourning coach a young smooth-shaven priest in a high waistcoat looked black as a cloud at the shopkeeper standing there.'

The whole of the story is handled with the greatest sympathy. We enter gradually but surely into the feelings of the protagonists. It is also constructed with great technical skill. There is no long narration of years but a series of scenes of past and present mixing in and out of each other, a true example of the modern short story.

Another of Hardy's best stories, also to be found in *Life's Little Ironies*, is 'To Please His Wife'. Here again there is a striking and dramatic opening, in which Captain Shadrach Joliffe appears suddenly in the church of a seaport town to give public thanks for his survival from a shipwreck.

Captain Joliffe, after his escape from drowning, is anxious to settle down, and soon gets to know two girls who are friends, Emily, who is quiet and submissive, and Joanna, who is tall and self-assertive, in fact, not at all a demure Victorian miss. Indeed, there is plenty in Hardy's pages to show us Victorian women in action in a way that is anything but conventional.

Shadrach is really drawn to Emily, but Joanna's jealous heart and combative spirit cannot bear to see him choose her friend. She wins him away even though she does not truly want him. Emily is at first terribly unhappy, but later she marries one of the most thriving citizens of the little seaport town. Shadrach, meanwhile, has left the sea and runs a grocer's shop in a very humble way.

As the years go by, Joanna becomes more and more angered by Emily's wealth, which is real, and by Emily's condescension, which is purely a figment of her own jealousy. She drives her husband and then her two sons to sea again, insisting on them making a trip which has dangers attached to it, but by which they may make a great deal of money out of a valuable cargo.

They fail to return. Hope fades and Joanna, now ageing and in poverty, is taken into Emily's home. Yet she lives in a room apart, and when she passes Emily on the stairs gives her these evil words: 'I know why you've got me here! They'll come, and be disappointed at not finding me at home, and perhaps go away again: and then you'll be revenged for my taking Shadrach away from 'ee!' And in the last scene in the story Joanna wanders out in a dawn mist dreaming that her husband and sons have returned, and knocks half-crazed at the door of her old home. This agony of hatred and self-induced jealousy is movingly conveyed in Hardy's vision. He does not condemn or moralize. He understands. He has seen the passion and suffering in Joanna's twisted mind. It is accomplished in a few thousand words, and gains from its brevity. No wonder A. E. Coppard picked out this story for his especial admiration, and found it an inspiration for the whole idea of short-story writing.

A writer of a later generation to whom these stories are surprisingly close is D. H. Lawrence. In 'The Son's Veto' we have a working-class girl giving comfort to a clergyman whose former wife has been ill and childless; then a self-conscious class struggle between a son and his mother; finally, the suggestion that Sam, the country worker, is leading a better, more genuine life than the young public school priest. It is a typical Lawrence theme. So is the jealous, destroying heart of Joanna, driven on to self-destruction by sexual and social rivalry. The very closeness of these themes to Lawrence makes one wonder how these stories might have both gained and lost had they been written by him instead of by Hardy.

Hardy has other resemblances to Lawrence as a short-story writer. Although they both wrote a large number of short stories, and among them some very fine ones, they neither of them seem to be greatly concerned with the short story as a form, but were apt to let short stories range and sprawl as they would. Both made a large contribution to literature through novels and poetry. In fact some of Hardy's best story conceptions take the form of short poems. As so often with Hardy, one is amazed that with such a perfect mastery of condensed form in his power he cared at times so little for the craftsmanship of the story.

Hardy could, on occasion, set a short story in a single scene, as in 'The Three Strangers', which is probably his best-known and most widely anthologized story. Here the arrival at one house of the hangman, the unfortunate man he has come to hang who has escaped, and the condemned man's brother, all seeking shelter from a tempestuous night, has perhaps too much of coincidence and remarkable situation. The emphasis is on the event, rather than on character, but the drama and the setting in the shepherd's house are typical of Hardy, though not of Hardy in one of his deepest moods.

A Group of Noble Dames is probably Hardy's heaviest collection of stories, and also his most morbid. It includes the horrible story of 'Barbara of the House of Grebe', a story which T. S. Eliot thought truly diabolic,[6] an ultra-Gothic romance that seems

[6] T. S. Eliot, *After Strange Gods* (Faber & Faber, 1934), pp. 56-7.

all the more dreadful for being treated with Hardy's broadcloth realism.

His best collection is *Life's Little Ironies*. This contains both 'The Son's Veto' and 'To Please His Wife', and also a group of linked stories, 'A Few Crusted Characters'. Here there are one or two stories of lighter mood, and the ancient device of the group of narrators is used in an unusually telling way, to build up one complete story. They combine to present the key story of John Lackland, the traveller returning to the village that he had left thirty-five years before. We saw in chapter III how closely this mood resembles an ancient prototype, a mood often repeated in the surviving fragments of Anglo-Saxon poetry, and found again among English short-story writers in later years, as the art of the short story becomes more fully realized. Hardy feels this mood if ever a man did; and Frank O'Connor's book *The Lonely Voice* deals with the same notion. In his view, the short story is especially suited to search out the separation and loneliness of the individual, people who through their experience are 'wandering about the fringes of society'.

Some critics have seen in Hardy's short stories a sharper, clearer experience than is to be found in the novels. Albert Guerard, in *Thomas Hardy: The Novels and Stories*, writes:

As a rule the women of the short stories and novelettes resist obvious classification more often than do those of the novels. It is hard to see why this should be so, unless a brief glance fixes an obvious individuality, while full exploration goes beyond it to type: to what has already been observed, and often.[7]

This is the very nature of the short story. It deals with the mystery of individual being. We may grow weary at the number of comparative failures in Hardy's short stories, and of the too often repeated contrivances. Yet at his most successful he is a poet of the short story. His creative writing began and ended with poetry, rather than with prose fiction.

[7] Albert J. Guerard, *Thomas Hardy: The Novels and Stories* (O.U.P., 1949), p. 145.

XI

American Critics
and Russian Writers

'The nineties,' said H. G. Wells in 1911, 'was a good and stimulating period for the short-story writer.'[1] The reason for this, he
tells us, was that short stories were reviewed and discussed, and
he goes on to regret that adequate criticism of short stories has
subsequently declined. 'People talked about them tremendously,
compared them, and ranked them. That was the thing that
mattered.'

It may seem a little surprising now to be told that the 1890s was
a golden age of short stories in England, and at first it conjures up
thoughts of *The Yellow Book*, of jewelled prose, and of con-
coctions such as Wilde's story, 'The Birthday of the Infanta.'
However, there are short stories of more serious interest in *The
Yellow Book*, by Henry James, Gissing, the young Arnold Bennett, and Mrs. Leverson, who wrote on her own level of lightly
witty, social comedy, to which Wilde might have given a far
keener cutting edge.

It is hard now to put one's hand on those discussions of the
short story that Wells found so exhilarating. We must remember
that Kipling's earlier stories had already been published, as well as
those of Wells himself. There had been a great deal of development and discussion in other countries; not only among the
Russians and French but also the Americans. A very well-known
article of Bret Harte appeared in the *Cornhill* in July 1899, in
which he modestly deprecated his own work, saying it was his

---

[1] H. G. Wells, *The Country of the Blind* (Nelson & Son, 1911), Introduction,
pp. iv–v.

American forerunners, Poe and Hawthorne, who had created the form, and all he had done was to give his stories a homely location in real American geography, and among real people. While Bret Harte is not the deepest of short-story writers, he perhaps underrates his own contribution in this comparison of achievement.

Meanwhile, in England, Stevenson and Hardy had carried the short story a long way through a transitional period. When they began to write, a short story in England was still apt to appear simply as a chain of incidents or to rely for its point on some violent, romantic, or spooky happening. Stevenson's contribution, as we have seen, was rather one of form and Hardy's of content. Hardy's last book of short stories appeared only a year before James Joyce's *Dubliners,* and Coppard pays tribute to Hardy as a direct influence. By 1922 the anonymous editor of an anthology of *Georgian Stories*[2] was already including the work of Katherine Mansfield and D. H. Lawrence. He expresses the hope that his collection is 'representative of the modern short story', but describes his own taste as old-fashioned, in still looking for the 'dramatic plot, and the surprise curtain'.

By the 1890s a point has been reached when comparative dates begin to be extremely interesting. Such questions as Chekhov's influence on Katherine Mansfield are only just over the horizon. Yet it becomes very plain that the newer conceptions of the short story had lagged behind in England and were going to go on doing so.

At this time it was the Americans who had most consciously explored and made articulate a theory of the short story as an art. By the end of the nineteenth century short stories had become a subject on which American professors of literature were expressing their views. In Chapters XV and XVI of *The Short Story in English* Professor Canby gives a systematic account of 'the discussion of the short story which has continued now for some twenty-five years'. He refers to a number of American critics and adds, 'I say American, for with few exceptions the attitude

---

[2] *Georgian Stories* (Methuen, 1922).

of the English critic has seldom been au sérieux.' He suggests also that already the field of criticism has become overworked.

Professor Brander Matthews harking back to Poe's often quoted distinctions, began the whole discussion with his essay on the *Philosophy of the Short Story*, first printed in its entirety in 1885. He defined the short story by its effect, a certain unity of impression which set it apart from other kinds of fiction, and he was the first, after Poe, to attempt an explanation of what our short-story writers had been accomplishing, the first to recognise that they had been accomplishing something new. Spurred on by an invaluable distinction, which made us see, as we had long felt, that fiction was upon a new trail, the present writer endeavoured to press onward into the matter, urging that a *conscious* impressionism, a *deliberate* attempt to convey a single impression of a mood, or emotion, or situation, to the reader, was a distinguishing characteristic, and that this, and not a chain of incidents, was the consequent sum total of the short story.

Canby's general summing up of the emergence of the modern short story is well worth quoting at length, though as we shall see presently, he has remarkably little knowledge of the work of Russian writers. He continues:

Our short story *is* sharply marked off from other forms. To be sure, it reveals itself as merely a special case, and particular development of the endless succession of distinctively short narratives which, since the world began, have dealt with those life-units that were simple, brief, and complete in their brevity. But it differs from them in degree if not in kind. This special case can show an infinitely higher measure of variety in narrative, of totality *in petto*, than had ever been sought consciously before.

Canby argues that the short-story form had a special rightness for the things it had to deal with.

Indeed, it was demanded by the characteristics of a period which supplied innumerable situations—significant nodes, as it were, where our attention clung. . . .
Once the climax and the climax alone was in the author's foremost thoughts, reproportioning, and a subordinating of all the elements of

I

the story to its desired result followed automatically, and produced the highly characteristic opening and most familiar end. . . .

Canby then continues to say that while earlier writers may have sought the macabre, the melodramatic, the over-comic, or even, with the natural-seeming Bret Harte, the over-simplified, it was Henry James who brought true naturalism, however long-winded, to the short story, although even he was dependent on situation rather than the sheer living event.

It is hard to give a short story its requisite point in an account of wash-day at the public laundries, or in a week from the life of a negro schoolboy. But one can work out an interesting situation, with a stern avoidance of sensation, and yet with aplomb.

All this is a sound and familiar account of the development of the short story in English during the nineteenth century. It has a danger, as Canby himself says, of being at this date already too self-conscious, and with all the new developments in form one may still prefer Chaucer. There is, however, a remarkable omission from Canby's view. He makes comparisons with the French, gives due reference to Maupassant, Merimée, and Daudet, but he ignores the Russians almost completely. His book is dated 1909, yet there is no mention of Chekhov. This might be explained by the lack of Chekhov translations, but there is no specific mention of Gogol, Turgenev, Tolstoy, or any Russian writer of the nineteenth century, except a brief reference to Pushkin. If Canby had been more aware of Russian short-story writers, to whom he makes only a passing reference, his analysis would surely have had a less self-conscious awareness of the employment of a technique. For with the Russians the form seems to come far more casually, far more as a matter of course, while what is new appears to be the subject matter of the stories. They are more completely absorbed in the human truth of what they have to say, and their short-story form seems to arrive naturally instead of being hammered out. That is merely the appearance it gives, because the short-story art, of all arts, does not, at its best, draw attention to its own skill.

To some extent the writers of American and of English stories too, give the theorists their lead. Poe's analysis of the process of short-story writing became a famous *ex cathedra* pronouncement, which Nathaniel Hawthorne duly took up. In an article which was based on his review of Hawthorne's *Twice Told Tales*, he refers to the need for creating 'a certain unique or single effect. . . . In the whole composition there should be no word written, of which the tendency, direct or indirect, is not to the one pre-established design.' Robert Louis Stevenson talks of three ways of constructing a short story; and in another, much quoted passage talks of the 'brutal and licentious public' who persist in 'thinking that shocking situations or good dialogue are got by studying life: they will not understand that they are prepared by deliberate artifice, and set off by painful suppressions'.[3]

Perhaps we should not take him too seriously, but his intention is to stress the importance of the technique, as against the content of the story. If Kipling does not provide explanations about the intricacy of what he is doing, he is apt to make certain that it will not be missed. Sheer jugglery of construction is at times the most interesting part of his short stories.

Chekhov's stories do not look so intricate as Kipling's, nor does he write about the art of the short story in the same way as Poe or Stevenson. In his notebooks and letters, we find he is far more occupied with the observation of human beings, far more concerned with the scenes and people that he feels can be captured in short stories. The form with him is the organic expression of each particular flash of vision. He remarks that there has been a great deal of talk about the development of the short story as an art form, but that all that has really happened is that 'Maupassant in France, and I in Russia began writing very short stories. There's your new movement in literature'. We have to remember that it was Chekhov and Maupassant who were writing the short stories that were really short: the implication is that not until the stories are really short do the especial insights of the form truly show themselves.

There are numerous other Russian story-writers of this date besides the best-known and most often quoted authors Gogol,

[3] Graham Balfour, *Life of R. L. Stevenson* (Methuen, 1901).

Turgenev, and Chekhov. Korolenko, for instance, whose dream-like writing verges towards the short-story form; Uspensky, who, unlike Korelenko, has a gift for putting down scenes and events with brevity and thrust, a style moving towards that of Hemingway; Garshin, who can write deeply imaginative and disturbing stories, stories of the limits of experience: of a soldier, for instance, lying desperately wounded, and managing to survive through changing realms of consciousness till he is found by his comrades on the fourth day; or Kuprin, who in range of subject and mood is a lesser Chekhov and whose study of Yass in 'The Slavonic Soul of Yass' is famous; Yass, the house servant to a doctor, dignified yet absurd, honourable yet at moments disgraceful, domesticated yet at the last horrific, is put before us with unforced sympathy and understanding.

These stories have a technique and a form that is very hard to find in English stories of the time. They deal with simple and at times undramatic lives; and the movement towards a climax is not over-emphasized. In the main, it is an impression of human understanding and of complete identification with their characters that these writers leave behind, rather than the notion of authors at work. Often enough the stories reveal themselves without any personalized narration or obtrusive remarks. In fact, the development of the Russian short story in the nineteenth century consists partly in the point of view of the narrator, and in the question, 'Who is the narrator?'

Frank O'Connor says of a passage in Gogol's famous 'The Overcoat':

If one wanted an alternative description of what the short story means, one would hardly find better than that single half sentence, 'and from that day forth, everything was as it were changed, and appeared in a different light to him'. If one wanted an alternative title for this work, one might choose 'I am your brother'. What Gogol has done so boldly and brilliantly is to take the mock heroic character, the absurd little copying clerk, and impose his image over that of the crucified Jesus, so that even while we laugh we are filled with horror at the resemblance.[4]

[4] Frank O'Connor, *The Lonely Voice* (Macmillan, 1963), p. 16.

These are striking words; and they imply also a self-abnegation on the part of the author, who eliminates his own personality, as far as that is humanly possible. It is a purity of intention. Referring to a short story written by his brother Alexander, Chekhov said, 'Be honest with yourself, throw your own personality overboard . . . renounce yourself for at least half an hour.' Chekhov is of course the master of them all. He saw people both as a writer and as a doctor; and his range and variety of observation is extremely wide. He has an unassuming touch even when he is at his most serious; yet an essential brightness of spirit, an aesthetic joy, mingles with his saddest moments.

When writing a letter to Grigorovich he is so moved by the beauty of the snow he says, 'It is a season when God himself it seems would go for a drive in a sleigh.'[5] Yet Chekhov spent most of that Christmas Day with a patient who died while he was with him; or again:

I have often been reproached, even Tolstoy has reproached me, for writing about trifles. I am told I have no positive heroes. . . .[6]

I haven't acquired a political, philosophical outlook on life. I keep changing it every month, and I therefore have to confine myself to descriptions of how my characters love, get married, beget children and talk and die.[7]

That is not to say that all these stories of the Russians are good stories. Chekhov himself wrote some worthless stories, but then, like Maupassant or Maugham or Kipling or a good many other authors, he wrote a great many stories—too many. Even with so small an output as Katherine Mansfield's, it is remarkable how seldom she reaches her own best level.

The general fault of the Russian writer of this period is that they overwork the minor key: too many of them are too predictably sad. Some authors, such as Schedrin, write stories that are so overloaded with hatred of the landowners and officials, and so full of grief for the mujeks, that the individuals become lost in generalized pictures of black and white. Though much of this may have been a true reflection of the sadness and pain of many

[5] D. Magarshack, *Chekhov* (Faber & Faber, 1952), p. 172.
[6] Ibid., p. 371.   [7] Ibid., p. 123.

individual lives, it does not make them good stories. One feels a certain dismay at seeing Chekhov drawn into discussions of a conscious revolutionary intention, and Gorky labours this point in his view of Chekhov.

Chekhov does at times explain that he had the intention of exposing the awful banality of many lives, and the boredom and vulgarity of some people's feelings: but his eye is on the individual, not on political reform. He began by seeing his stories as humorous sketches of people's absurdities, though he may at times be scathing. Yet he soon becomes far too deeply interested in his characters to see them merely as absurd. He knew, as Gogol knew, that poor timid clerks are not comic spectacles; nor are drunken workmen, nor over-romantic gushing young women, nor pretentious young men who lay down the law. He knows that they all have moments of delight, and moments of despair, and that they cry out not to be satirized or exposed or exaggerated, but to be seen with sympathy and loving-kindness. Yet his care for the inner truth of the individual makes the people in his stories points of irradiation which shed light on the conditions of their lives and of other people round them. The discursive background is contained in the truth with which the individual is seen.[8]

In this way, as was suggested with Hardy's portrayal of character, a short story may by its isolation be more effective, have more intense individuality, than a novel. The insight develops with the form. Cleanth Brooks and Robert Penn Warren use the image of a prism reflecting its rays on a surrounding area, and they compare a typical 'discursive' style with the 'concentrated' style. Their book contrasts a discursive passage from *Vanity Fair* with a scene from James Joyce's well-known story 'The Two Gallants'—and they show what a wealth of discursive background is concentrated in the depth with which the characters are seen by Joyce.[9]

[8] See *Notebooks of Tchekhov with Reminiscences by Maxim Gorky*, translated by S. S. Koteliansky and Leonard Woolf (Hogarth Press, 1921).

[9] Cleanth Brooks and Robert Penn Warren, *The Fundamentals of Good Writing* (Denis Dobson, 1952), pp. 270-1.

This is not the place to dwell at length on Chekhov's methods, which are simply subservient to his central purpose. Some of his best-known stories, such as 'The Bishop', or 'The Chorus Girl', are accomplished in a single scene. Sometimes the single scene does not even, ostensibly, use any flashbacks to cover other points of time. In other stories, however, such as 'The Darling' or the most famous of all, 'The Lady with a Dog', the construction is not cut to pattern: these stories could almost be described as a chain of incidents, and it is simply the integral unity of thought and feeling that provides the form and moves towards the climax.

Occasionally, though not often, Chekhov himself appears as the narrator. 'Easter Eve', for instance, published in 1886, begins with the words, 'I was standing on the bank of the River Goltva waiting for the ferry boat from the other side.' The story of the young monk that follows, and his feelings for his dead friend, who had been neglected and unappreciated, is observed by an 'I', Chekhov himself, conveying to us his own sensations on hearing the story. Katherine Mansfield, following Chekhov in some ways, treated the elimination of the direct narrator more strictly than he did.

The movement away from personal narration during the nineteenth century is gradual and by no means steady. Gogol is apt to keep any mention of 'I' or any personalized angle of comment out of his stories, yet small touches appear, such as 'In our little town' or 'It's a pity I can't remember what made the brigadier general give his big dinner.' Such a remark is sometimes the one mention of the author in the course of the story.

Unexpecteldy, Turgenev's *Sketches of a Sportsman*, one of the most truly poetic books of short stories ever written, is conveyed to the reader as a series of stories and scenes which all come within the author's own experience; this, surprisingly enough, was also Somerset Maugham's favoured method.

It is Turgenev himself who is talking and who tells us at the beginning of one story that he was delayed for the best part of a day at a posting house; or that he caught a cold in an out-of-the-way town and sent for the local doctor, and that this is the way in which he heard the story. Or he may start off in the traditional manner with a few essay-like observations about drawing a covert. But he carries the form, in which the story emerges from an essay, to the highest degree of refinement: the causerie does not develop, but the story does.

His most moving and intimate story of all, 'The Living Relic', which tells of a once beautiful peasant girl wasting away with illness, begins with two or three pages of opening, which the strict theorist might say were irrelevant, and serve no purpose other than to describe the discomfort of Turgenev and Ermolai on being drenched in the rain: however, others feel as I feel myself, that this apparent digression, this excursion into personal and minor discomforts, is in this story an integral part of the whole.

Turgenev's work was epoch-making not only in the history of the short story but also as a historical event in itself. Quiet and restrained though the stories are, Alexander II told Turgenev that from the time he read *Sketches of a Sportsman* he constantly dwelt on the necessity of liberating the serfs: and that Turgenev's stories became the forerunners of the Act of Liberation of 1861. One cannot say that even Kipling's brass and percussion had so powerful an effect on events.

Turgenev's practice, like that of Chekhov, seems to repudiate too much analysis; their part was to create the art form rather than to discuss it. Although Turgenev introduces himself, and then introduces his story, he is the most unobtrusive of narrators. If he tells us of his own thoughts we find his eye is all on the landscape or the character he is observing. He himself recedes. When David Richter wrote an Introduction to an English translation of Turgenev's stories, published in 1895, nearly forty years after their original appearance, he said, 'We lose sight of the author in these tales. We feel as if actual life were being enacted before our eyes, as if for the first time we saw and grasped its meaning and felt all its imperfections.' This is remarkably close to Somerset Maugham's first thoughts on reading Chekhov. One has to remind oneself that Turgenev was practising the art of the short story, and that he was not simply recording the life around him.

We may lose sight of the author, yet when we have reached

this degree of insight and intimacy, the personality of the author still remains all important. If we turn back to Elizabethan story-telling, we shall find that in spite of varying degrees of euphuism, there is not really a great deal of difference between the way two Elizabethan story-books set out 'a noble heroical and marvelous discourse' or tell 'a mad and merry prank withal'. Yet if Kipling had written the story of the last day of a bishop it would not have been much like Chekhov's story 'The Bishop'; or if Chekhov had written the story of a Warrant Officer who deserted the service for the sake of a woman, it would not have been much like 'Mrs. Bathurst'.

Some people see very little in Chekhov, and this is a perfectly valid and genuine response. Kipling, too, has become a positive battleground of disagreement, and those who feel instinctive like or dislike of him are apt to regard each other as hopeless cases. While Chekhov seems to cause irritation among people who do not agree about him, Kipling causes positive anger. Critics may be able to account for and analyse these personal responses that well up unbidden in people who are readers rather than critics, but it is very hard indeed to alter them. There is in fact no getting away from them. It is not a question of brainwork or knowledge or perseverance, but of personality. Reading a short story is a brief encounter between two people, and it is an intimate en-counter. Because the short story cannot have padding, the human values are extremely active, although they are not plainly ex-pounded. Even though the author may eliminate all intentional comment or display of his own personality, his individual vision remains all the more clear. Sean O'Faolain, in his book *The Short Story*, stresses the point that short-story writing is one of the most personal of arts.

XII
Kipling

I

The criticism of Kipling has been through many phases. His work arouses such strong feelings, and so much has been written ardently praising him or angrily attacking him, that Kipling controversy has become nowadays something of a specialized subject. One could write a book on what people think about Kipling.

Some of Kipling's greatest admirers are apt to dwell on the amount of specialized knowledge one needs in order to appreciate what he is doing: one should know about life in an officer's mess, one should know one or two Indian languages, one should know something about sail, about steam, about Freemasonry, about the Koran, about India at the time of Kipling's youth: all this knowledge and experience will enable one to understand and savour Kipling's achievement to the full. Yet such considerations tend to put a hedge round Kipling, to suggest, as he suggests himself, that he is speaking to initiates.

However, neither Kipling nor Kipling exponents invented his amazing early success. This came from the reading public at large, and it came with the most dramatic speed. If ever a youth blew his trumpet before the walls of Jericho, and saw them fall flat, it was Kipling. He tells us in *Something of Myself* that editors whom he met in London, in the early days of his fame, could hardly believe that he was so young. Though a book of verses had a great deal to do with this success, it was his early short stories that clinched the matter. 'And in the autumn of '89,' he writes, 'I stepped into a sort of waking dream when I took, as a matter of course, the fantastic cards that Fate was pleased to deal me.'[1]

[1] Rudyard Kipling, *Something of Myself* (Macmillan, 1936), ch. IV.

Kipling, like Chekhov, had known great unhappiness in his childhood, though of a different kind. He was for a period separated from his parents, and suffered from loneliness and cruelty. Chekhov's unhappiness was more prolonged, if more diffused. Kipling tells us of his great and sudden happiness when he was able to rejoin his parents in India at the age of sixteen. Chekhov's unhappiness came not from the absence, but the presence of his father. Chekhov, also, was thrashed, but he suffered within the family circle, enduring what they all endured, and he escaped by growing up into a patient character with a great deal of quiet strength, and probably a more balanced emotional nature than Kipling's.

Like Kipling again, Chekhov achieved fame through short stories, though far more gradually. Both had the experience of seeing a comparatively few short stories create their literary success. When Chekhov wrote his 'Happiness', which is only a few thousand words long, and 'The Steppe', which is a 'long short' story, he took the artistic world of Moscow by storm, though his fame was not so popular or reverberating as that of Kipling. There are very few authors who have achieved a stature in world literature mainly by short stories, and it is interesting that there should have appeared almost simultaneously in three different countries three writers whose fame would have been created by their short stories even if they had written nothing else. Of these three, Kipling was also a poet, Maupassant a novelist, and Chekhov a dramatist.

Kipling, like Chekhov, could not really write novels. Chekhov tried hard enough, and on more than one occasion speaks of a novel on which he is working, and talks of training himself to see affairs in a more narrative and generalized way. He thought of using 'The Steppe' as the opening of a novel, and it may well have been his artistic guardian angel that stopped him, because the small boy's journey across the steppe with the team of wool waggoners is wonderfully complete in itself, and to add anything might well have spoilt what is already there.

Kipling achieved length in some of his books, but not novel

form. *Kim*, which is often thought to be his masterpiece, is episodic, and when he told his mother that he had chosen this form consciously, with his thoughts on *Don Quixote*, she laughed at him. 'To whom the Mother: *Don't* you stand there in your wool-boots hiding behind Cervantes with *me*! You *know* you couldn't make a plot to save your soul.'[2] In due course Kipling, like Chekhov, gave up the attempt to be a novelist, but his later stories, such as 'Dayspring Mishandled', grow more and more complicated, deal with long interweavings between several lives, and in fact suggest whole novels. Perhaps even 'the Mother' would have agreed, if she had seen 'Dayspring Mishandled', that he had made a plot after all.

However, unlike Chekhov, Kipling is not the man to disappear within his own short stories; far from it. We do not lose sight of the author. He likes to narrate in a strongly personal tone of voice and with plenty of his own asides and comments. He tends to see people and events violently and dramatically. If he wants to be funny he goes in for rip-roaring farce. He spells Fate with a capital 'F'. His characters move in a world of Powers that are dominating and revengeful. He expatiates upon a Law— a harsh law of 'the Gods' standing behind the harshness of human empires, and often seems to relish being the official spokesman of these Powers. Though he was gentle and kindly in his family life, this strange loud voice is apt to appear all through his work. A Nobel Prizewinner, spokesman of an Empire, and friend of the mighty, with a strident political voice, he makes a paradoxical use of the modest art.

It is in the earlier stories of Kipling that he appears least prominently as the personal narrator. This is partly because they were originally written for *The Civil and Military Gazette* and *The Pioneer* and they had to be pared to the bone, although some of them were afterwards expanded for collection in book form. In contrast with this, he tells us that some of his later stories were distilled from much longer versions, and one receives the impression that a digressive and talkative style came naturally to him, and that he arrived at shortness by skill and by the practice

[2] Kipling, *Something of Myself*, ch. V.

of his own craft; a discipline of which he had complete understanding and mastery.

Some of his early short stories are written without any narration at all. 'The Story of the Gadsbys' is revealed entirely in
dialogue, though stage directions give hints of descriptive
passages that might have been written. The Gadsbys' story is
played out in the officer's mess, at the tea parties of the mem-
sahibs, and in the home of Captain Gadsby and his bride. It is
one of the few stories in which Kipling enters closely into a
relationship between a husband and wife, and in which the needs
of the wife and home are set against the man's world. When
Gadsby first sees his future wife, he says, with a professional eye,
'The filly, by Jove! Must ha' picked up that action from the sire.'
Yet in the end it is home life that wins. Fortunately Captain
Gadsby has a fine estate to retire to in England, which cushions
his self-sacrifice in leaving the regiment.

Stripped of surrounding narration and comment, the situation
and conversation in 'The Story of the Gadsbys' often appears
violently stagey and sentimental. At one point, for instance, Mrs.
Gadsby lies in a high fever after her baby dies.

Voice: Can't they do *anything* to help me? I *don't* want to die.
Captain G.: Hush dear. You won't.
Voice: What's the use of talking? *Help* me. You've never failed me yet.
  Oh Phil, help me to keep alive. (*Feverishly*) I don't believe you wish
  me to live. You weren't a bit sorry when that horrid Baby thing
  died. I wish I'd killed it!
Captain G. (*drawing his hand across his forehead*): It's more than a man's
  meant to bear—it's not right.

It is in much the same manner that Captain Gadsby expresses his
misery and his feelings of treachery when he decides to give up
the army and return to England. His friend's aside at this point,
'Couldn't conceive any woman getting permanently between me
and the Regiment', runs on traditional, in fact, Ouida-esque
lines. *Under Two Flags* had set the model twenty years before.
Wives, the troublesome little angels, are not really a possible
part of life, except for certain heartbreaking set pieces, and when

Captain Gadsby goes off to his home estates, we are left to the man's world.

Kipling does not appear in person in the Gadsbys, but his identification with the officers' lives is one of the notable sources of his peculiar style. In another of his earliest collections, *In Black and White*, he skilfully absorbs the loquacious manner of various Indians. This Urdu and Hindi English is another of the sources of Kipling's style, and was to be used with great effect in more serious later stories, such as 'A Sahib's War'.

Another of Kipling's earlier groups of stories is the famous *Soldiers Three*, in which he develops his admiration for three seasoned and inseparable soldier friends, telling us that he was proud to be one of the few civilians to win their trust, and treating their exploits from endurance in battle to dog-stealing, drunken fighting, and practical jokes in Hindu temples as altogether laughable and splendid. He writes in 'Krishna Mulvaney', a short story from *Life's Handicap*:

Through no merit of my own it was my good fortune to be in a measure admitted to their friendship—frankly by Mulvaney from the beginning, sullenly and with reluctance by Learoyd, and suspiciously by Ortheris, who held to it that no man not in the Army could fraternise with a red coat. 'Like to like,' said he. 'I'm a bloomin' sodger—he's a bloomin' civilian. 'T'ain't natural—that's all.'

But that was not all. They thawed progressively, and in the thawing told me more of their lives and adventures than I am ever likely to write.

In *Plain Tales from the Hills* and *Life's Handicap* the Kipling manner is in full flower. The narrator is often 'I', the persona assumed by Kipling, the man with the inside knowledge. We find the appeals to Allah; the asides suggesting that there are still better stories that cannot be told to the public; the assumption that there are certain Laws and Powers which are understood among the initiates, to whom Kipling belongs, but to whom the reader may or may not belong.

Some dreadful things happen in these early stories. An Indian girl who has been meeting a white man at a window has her arms severed at the wrist. Next time he goes to the window the mutilated stumps are thrust through for him to see. A villainous white man who bullies his wife and bribes false witnesses against her is duly exposed and flogged by the man he has tried to involve. In another story Strickland, the police officer, and 'I' together capture a leper, and burn him with the red hot barrels of a gun in order to make him remove a supposed spell. There are other stories of young men breaking down, or breaking out; saving their reputations, in the nick of time, or losing them for ever. There are stories of sorcery, sometimes treated as a mere trick, sometimes linked with black magic. 'Georgie Porgie' and 'Without Benefit of Clergy' are both stories of mixed marriages: in one, the white man is crudely heartless, in the other, he is shattered by self-reproach. There is heartbreak, tenderness, agony. There are wonderful descriptions and a wealth of story invention, all told in the same loud voice.

There can be no wonder that Kipling's early stories were a huge success. The material was new and surprising: the life of the British in India had never been seen before in these terms. The hard shades and colours of human affairs imposed by the life itself, and brilliantly focused by the use of the short story, glittered like new-minted coins. Kipling's stories have the force, the punch, the climax developed by Bret Harte in dealing with his mining camps and towns, but they have a far wider range of theme and depth of creation. There had been nothing like them in English literature.

From these early flashes of genius onwards, Kipling's stories gradually develop in depth. He himself left India, and returned only once. He married; travelled; lived in America; found a beautiful old house in England; became a prophetic mouthpiece of the ideals of Empire; spoke of dangers to come; lost his only son in the First World War; published his last book of stories in 1932.

All these experiences are reflected in the stories. His knowledge of the world becomes enlarged, and boosted by his wonderful success, he naturally begins to 'feel his oats', as Captain Gadsby would have put it. We may say, roughly, that Kipling passed through a middle stage, in which he wrote of many trades and callings, from the fighting services to the age-old crafts of the countryside. In this phase he refers with increasing authority to the notion of higher powers which rule men's lives, and seem to be interpreted through the discipline of worldly might. He expounds, as in 'The Brushwood Boy', his ideal of the serious-minded English soldier, born for command of other people, with a melodramatic shiver of strange dreams and portents guiding his life.

Then, roughly again, we may say Kipling's stories develop into a later and final phase, when he becomes the friend and intimate of men in high places. He sums up his life's experience, probes deep into men's lives and motives, struggles always to fathom the mysterious Law and Will. Meanwhile the craftsmanship becomes more and more complicated. Sometimes he refers to himself openly as a prophetic figure, and 'Uncovenanted Mercies', the last story in his last volume, opens with these words: 'If the Order Above be but the reflection of the Order Below, as that Ancient affirms who has had experience of the Orders, . . .' In a footnote we are told that these words are quoted from his own previous story, 'On the Gate', which opens with precisely the same sentence. Here he seems to be claiming experience not merely of men and women but of 'Orders'. The use of the capital letters is interesting, the 'Ancient' (who is Kipling) getting his capital along with the Orders. It is striking, too, that the Order Above is a reflection of the Order Below, and not, as most people would have thought, the other way round. Is the Order Above, then, an emanation of the world rather than a pre-existing entity?

Both these stories deal with angels and archangels, and we see these higher powers discussing human affairs as if they were so many top administrators dealing with staff reports—and deciding whether to use severity or sympathy, the main idea of 'Uncovenanted Mercies' being a 'full test for breaking strain'. This story has the authentic Kipling 'frisson'. The talk among the archangels may strike people as inspired, repellent, pretentious, or perhaps just advanced fooling.

Kipling's admirers are apt to steer one away from the early

work to the 'greater depth' and insight of the later stories, 'The Gardener', 'The Wish House', 'The Manner of Men', 'The Church that was at Antioch'. Others may prefer the more simple dramatics of the young writer to the prophetic overtones of *Limits and Renewals*. Yet throughout forty years, certain inalienable aspects of Kipling's art continue to emerge. These may have been heightened by his Indian experience, by his intense concentration on a journalist's job, yet they belong to the man himself, who one senses could not have felt otherwise, and would have developed his own full head of writing steam without the journalist's training. What are these characteristic traits?

II

At the outset, and always, it was part of his nature and his gift to see the world in heightened and often glaring colours. His tone is almost the exact opposite of the quiet voice of Somerset Maugham. He is immensely impressed, whether it is by a drunken prank, the peace of the countryside, the shop talk of a surgeon, or the raging of a battle.

Among the aspects of the world that impressed him most of all was the notion of men in action: men doing their jobs, privates, captains, craftsmen; linked with this he enjoys using the jargon of men's trades. He is always wonderfully skilful at mastering documentary material, and takes a great pride in doing so.

Sometimes he practises this mastery of documentary content to the detriment of his stories. The material dominates the human characters. Rather as an intricate rhyme scheme may establish that a composition is a poem, so the prodigious display of inside knowledge deftly woven into conversation and action may establish that this is indeed an achievement as a story.

Linked with the idea of perfection in craftsmanship is the idea of turning men themselves into perfect parts of a great craft: licking young men into shape; turning the raw into the mature; breaking men in the process if they are not fit material. In this simplified moral code, duty may be hard, but it is plain. Liberals are apt to be presented as traitors and poltroons.

Linked with this again is the notion of retributive punishment,

K

and revenge. It crops up repeatedly in the stories: in 'The Mark of the Beast'; in 'A Friend of the Family', where an ingenious Australian carries out a long and intricate scheme to harass a mean-minded opponent; in 'Sea Constables', where the Skipper of a neutral oil tanker who has been trying to make a rendezvous with a German submarine falls desperately ill, and in a mood of cold-blooded revenge is refused the entry to a port, on which his life depends. Fair enough, some might say; and this story has been a bone of contention. One can argue that Kipling is merely reporting the conversation of the men who take part in such things. Yet the theme is recurrent, and the whole climax of 'Sea Constables' is the revenge. This is the point of the story, masked to some extent by the customary brilliance in conveying the work of the patrol boats.

Another recurrent thread in Kipling's stories comes from his passion for the mysterious and the magical. Often enough this takes a nasty form, as if the narrator means to make the reader's flesh creep. Yet there is also white magic, as in 'The Wish House', where loving self-sacrifice leads to the transference of a fatal disease from the selfish beloved to the unselfish lover—a moving story; yet it is none the less magic, not psychology nor Christianity. It is made very plain that her action comes from knowing an old gipsy trick, creepy and frightening and danger-ous. I can hardly believe that in 'The Wish House' Kipling was at this point simply reporting the antique superstition of two elderly country women. The whole thing is too much of a piece with his own point of view, as expressed in *Letters of Marque* and *Something of Myself*. He himself is stating that this white magic exists and is the point of the story. In fact, when he says, 'A Token is a wraith of the dead or, worse still, of the living', he breaks into the narration of the story with information that comes from himself as the author and not from the characters. The story 'They' with its ghost children also has an element of white magic as a balm for suffering and loss, and 'Unprofessional' suggests that there are strange, unknown tides affecting our sanity.

Another characteristic of Kipling's stories is, as we have seen, the relative absence of wives and families. After Captain Gadsby

yields to his wife's wishes and leaves the regiment, women as
ordinary people more or less vanish from the stories, only to re-
appear as portents: breaking men's lives, ministering to men's
dreams; priestesses and acolytes of the higher sacrifice or the total
prostitution. The mother of 'The Brushwood Boy' discusses
with him his dreams of Empire 'as a mother and son should'.
The blind lady in 'They' attracts the ghost children because she,
like the author, 'understands'. The whole affair of running a
home, the everyday bravery and labour of the working-class
mother, the views of a Mrs. Mulvaney, are not mentioned. There
is almost nothing about Indian women, except as dumb sacrifices
and devoted adorers, no hint of a suggestion that within thirty
years of Kipling's death India would have sent a woman am-
bassador to Moscow and London and would have a woman
Prime Minister.

The relationship of Captain Gadsby and his wife in later life,
at the age of forty-five, say, does not appeal to Kipling, and in
the opening paragraph of 'A Deal in Cotton' this is how he
portrays the redoubtable Strickland after he had married, and
grown a bit heavy.

Long and long ago, when Devadatta was King of Benares, I wrote
some tales concerning Strickland of the Punjab Police (who married
Miss Youghal) and Adam, his son. Strickland has finished his Indian
Service, and lives now at a place in England called Weston-super-Mare,
where his wife plays the organ in one of the churches. Semi-occasion-
ally he comes up to London, and occasionally his wife makes him visit
his friends. Otherwise he plays golf and follows the harriers for his
figure's sake.

The scorn of 'a place called Weston-super-Mare' is withering,
and Strickland, left over, so to speak, from 'The Mark of the
Beast', is now put into the picture, merely in the role of listener
and prompter to a story told by his son—poor old Strickland,
one feels, puffing a long way after those harriers.

The above opening paragraph is a further sample of Kipling's
use of a flamboyant narrating style. Though he did at times
eliminate this narrating self, he was always fascinated by the
thought of the story that is told personally to a listening audience,

the antique spoken story of the bazaar. This is a feature of his art throughout, this notion of the bazaar voice, and of men who say that they have seen the story for themselves and are passing it on. Sometimes he is part actor in the story himself. In *Life's Handicap*, one of his earlier collections, he writes a Preface telling how he met an ancient Saddhu, Gobind the one-eyed, who in the last days of his life discussed with Kipling his 'honoured craft' of story-telling. This Preface itself takes the form of a story, an unusually gentle one for Kipling, having a kindly humour, and the dignified melancholy of the closing days of a long life.

Gobind himself has been a story-teller, and he and Kipling touch on the difference between the story told to a live audience, who may be required to offer more money before the end is revealed, and the story written and printed in a book. Kipling speaks of critics who may even doubt that the tale is true, and Gobind replies that 'A tale that is told is a true tale as long as the telling lasts.' This is as much as to say that a great deal depends on the personal powers of the live narrator to cast a brief spell on his listeners.

Kipling promises that he will honour Gobind by recording their conversation in the forepart of the book, and Gobind mildly exults before the priests of various faiths who are gathered together in the old Chubára.

Having created this surface of verisimilitude, Kipling then goes on to tell the reader:

These tales have been collected from all places, and all sorts of people, from priests in the Chubára, from Ala Yar the carver, Jivan Singh the carpenter, nameless men on steamers and trains round the world, women spinning outside their cottages in the twilight, officers and gentlemen now dead and buried, and a few, but these are the very best, my father gave me. . . . The most remarkable stories are, of course, those which do not appear—for obvious reasons.

Thus from his early days we see that Kipling was master of all the tricks of suggesting that his stories were 'really true'. He poses as a reporter, passing on the tales that he has gathered. One would not doubt a woman at her spinning wheel in the twilight; one could not question the word of Kipling's own father; the best stories 'of course' and 'for obvious reasons' cannot be told.

This is, in the main, Kipling's solution of the problem of 'who is the narrator?' He is usually the narrator himself, and he is apt to allege that the story has really happened. Yet this is the method that confuses historical truth with the truth of fiction. Kipling is an author of fiction, and although he may use the skill of Daedalus in building up the verisimilitude of the narration, these tricks of the trade do not contribute in the slightest degree to the inner truth of the story.

Sometimes he uses two or three narrators, who each know part of a story and discover the whole drama almost casually by comparing their knowledge. That strange story, 'Mrs. Bathurst', arises because of a chance meeting between Kipling himself, an old friend of his, Hooper, who is an inspector of railways, another old friend, Pyecroft, a naval petty officer, and yet another man, Pritchard, a sergeant of Marines, whom Kipling has not met before. They begin to exchange reminiscences. All this in itself is quite a story, but out of numerous anecdotes there comes the story of Mrs. Bathurst and Vickery, the Warrant Officer, who sacrificed everything because of his infatuation. In the meanwhile a tense situation arises between Hooper and Pritchard, as Pritchard suspects Hooper's motives in asking too many questions. 'I' has to vouch for Hooper's friendliness. The mistrust is finally resolved when Hooper is able to fit his startling knowledge of Vickery's final fate into the picture. Thus the fiction emerges from a conversation between several men who by now seem so real that we are apt to forget they also are fiction. Indeed, Pyecroft, Mulvaney, and others have had the reality of true friends to many people.

A remarkable *tour de force* of ingenuity, even by Kipling's standards, is 'Dayspring Mishandled'. It must be one of the most richly compacted short stories ever composed, a mixture between a kind of literary murder and Father Ronald Knox's fascinating mock-proof that Queen Victoria was really the author of *In Memoriam*. It is yet another revenge story, Kipling's most subtle revenge story of all.

At the beginning of 'Dayspring Mishandled' we are shown the mysteries of a cheap literary factory, a group of young men at work for a weekly wage on various fictional projects. The story starts with a typical Kipling flourish.

In the days beyond compare and before the Judgements, a genius called Graydon foresaw that the advance of education and the standard of living would submerge all mind-marks in one mudrush of standardised reading-matter, and so created the Fictional Supply Syndicate to meet the demand.

The seeds are sown of the lifelong hatred for Castorley felt by Manallace, 'a darkish, slow northerner of the type that does not ignite, but must be detonated'. Manallace cannot forgive Castorley's insulting treatment of a woman whom they both once loved.

In the course of years Castorley leaves the literary syndicate, and by dubious methods rises to the eminence of a great Chaucer scholar. A satirical portrait is given of Castorley and his behaviour that has all the bite and amusement of Angus Wilson. Manallace, however, keeps on visiting Castorley, picks his brains about Chaucer, and prepares an elaborate hoax, designed to explode his reputation; in fact, he prepares a false 'discovery', a page from an unknown Canterbury Tale, all done on contemporary vellum with ink made to a medieval recipe and penwork in the style of a known scribe using a certain kind of faulty quill pen. Manallace takes years to do this, then binds it up into the back of an old book as a stiffener, in the authentic manner, and contrives to insert it into a job lot of books which is about to be sent to an American firm. In due course the fragment is 'discovered' in America, Castorley is sent for as the great expert, clinches his reputation, and wins a knighthood by his irrefutable confirmation of the authenticity of the manuscript, which is, of course, ready-made for his own specialized knowledge at every point.

It is the 'I' of the story who, having observed Manallace's peculiar hobbies over years, now ferrets out the secret from Manallace, and ask what he intends to do by way of springing his trap. Interestingly enough, Manallace delays the exposure and the revenge is never completed. Castorley has fallen ill but has a great book coming out, with which Manallace, his apparently faithful old friend, is helping him. Manallace now realizes two things. Castorley's wife has also guessed the secret but awaits complete confirmation; and she is the lover of the doctor who is treating Castorley. A position of Jamesian *double entendre* arises between her and Manallace, who have each guessed a secret about each other.

It is now Lady Castorley who begins to torture her husband, and Manallace who comforts him in the closing months of his life, by assuring him that 'It's *your* find—*your* credit—*your* glory and—all the rest of it.'

It is amazing how much this story contains. The plotting, the documentary information, the ironical twists, the satire of literary pomposity are carried off with extreme bravura. Yet is it really to be swallowed? Could Manallace really have behaved, over a long period of years, with such sinister melodramatic secrecy? Kipling presumably believed that he could. Yet if he really believed in it heart and soul, why did he put in two footnotes, one of which pretends that Castorley was a real authority of whom educated readers must have heard, and the other of which links the woman whom Manallace loved with a character in one of Kipling's most absurd farces (another revenge story), 'The Village that voted the earth was flat'? Writing this kind of footnote to one's own short stories is indeed a curious trait, suggesting that the truth of fiction is a kind of three-card trick. Which is fact? Which is fiction?

These, then, are the characteristics that run through all Kipling's stories: the highly dramatic vision; the intense interest in men at work together; the gift for absorbing information about jobs and crafts; the conception of men as parts of a vast work to be achieved, while the human stuff is hardened or broken in the process; the theories of a harsh punitive justice and the recurrence of personal revenge; the outcroppings of sheer magic; the near absence of women, of home and married life; and present throughout it all, the personalized narrator, the man who is in the know, the narrating 'I', who impresses on the reader that he has it all 'from the horse's mouth', whether that means simple private soldiers or archangels. Finally, holding these elements together, there is the superb craftsmanship.

Let us, however, turn to some of the stories written late in Kipling's life.

III

Among Kipling's later stories that are praised for their compassion and insight are 'The Church that was at Antioch' and 'The Gardener'. 'The Church that was at Antioch' shows Kipling's skill in writing with authenticity of a historical moment. The scene is the city of Antioch at the time of one of the early and mysterious meetings of Christians at Antioch. The whole story gains considerably because there is no elaborate conversational framework, no narrating 'I'. It comes straight on to the page as pictures, dialogue, and action.

Kipling gives us one of his most emotional delineations of a soldier going about his duty. Valens, the young Roman officer, is a man after Kipling's own heart; fearless, conscientious, curt of speech, roughly kind-hearted. Valens, who is a follower of Mithras, is stabbed in the back during a riot in which he has done a great deal to protect the Christians, among whom are St. Peter and St. Paul. While dying he forgives and pleads for leniency for his assassin.

There is certainly a mood of compassion here, both for the young officer and for the murderer, but Kipling goes on to labour a message of his own, and by the time we find St. Peter saying, in effect, that there is no need to baptize a man of Valens's forgiving spirit, we realize that the whole purpose of the story from the beginning was to score points for Mithraism. Valens has little depth of individual creation. We find to our disappointment that he has simply been invented as a mouthpiece for an argument.

'The Gardener' is another of Kipling's most famous later stories, and this again seems more of a deliberately constructed theory than a story. In 'The Gardener', Helen Turrell, a spinster, brings up a boy who is said to be the illegitimate son of her dead brother. The boy gradually realizes his illegitimacy, and there are one or two painfully hysterical scenes, in which the child is allowed to address Helen as 'Mummy' at bedtime.

The boy grows up and is killed at Ypres; and later Helen goes to seek his grave in a vast graveyard of war dead. As she is looking down the bewildering rows of graves, a mysterious gardener appears to her, and 'with infinite compassion' says, 'Come with me and I will show you where your son lies.'

This story, like Stevenson's 'Thrawn Janet', seems to ignore its own true point in favour of a magic climax. We are surely not expected to take the word 'son' as a surprise at the curtain drop. Any reader, and especially any reader used to Kipling, must have a strong suspicion that the boy is Helen's own illegitimate baby, almost from page one of the story. Anyhow, if this is to be a matter of guesswork, with a climax in the last line which consists of the author saying 'You guessed right' or 'I fooled you', it is not a very serious story.

The interest of the whole story surely consists in the heroic Miss Turrell's effort to bring her own baby up as her nephew, never allowing her friends and neighbours in the village to break openly through her pretence, whatever they may really have thought. In 'A Habitation Enforced' Kipling shows that he knew how people in English villages will ferret out family news and connections that spread out to America and back.

Helen Turrell's story is a deeply domestic and down-to-earth theme, which Kipling touches only at the melodramatic moment when the child in a fever addresses Helen as 'Mummy'. The story not only lacks ordinary verisimilitude, but it makes almost no attempt to search out the kind of daily unpretentious truth in which Chekhov was chiefly interested. Once again it seems to deal with a pre-cast message rather than with human beings, and the message is that there may be apparitions suggestive of a higher sympathy and that such apparitions may appear to be seen by unmarried and bereaved mothers at dramatic moments, assuring them that 'illegitimacy' is only a man-made idea and that motherhood is real.

Frank O'Connor has much the same view of this story. He begins by saying it is an admitted masterpiece, 'a most moving piece of writing'. He tells us it always makes him want to weep, yet something about it makes him uneasy. He goes on:

As a writer I can put up a very good case for the form of the story as Kipling wrote it. I can say that this is a story of hypocrisy that has blasted the life of an innocent child and that it is proper that the form of the story should be the external representation of all the hypocrisy up to the supreme moment when it is confronted by God and collapses. But really, I don't believe a word of it. Instead I have found myself rewriting the story as it might have been written by Chekhov or Maupassant, just to see what would happen: if instead of beginning, as Kipling does, with 'Everyone in the village knew that Helen Turrell did her duty by all her world, and by none more honourably than by her only brother's unfortunate child' I wrote, 'Helen Turrell was about to have an illegitimate baby'; and, instead of the fine irony of 'She most nobly took charge, although she was, at the time, under threat of lung trouble which had driven her to the South of France' I wrote, 'So as to have the baby she had to pretend that she was suffering from lung trouble and had been ordered by her doctor to go to the South of France'.

Having written these words, Frank O'Connor loses all faith in Kipling's version and compares 'sharing a real human experience' with 'having one's brains battered in by a celestial gardener'. He then goes on to say:

Now if I could say straight out what is wrong with Kipling's treatment of 'The Gardener', I could put my finger on what is wrong with Kipling as a writer, but it is not enough merely to point out how somebody else could have done it better. What does emerge from the rewriting is that Kipling does not keep his eye on the object. He is not really thinking at all of that mother and son but of an audience and the effect he can create on an audience.[3]

He sums Kipling's method up as an 'oratorical approach'.

IV

Frank O'Connor opens his chapter on Kipling by saying that he feels a sense of embarrassment in dealing with Kipling, because while he admires the work of Kipling he feels that if Chekhov and Maupassant are 'real writers then Kipling is not; if, on the other hand, Kipling is a real writer there is something obviously wrong with them'.

[3] O'Connor, *The Lonely Voice*, ch. IV.

The difference is in the end simply one of personalities. Chekhov is a complete contrast to Kipling. Chekhov did not travel outside Russia. He felt no call to lecture the Russian people about their public duty. He had no upper-deck standards to preserve. He revelled in the life of artists, writers, and theatre people in Moscow, was easy-going and kind-hearted, though tenacious and hard-working in using his own gifts and helping his family. He was also a practising doctor. The successful and courted writer did not give up his medical practice till near the end of his life. He did not seek out or favour fashionable patients, but saw an endless number of poor people who could pay him very little. His sympathies and thoughts were drawn to the joys and sufferings of ordinary people in everyday life. He did not like discussions and social theories, which he once referred to as 'parading in peacocks' feathers and fishes' teeth'. Notions and opinions appeared to Chekhov to be absurd excrescences on human beings in the nature of warts, boils, and hunchbacks.

Preaching and propounding is as far from his nature as from his artistic practice. He wanted simply to see and portray individual people with sympathy and understanding, and above all truth. If we are to see Kipling with sympathy and understanding, we must accept the fact that he is a preacher and a moralizer. It is his very nature. His whole manner is shot through with points of view and messages, implied when they are not stated. At times he seems to have a private religion up his sleeve.

As a purely personal reaction I enjoy most some of the simplest of his stories. I prefer the story-teller to the preacher, the man who builds up an empire of his theories. When I was a child I used to pore over the pictures of Mowgli in *The Jungle Book*, with hopes of delight. When I tried to read the stories I was repelled by the fearsome pi-jaws, the priggish jungle civics, put into the mouths of bears and pumas. Wolves talking about 'the honour of the pack' struck me as the last dregs of grown-up moralizing.

My great joy, on the other hand, was the story of Rikki-Tikki-Tavi, the mongoose who slew two cobras and a poisonous little brown snake, and saved the lives of a boy and his father and mother. Here all Kipling's skill is at work, simplified and chastened. Though Rikki is given some human aspects, he does not talk about 'Mongoose law'. There is a splendid scene where Rikki seizes Nag the cobra by the neck, and the big snake goes thrashing round the bathroom, while Rikki hangs on for dear life. For dear life, that is the point, yet even at this moment Kipling cannot resist saying that if Rikki-Tikki-Tavi were killed he preferred to be found with his teeth locked 'for the honour of the family'.

'The Bull that Thought' is another animal story, written for adults this time, which exhibits all Kipling's gift as a poet crafts-man, while almost eliminating the Kipling *persona*. There is a typical opening in which Kipling so impresses Voinon, a French general merchant of the Camargue district, with his splendidly powerful car that Voinon gives him some special champagne kept only for the true cognoscenti. Then it is Voinon who tells the delightful story of 'The Bull that Thought'. Kipling on this occasion follows the advice that Chekhov gave his brother, and forgets his own personality, yet gives a wonderful display of his own genius in understanding and portraying another man's world with complete authenticity: it is an appealing small world too, of herdsmen and bulls who recognize a friendly kinship in bull-rings where the bull is never killed, and only the man is in danger. That Roy Campbell praised its authenticity is praise indeed.

Strangely enough, it is Kipling himself who makes a haunting comment on the endurance of these smaller, more modest themes, and the passing nature of mightier affairs.

> Of earth-constricting wars,
>   Of Princes passed in chains,
> Of deeds out-shining stars,
>   No word or voice remains.
>
> Yet furthest times receive
>   And to fresh praise restore,
> Mere flutes that breathe at eve,
>   Mere seaweed on the shore.[4]

[4] 'The Survival' (Horace, Ode 22, bk. V), in *Debits and Credits* (1926).

XIII

Edwardian Developments: Who is the Narrator?

I

It was pointed out in chapter XI that the influence of the Russian and French short-story writers came late to England, where the form of the short story was moulded by the strong hand of Kipling. Many people who disliked what he said still thought of his stories as models of form. Though George Moore's *The Untilled Field* (1903) and James Joyce's *Dubliners* (1914) were written during the first decade of the twentieth century, there is little sign that any already well-known and established author had read or admired Chekhov, and there was much in the Edwardian period that was inimical to the quieter, more private stories of the Russians. The coming changes were dammed up by various factors.

First was the personality of the period itself, both massive and public. The working class were at times just as jingoistic about the exploits of leaders like Kitchener as were the politicians. An atmosphere seemed to emanate from the opulent personality of the king himself. It was a time when fashionable taste thought the formalized slaughter of thousands of pheasants was a most delightful pastime, and the aura of cigar smoke, diamond tie-pins, and champagne lunches spread over the moors with the gun smoke; all a little different from Turgenev's *Sketches of a Sportsman*.

It was true that the set-piece moral earnestness of the Victorians was departing, giving place to doubts and theories about society itself. Famous authors had sport among the arguments, and

Shaw, Chesterton, and Wells enjoyed shooting down high-flying notions. Yet this all seemed to take place within the barriers of Britain's impressive insularity, and within the realms of debate. It did not seem that anybody would really knock down the property world of the Forsytes of Galsworthy, or the Wilcoxes of *Howard's End*.

Short stories could not amount to very much amidst this clatter of argument. The Russians, the French, and the Americans had all been discussing short stories as an art form, and this in itself ran counter to a deep-rooted British feeling that to be conscious of form in matters of authorship was in itself bad form. As Professor Sutherland puts it in his essay on English literature in *The Character of England*, the common reader is apt to be 'secretly convinced that a care for such matters is almost certainly symptomatic of a want of creative energy'.[1] Conversely, and this applies particularly to short stories because of their relationship to informal narration, the outward appearance of the straggling or the racy improvisation is often welcomed as something which is sure to be genuine even when it is carefully contrived; the manuscript found by chance, for instance, or a man of action telling in his own blunt way a yarn which of course 'really happened'. In his autobiography, H. G. Wells, as Professor Sutherland points out, laughs at Henry James for his interest in the novel as an art, and writes, 'I was disposed to regard the novel as about as much of an art form as the market place or the boulevard.' Wells was deliberately playing down to the popular notion that form is irrelevant and in fact suspect.

II

While the influence of Kipling was at its height, two world-famous novelists, Joseph Conrad and Henry James, were also bringing their weight to bear on short stories; but while they both discussed the forms of fiction, they were not particularly interested in brevity. Clearly, Conrad is a writer who needs space. He is at his best when the brooding intensity of his visual scenes run on for page after page. In such famous long short stories as

[1] *The Character of England*, ed. Ernest Barker (Clarendon Press, 1947).

'Youth' (1902) and 'Typhoon' (1903), he gives us magnificent seascapes, raging storms, the inner personality of ships and of men fighting the elements. Dangers are piled up and words come flooding like the tempests. 'Youth' is a story of indomitable persistence, yet it is any brave young officer's story. We know that the 'I' of the story will fight disaster upon disaster to the end. It is a story of action and event. 'Typhoon' is the deeper, the more satisfying work of art. It gives us the single incident of the typhoon wonderfully portrayed, and with it the intense reality of the stubborn Captain MacWhirr, a man so solid that his officers think him very stupid. In the height of the hurricane he sends for a book of reference and studies the nature of typhoons. Yet it is he who insists on protecting the small possessions of his Chinese passengers at a time when it seems almost certain that the whole ship will founder at any moment. He has the complete integrity and honour of his calling—not merely a will to conquer.

Like Kipling, Conrad moves mainly in a man's world. Judging from his short stories, he seems to feel that it is the sea which forges character, while the lonely trading outposts bring dissolution. This is the theme of both 'Heart of Darkness' and 'An Outpost of Progress', which are also 'long shorts' rather than short stories.

In *Tales of Unrest* (1898) and *A Set of Six* (1908) we can see something of Conrad's art when it is applied to shorter stories. 'The Idiots' (in *Tales of Unrest*) is an extremely horrible and effective story in which Conrad for once takes a situation which is pitched in the home. It is set in the French countryside and has a link with the dark side of Maupassant, whose influence Conrad acknowledges. The tendency in his shorter stories is for the skeleton of a melodrama to stick out too clearly. 'The Brute' (one of *A Set of Six*), for instance, is the story of a ship which was destined to kill a man on every voyage, and though it is told with all Conrad's authority, it is just an old salt's yarn, a tall story.

A preoccupation with the personality of the narrator is sometimes an embarrassment. Conrad occupies several pages at the beginning of 'Heart of Darkness' in building up the verisimilitude of the speaker, Marlow. In 'Youth', also, the story is told by

Marlow, 'at least I think that's how he spelt his name'. That, surely, is overdoing the mechanical device of pretending the story comes from somebody other than the author—in this instance somebody with 'sunken cheeks', somebody who 'resembled an idol', in fact, a kind of witch-doctor image of Conrad himself.

Is there anything artistically dubious in building up a narrator who is supposed to vouch for the truth of the story? The danger is that it becomes a mere trick. One cannot believe that Marlow spoke whole stories in wonderful Conradian prose. It destroys the very conviction that the yarn spinner is supposed to maintain. As if Conrad himself felt uneasy he developed a strange habit of telling his readers in forewords and postscripts how much of his stories he claimed to be fact, and how much he invented. He tells us, for instance, that the story of 'Il Conde' in *A Set of Six* really happened to a charming old gentleman, whom he knew. The general situation, however, turns up in Harman's *Common Cursitors*, and was probably not original even then. He says, on the other hand, that Captain MacWhirr in 'Typhoon' is entirely the product of his own imagination, but that he feels the character must really have existed. Yet it is quite unnecessary to tell us this. The 'imaginary' Captain MacWhirr possesses the only kind of reality that matters.

The narrator approach also encourages Conrad to interrupt the story and address his ideas on the problems of authorship to the reader. He breaks off in the middle of 'An Outpost of Progress' (in *Tales of Unrest*) to tell us:

Everybody shows a respectful deference to certain sounds that he and his fellows can make. But about feelings people really know nothing. We talk with indignation or enthusiasm; we talk about oppression, cruelty, crime, devotion, self sacrifice, virtue, and we know nothing real beyond the words. Nobody knows what suffering or sacrifice mean—except perhaps the victims of the mysterious purpose of these illusions.

If we look strictly at dates, it is perhaps unfair to say that Henry James seems old-fashioned for his day. He was born only three years after Hardy, and 'Daisy Miller' was published in 1879, well before Hardy's earlier stories; but it is the famous later style of James that seems most remote from the more modern short-story form. In the later stories, James, at his most longwinded, is at the reader's elbow the whole time like an over-attentive guide, nudging him, and telling him how to look at everything. In some ways he is the very reverse of a short-story writer; he is a producer of elaborate discussions about stories.

'The Turn of the Screw' is often referred to as a short story. It is certainly shorter than some of James's novels and it has the singleness of theme that is suitable for a short story. It is, however, about 50,000 words long, ten times longer, for instance, than such well-known modern short stories as Francis Tuohy's 'The Admiral and the Nuns', Mary Lavin's 'The Will', Kipling's 'Mrs. Bathurst', Elizabeth Bowen's 'Joining Charles', or Chekhov's 'Happiness'. 'The Turn of the Screw' approaches the length of a novel, and the tremendous paraphernalia of establishing the narrator occupies nearly half the length of the short stories just mentioned.

Let us look at this in detail. A group of friends of whom 'I' is one are gathered round a fire in an old house at Christmas time. A very remarkable manuscript is mentioned by one of the friends, Douglas, and 'I' asks some questions, aimed to build up its authenticity. Douglas explains that it 'is in old and faded ink and in the most beautiful hand'. It was written long ago by the governess of his sister. Douglas's sister sent it to him before she died, and it has been lying in a bureau for many years. Douglas is now persuaded to write and ask for the manuscript. A few days later it arrives, but even then it still needs a 'few words of pro-logue'. So 'I' tells the reader that years after the occasion on which the story was told to the group of friends, Douglas handed over the manuscript so that 'I' could make an exact transcript. The 'few words' of prologue (three pages) then follow before we are able to begin on the manuscript itself. We do not, of course, see the exquisite handwriting, but we very soon perceive that this second 'I', the governess, writes in the same style as Henry James himself.

L

One could hardly imagine a more complicated set of knotted strings and pulleys to set a short story going. It is an extreme example—perhaps it is *the* extreme example—of the lengths to which a short-story writer can go in establishing the narrator. All the accounting for the existence of the manuscript rubs in the fact that there never was such a manuscript. It simply demands disbelief. Yet the story itself is a fascinating example of James's drawn-out skill in disturbing suggestion. It is truly nasty, whether we think the children were really corrupted by vicious ghosts, or destroyed by the morbid hallucinations of the governess with the beautiful handwriting.

James's complete output of short stories is prodigious, and some of the best and most typical are to be found in *Fourteen Short Stories*, introduced by David Garnett.[2] They range from 1879 to 1908, and this selection conveys the characteristic art of his short stories. They examine at extraordinary length the refinements of social situations among well-to-do Americans and English people. They are intricate, involved, and nebulous; they tend to arouse attentive curiosity rather than joy or sorrow.

Let us take one typical James situation. In 'The Tree of Knowledge', Lancelot Mallon, a talented young man, grows up to the realization that his father, who is a sculptor, is a nincompoop; that his mother knows this, but is keeping up the fiction that he is a genius; that his godfather, whom he trusts, has been involved in the most delicate situation with his mother. Nothing can be put into words, but doubt rustles around in a thicket of innuendo.

The whole situation, among these good people, was verily a marvel, and there was probably not such another for a long way from the spot that engages us—the point at which the soft declivity of Hampstead began at that time to confess to the broken accents of St. Johns Wood. He despised Mallon's statues and adored Mallon's wife, and yet was absurdly fond of Mallon, to whom in turn he was equally dear. Mrs. Mallon rejoiced in the statues—though she preferred, when pressed, the busts; and if she was visibly attached to Peter Brench it was because

[2] Henry James, *Fourteen Short Stories*, ed. David Garnett (Rupert Hart-Davis, 1947).

of his affection for Morgan. Each loved the other moreover for the love borne in each case to Lancelot, whom the Mallons respectively cherished as their only child, and whom the friend of their fireside identified as the third—but decidedly the handsomest—of his godsons.

As with the descriptive atmosphere in Conrad, it is surprising sometimes when we remove these long explanations and intricacies of thought to find how obvious and even 'magaziney' the situation and sentiments of the characters are. Here, for instance, are the closing words of 'The Jolly Corner':

Then, 'He has a million a year' he lucidly added. 'But he has'nt you.'
'And he isn't—no he isn't—*you*,' she murmured, as he drew her to his breast.

Strangely enough, James himself seemed to hanker for a more succinct form of presentation. 'I come back, I come back to my only seeing it in the dramatic way,' he writes in his Notebooks, 'as I see everything nowadays.' Yet he progresses further and further towards presenting his material in the abstract, discursive way.

One of his most sympathetic stories, 'Brooksmith', is also one of his shortest. 'Brooksmith' is an unusual venture for James, for it examines life outside the drawing-room classes. It studies the decay of an epicene young butler who for some years had handed the cakes and almost shared the conversation at his bachelor master's literary tea-parties. When his master dies, Brooksmith is lost and unhappy. He can never find such a place, such an employer again. He drifts, declines into sordid surroundings, and finally disappears. This is a story in which James simplifies his own discussion and more nearly approaches a modern form.

In the Edwardian period there was at times an obsession with the idea of a personal narrator in fiction. James, Conrad, and Ford Madox Hueffer exchanged views on this subject. *Lord Jim*, for instance, is supposed to have been largely spoken by Marlow in a few long sessions to a small group of people. Ford Madox Hueffer, in *The Good Soldier*, tells the whole novel through the mouth of an 'I' who is one of the leading characters in the story. This 'I' repeatedly protests his lack of story-telling skill, repeatedly reminds us that it is a 'real' story. He is trying to tell it as if he was alone in a cottage with a sympathetic friend. This lack of arrangement, he insists, demonstrates its reality. 'I console myself with thinking that this is a real story and that, after all, real stories are probably told best in the way a person telling a story would tell them. They will then seem more real.'[3] This brings to a point the whole feeling that simulated unskilled speech is in itself the best approach to the truth, and that this fact ought to be rubbed in to the reader. The theory of using a spoken style of narrative for short stories was later made fully explicit by Somerset Maugham, and we will return to it in discussing his views.

III

There were other influences that continued to act against the development of interest in the art of the short story as practised on the Continent. H. G. Wells, perhaps the most famous short-story writer of the period after Kipling, used the short story mainly for exploring strange ideas. One of the founding fathers of science fiction, Wells has an extraordinary gift for realizing his notions rapidly and readably. It is a pity that he never tried to crystallize his *Kipps* vein of insight and creation in the form of short stories. In fact, he fostered the old idea that a short story must contain magic. 'Let's pretend' is his approach.

Then there are the wits who are also a strong influence. The inimitable cleverness of Max Beerbohm must have turned many thoughts to the attractions of the polished social extravaganza. His single book of short stories, *Seven Men*, is the quintessence of *salon* entertainment. He himself repudiated the notion that he was a satirist, and if there is any rebuke in *Seven Men* it is of the most urbane kind imaginable. He is simply indulging in some inspired fooling at the expense of some very silly people. Not only the situations, but the delicate precision of the prose give *Seven Men* the status of a classic. R. A. Scott James says of him very aptly that 'his is the kind of writing which English literature is supposed not to have'. But certainly, if we compare his vein with Voltaire or some other Gallic spirit we shall see that something

---

[3] Ford Madox Hueffer, *The Good Soldier* (John Lane, 1915).

very English has crept into the conception. He is more comparable perhaps with the spirit of Horace Walpole or Matthew Prior. Paradoxically, *Seven Men* was not published till 1919, although some of its separate pieces appeared far earlier.

Another leading wit was Saki (the pen-name of H. H. Munro). His amusing sardonic stories were used to cover up and yet to express his deeper feelings in a vein of laughable, anti-moral inventions. Here the satire is more openly stated. The world of his short stories has a deceptively natural appearance of Edwardian family life. That is the essence of the joke; within this natural seeming world the flippant and the young score delicious victories over the middle-aged. There is a strong serious intention behind this kind of flippancy, but Saki was satirizing personal relationships, and the attitude of grown-ups to children as he had experienced it, and not any larger social themes.

E. M. Forster, in his early book of short stories, *The Celestial Omnibus* (1911), also creates worlds of fantasy, more obviously allegorical than those of Max Beerbohm or Saki. His intention is to discuss aspects of human beings and society, though his touch is light and he is the most sympathetic of moralists. The title story, 'The Celestial Omnibus', which contrasts a boy's strong imaginative experience in the face of literature with the stereotyped lip-service of the elders, is characteristic and famous.

All these polished artists, who were pursuing their own personal side-tracks in the use of the short story, are antidotes to an over self-conscious high seriousness; they do not pontificate and they do write shortly. In fact, when we turn to Forster's early novels we find in the slightly breathless vivid prose interesting glimpses of the coming style of Katherine Mansfield.

In one of his short stories, 'Other Kingdom Wood', E. M. Forster handles a theme which might well have come from Katherine Mansfield: a young girl, sensitive, natural, and rather ignorant, is engaged to a well-to-do, dominant man who wishes to lavish everything on his bride, and yet abrades her with his over-assured education and wealth. Forster solves the problem, as Katherine Mansfield would never have done, by turning the girl into a dryad, in the very wood which her husband has given her. Katherine Mansfield would have let us see how very much Evelyn Beaumont wanted to turn into a dryad.

IV

Meanwhile there were other writers of short stories, not nearly so much acclaimed as Wells or Conrad, and whose work was on a smaller scale, but who were nevertheless preparing the way for a changing conception of the art of the short story.

George Moore, in *The Untilled Field*, published in 1903, gives us stories of natural and unforced humanity, which he himself counted among his best work. Unquestionably they are nearer to Russian and French models than English, and are very different, too, from the famous yarn-spinning of his Irish predecessors Somerville and Ross. He refers to himself as 'Zola's ricochet'. Murray Gilchrist's Derbyshire stories, *A Peakland Faggot* (1897), were picked out by some critics, but had no reverberating success. In their moods of quiet realism among the dales and farms they vary from the humorous to the sad and occasionally to the angry. Eden Philpotts noticed the relationship of Gilchrist to Turgenev. However, the comparison is not very close and leaves Gilchrist looking an unskilful and minor performer, although he has three or four stories that seem strikingly above the level of the rest.

Mad Shepherds (1910), by L. P. Jacks, is a book of remarkable originality and power, and that cross-grained, violent, and at times prophetic genius of sheep-breeding, 'Snarly Bob', is a true short-story creation, strikingly alive and real. The book, however, is presented in the form of essays and discussions, as well as stories, and makes no more than a chance contribution to the development of the short-story art.

Another writer of this period was Pett Ridge, with his unforced and kindly stories of ordinary London life: a typical story shows us simply the journey of a cheerfully drunk young sailor in a bus crowded with people, some of whom are helpful and sympathetic and some of whom are hostile: the kind of trifle of a story that often turns out to be extremely hard to do. Pett Ridge is sometimes apt to sentimentalize the brutal truths of poverty, and to overplay his characters as indefatigable Cockney humorists.

Here he is the reverse of Arthur Morison, who overemphasizes the sub-human brutality of delinquent men and hopeless women, who are doomed to disease and child-bearing amidst appalling squalor. Arthur Morison puts these harsh scenes across in brief, bald sentences. His *Tales of Mean Streets* are statements of cases as much as stories, almost as if parts of Mayhew had been given a spasmodic life and movement. Morison's first and probably best-known book of short stories was written in 1894, but it remained as an influence throughout the earlier years of the twentieth century. Gissing's drab stories of seedy respectability merging into bitter poverty are another sincere attempt to see the truth; perhaps he allows the utter dreariness of some of his feelings to reflect itself too effectively in his own prose style.

As V. S. Pritchett has pointed out, the slum life of the great cities was a terror to the respectable classes—'the abyss just beyond their back door. The awful Gothic spectacle of hunger, squalor and crime was tolerable only as nightmare and fantasy—such as Dickens provided.'[4] These authors had tried to write about the truth that was largely missing from English fiction, and they used the short story to do it. There was a good deal of discussion during this period about the implications of French realism, naturalism, symbolism, and the scientific novel. American critics have in the long run paid more attention to the use of such classifications than the English. It is hard to tie labels on to good short stories, which tend to move towards a single centre, but some of the lesser known short-story writers of these years un-doubtedly made use of their understanding of the 'realist' and 'naturalistic' schools to penetrate towards the truth.

Stacy Aumonier is another example of an outstanding though variable short-story writer. He was at times too easily drawn from a sincere vision into slick situations, though these are at least a tribute to his deliberate professional mastery. At his best he wrote a few truly memorable stories. 'Them Others' from *Love-A-Duck* (1924) was written during the First World War, and is a sympathetic study of the gradual perception of the human reality of the enemy by a simple middle-aged woman. Her son is

---

[4] V. S. Pritchett, *The Living Novel* (Chatto and Windus, 1946), p. 153.

taken prisoner and painfully she gropes her way through the murk of propaganda to her memories of a German family who used to live in her own street. ' "She used to make a very good fruit puddin'," Mrs. Ware said suddenly at random. "Dried fruit and that. My Ernie liked it very much." ' 'Them Others' challenges comparison with Katherine Mansfield's 'Ma Parker', although the technique shows some striking contrasts.

Aumonier's 'The Great Unimpressionable' was in its day a famous story. It tells of a British soldier who passes through the most terrifying experiences, but whose thoughts are all the time with his home, his village, and especially his dog, and whose laconic letters after shattering adventures contain such news as 'The grub is better now'. The disasters that overwhelm Ned in his service are exaggerated to the point of grim farce. Yet the home-coming, when having endured everything stoically Ned breaks down on finding that his dog has died, is in a mood of truth that is moving because it is matter-of-fact. Once again we see the old Anglo-Saxon story of the exile, grief-stricken by the return for which he had longed.

Stacy Aumonier's best story is probably 'The Two Friends' from *Overheard* (1924)—an almost horrifyingly exact study of the self-indulgent emptiness of two middle-aged men. They form an apparent friendship entirely on the basis that they both drink too much every day at lunchtime, and treat themselves far too well at expensive restaurants. To others they appear to be close colleagues in some weighty business. However, their business affairs are almost non-existent. When one of them dies, and the other goes to his funeral, he finds his wife and family living almost in poverty. No drink is offered to him at their poor home and, unable to resist stopping the mourners' carriage at a pub on the way to the funeral, he ends by becoming shoutingly and despairingly drunk. The story moves towards agonies of farce, although heightened, yet convincing; it is reminiscent of Gogol rather than Chekhov, and not unlike some of the scenes to be created by William Sansom thirty years later.

It was these writers, rather than Kipling, Wells, or Conrad, who were helping to form the art of the short story that was to

appear in the 1920s. D. H. Lawrence's 'Odour of Chrysanthemums' was published in the *English Review* in 1913. Katherine
Mansfield and Coppard were already struggling to give form to
their invincible urge to express their vision of human beings in
the form of short stories.

Some of the lighter humorous writers, whose works reached a
wide public, were also contributing to the form of the short
story. The *Dolly Dialogues* of Anthony Hope, in the 1890s, which
are told almost completely without narrative, and the 'Eliza' series
of Barry Pain, in the Edwardian decade, have a serious depth of
feeling behind them. The stories of W. W. Jacobs about rustics
and sailormen are more farcical, but the craft of all these authors
in itself verges upon artistry, and may well have given lessons to
more serious writers. These light-hearted diversions came to a
brilliant late flowering in the 1920s with P. G. Wodehouse.
Bertie Wooster and Jeeves, known in many languages, are a most
unexpected Anglo-Saxon version of Don Quixote and Sancho
Panza, and convey with feather-light satire a departed state of
affairs, and a kind of laughter that seems to have died away with
it. *Innocent Amusements* was in fact the title of one of Barry Pain's
collections.

XIV
Katherine Mansfield

I

Katherine Mansfield, like Chekhov, like Stevenson, and like
D. H. Lawrence, was under the influence of tuberculosis. Her life
became a race against death; at the end an agonized race towards
clarity and enlightment as well as towards her point of departure.
She was only thirty-four when she died.

If she had lived to an old age, which is nowadays quite normal,
Katherine Mansfield would be with us still, in her late seventies,
rich, perhaps, in honours and film rights, and a redoubtable observer of the sixty years of literature in which she had played a
part. Yet the thought of Katherine Mansfield, alive in the 1960's,
is perturbing. We are still in the midst of a discussion about the
intensely living woman of the 1920's.

In whatever way we may answer speculations about her inter-
rupted achievements, her performance is unique. She is the only
author who has placed herself in English literature, and indeed in
Western literature, by a few short stories alone; and even her
output of short stories is small compared with Kipling's.

It is a fact, and a stubborn fact for those who dislike one or
other of these two, that Katherine Mansfield and Kipling are the
two most famous British short-story writers. They could hardly
be more different. Kipling wrote of action and of men in their
jobs. Katherine Mansfield is extremely feminine, writing of
ingénues, of girls left alone, of husbands and wives loving or de-
ceiving each other. Kipling talked of the greatness of Empire and
Commonwealth, and called readers to a realization of geopolitics.
Katherine Mansfield, coming from the farthest point of British
colonization, immersed herself in a struggling literary life in the

middle of London. Kipling was the master short-story writer of Katherine Mansfield's early days. Yet out of her dedicated and ruthless labour she evolved by uncertain steps her own short-story art, and she wrote as if she were completely unaware of Kipling's existence. To speak of a 'new art' of the short story at this stage may seem an exaggeration. Critics in the 1890s had already been talking of the new art of the short story. Yet this is how Anthony Alpers, himself a New Zealander, and author of the most comprehensive and well-balanced book about Katherine Mansfield, sees it.

In 1920, when *Bliss* and other stories first appeared, the short story had virtually no status as a literary form in English writing. With Saki prematurely dead—and Kipling too, in any creative sense—and Somerset Maugham a novelist and playwright as yet, there existed no English writer of any stature, who used this as a principal means of expression. . . . The short story as perfected by the Russians and Maupassant, with its own exacting principles having no relation to those of the novel, was not an English product.[1]

Bliss was in fact an epoch-making book, and it was no sooner published than Katherine Mansfield's reputation was established. *Bliss* attracted attention far more rapidly and dramatically than James Joyce's *Dubliners*, which was first published in 1914 and hardly noticed at the time. Lest Anthony Alpers should be considered partial, let us turn to a more general literary historian: R. A. Scott James. He says of Katherine Mansfield, in *Fifty Years of English Literature*:

She owed much to French writers, but the most obvious influence in her writing was that of Tchecov. *In a German Pension*, a collection of short stories published in 1911, did not yet show how great her talent was to be. But in *Bliss*, a volume of short stories published in 1920, she proved her power, and the triumph was repeated in *The Garden Party* (1922) and in the posthumous collection *The Dove's Nest* (1923) and *Something Childish* (1924).

It seemed that any significant fragment of life was enough for her. She observed it minutely, described it simply and objectively, and at the end the point had been made without apparent effort, leaving the

---

[1] Anthony Alpers, *Katherine Mansfield* (Cape, 1954), p. 295.

reader thrilled, disturbed or emotionally enlightened. Her early death deprived her country of a writer of short stories belonging to a kind which, in English literature, had never before been done with so much skill and subtlety of perception.[2]

Two interesting points arise from this passage of Scott James. The first is that in dealing with Katherine Mansfield at the very opening of his chapter on the fiction that followed the First World War, he emphasizes the earliness of *Bliss*. It is part of a new dawn. Katherine Mansfield belongs to the company of those writers, such as Eliot, Joyce, and Virginia Woolf, who were coming to full maturity during the First World War. *Bliss* was being acclaimed before the publication of *The Waste Land*, before *Ulysses*, before the books in which Virginia Woolf explored the methods of interior vision. *Bliss* was not, of course, published before *Sons and Lovers*, or before some of Lawrence's earlier short stories. Katherine Mansfield knew D. H. Lawrence during the war and he gave her a good deal of advice, some of it highly patronizing. However, she worked out her own art without the aid of Lawrence and his theories.

The second interesting point is Scott James's reference to the influence of Chekhov as a matter of accepted fact. The degree of that influence has always been under dispute. Middleton Murry played it down. Her detractors, on the other hand, have leapt on her close imitation, in fact, plagiarism, of one Chekhov story and have suggested that she was little more than a Chekhov despoiler. This is utterly unfair, although at least two other rather close similarities to Chekhov stories can be seen.

We may, however, truthfully say that Katherine Mansfield represents the transference of the Chekhov influence to English stories. She collaborated with Koteliansky in translating Chekhov's letters, and there are frequent admiring references to him in her journal. Yet the differentiation between Katherine Mansfield and Chekhov is of more interest than their resemblance. Anthony Alpers makes a perfectly sound point when he maintains that Katherine Mansfield achieved something very like her mature method 'by a fluke', when she wrote 'The Tiredness of Rosabel' at the age of nineteen. This was before she first came to know Chekhov's stories, which Mr. Alpers thinks were shown to her by some Polish friends, in German or in Polish translations.[3]

II

The contrast between Chekhov and Katherine Mansfield is curiously well shown in comparing the nature of two real events. The first is Chekhov's funeral, which Gorky describes with a certain anger at the lack of dignity and of public tribute to his old friend; Chekhov's funeral became mixed up with that of a general and people began to laugh. 'It was a very hot and dusty day. In front of the procession a fat police officer rode majestically on a fat white horse. . . .' One feels Chekhov would have smiled himself. The scene might have been written by him, and has exactly that touch of absurdity mixed with sadness, just that degree of colour and sense impression that he would have given it. In fact, it is remarkably close in feeling to the closing pages of 'The Bishop'. This famous story tells how after the Bishop's death the bells of six monasteries and forty churches rang out with joyful clangour, because it was Easter: and the bishop's aged mother returned to her one cow, in her little town where some people did not 'even believe she had a son who was a bishop'.

With this one might compare a certain very unhappy incident from Katherine Mansfield's life. When Middleton Murry and Katherine first met Gaudier and Sophie Brzeska, they were all four enraptured with a feeling of mutual sympathy and happiness. Their friendship flowered rapidly, and plans were made for the sharing of a country cottage where they were all going to be happy together. Then doubts began to arise; Sophie was the older woman, and Katherine found her rather overwhelming. One day Brzeska travelled from London to see the Murrys at their cottage. He arrived hot, weary, and aching for the welcome of his friends. He saw them through the open window without being seen himself, and heard Katherine discussing Sophie, and it seems Katherine was being witty and acid. The sensitive Gaudier

[3] Alpers, pp. 107, 132.

was deeply wounded and returned to London without revealing himself. Thereafter the Brzeskas, for reasons unknown to the Murrys, became their bitter enemies. Murry tells this story in his autobiography, *Between Two Worlds*,[4] in so far as he was able to piece it together, for at first he and Katherine did not know what had happened. They knew only that the Brzeskas suddenly changed from affection to hatred, and all four of them were needlessly confused and agonized.

Just as Chekhov's funeral is typical of Chekhov's art, this tense, unhappy affair is typical of Katherine Mansfield's. Chekhov was a sensitive man, helped in the long run by an admixture of common sense; but Katherine was hypersensitive. Middleton Murry himself says of his beloved Katherine, 'And, alas, I wasn't made like Katherine. I could not surrender myself wholly to the emotion as it came. I could not pass from total confidence to total despair and back again.'[5] Her stories also are full of joy and agony fluctuating. Even joy itself is agonizing. 'Oh, God!' exclaims the lover in 'Poison', 'What torture happiness was—what anguish!'

In the early story, 'Honeymoon', we see the ecstatically happy young couple confronted suddenly by sadness of the faded elderly singer in the café:

'Good Lord!' said George. It seemed that everybody was equally astonished. Even the little children eating ices stared with their spoons in the air. . . . Nothing was heard except a thin faint voice, the memory of a voice singing something in Spanish. It wavered, beat on, touched the high notes, fell again, seemed to implore, to entreat, to beg for something, and then the tune changed, and it was resigned, it bowed down, it knew it was denied.

Almost before the end, a little child gave a squeak of laughter, but everybody was smiling—except Fanny and George. . . .

And she looked at that gorgeous sea lapping the land as though it loved it.

Or there is Bertha in the famous 'Bliss':

What can you do if you are thirty, and turning the corner of your own street, you are overcome, suddenly, by a feeling of bliss—absolute

---

[4] J. Middleton Murry, *Between Two Worlds* (Jonathan Cape, 1935).
[5] Ibid., p. 459.

bliss!—as though you'd suddenly swallowed a bright piece of the late afternoon sun. . . .

Or Bertha again, enraptured by the appearance of some fruit in a bowl:

For the dark table seemed to melt into the dusty light, and the glass dish and the blue bowl to float in the air. This, of course, in her present mood was incredibly beautiful. . . . She began to laugh.

'No, no. I'm getting hysterical.' And she seized her bag and coat, and ran up to the nursery.

One of the chief points of 'Bliss' is not merely that a wife sees her beloved husband embracing another woman, but that she has throughout the whole evening been in a state of almost hysterical happiness. Again, Miss Brill, the withered spinster who over-heard the young couple on the park bench laughing at her, has a kind of ecstatic overtone of experience in which she feels she is watching herself and the whole scene from outside. These are typical moods, and it is not surprising that the young girl in 'The Garden Party', when she learns of a violent death in the home of a poor family on the day of her parents' garden party, undergoes a series of emotions which are almost inexpressible; after making her painful, inadequate visit of sympathy to the stricken family she can only stammer incoherent words to her brother.

'Was it awful?' he asks her.

'No,' sobbed Laura. 'It was simply marvellous. But Laurie——' She stopped and looked at her brother. 'Isn't life,' she stammered. 'Isn't life. . . .'

But what life was she couldn't explain. No matter. He quite under-stood. '*Isn't* it, darling?' said Laurie.

She is often thinking of a man or woman with a hidden sorrow or incoherent happiness, or a knowledge that will not come to birth. We must remember that as she grew older, as her own art matured and she lost her much loved brother, she passed into an experience beyond the obvious manic-depressive category of the psychologist. Increasingly she came to live with the foreknow-ledge of her separation from Murry and her approaching death.

Often she was alone with her illness and her feelings, in *pensions* in France or Switzerland, while he had to work in London.

Even apart from this flying up and down the scales of emotion, Katherine was a very complicated personality. Fastidiousness and a desire for breadth of experience fought within her; she was courageous in the long run, yet often shrinking over small disturbances. Some people found her alarming and too clever, yet Murry says that the timid, betrayed *ingénue* revealed in the character of Mouse, in 'Je ne parle pas Francais', was 'the secret Katherine', and he tells us that when the second part of the story reached him it 'struck me numb and dumb with pain'.[6]

Nor were these mere variations of mood. She became her moods. When she was young she would try out different personalities self-consciously, and she did some strange things as a result. In her stories she is extremely good at depicting young girls, difficult, sentimental, spoilt, and as the middle-aged might see it, impossible, yet from whom one feels a deeper, more serious, more lovable self is going to emerge.

Beryl Fairfield, who appears in 'Prelude' and 'At the Bay', stares into the glass wondering how she can discover and show her true self, and she mocks at the chatty and amusing letter she has just written, saying that none of it is *true*; just as Katherine herself writes in her journal (October 1921), 'I try to pray—and I think of something clever.'

This brings us to another quality, that is, the very essence of her art, and gives it a unique place in English fiction. That quality is the sheer intensity of her vision. She has a sensitivity to the external world so vivid that it seems to pass beyond normal experience to a point at which one feels a door is about to open into a more luminous state of knowledge. It seems that she and her characters see the whole world as a burning bush, and listen for the voice within; and it is this unique intensity of experience that she can impart to some readers, if not to all.

This Traherne-like quality of perception does not apply merely to aesthetic impressions, to the sight and sounds of the external

[6] Middleton Murry, *Between Two Worlds*, p. 463.

world; it is a vision of people, framed in their lives, and it impels her throughout all her shifting moods to write stories, and not merely to record rapturous descriptions. In fact, in her middle period she often concentrates on a portrayal of character and personality without visual description. 'And the passion I feel,' she wrote in her journal, 'It takes the place of religion. It *is* my religion of people.'[7]

Chekhov, both in his art and in his own personality, achieved more easily an artistic balance for which Katherine Mansfield had to struggle. Though he had suffered as a child from a physical violence and degradation that Katherine did not know, he had not suffered as an adolescent from a feeling of alienation within a family group to which he owed love. He knew moods, but not a violent wrestling with his own personality. Though he detested banality and said it was the great enemy, yet as a young adult he took gaily enough to a bustling world which he found comic as much as distressing.

Chekhov and Katherine originally approached short stories from almost completely different points of view. Chekhov's early stories are little comic pieces. Gradually he grows more serious. Katherine's earliest work, on the other hand, tends to be extremely earnest and lacking in humour. She pored over Marie Bashkirtseff. It is almost impossible to see her future talent in, say, 'The Death of a Rose', which is just an outpouring. 'It is a sensation that can never be forgotten to sit in solitude and semi-darkness, and watch the slow sweet sorrowful death of a Rose. . . .' Is this really Katherine Mansfield?

Surprisingly enough, the young Katherine Mansfield shared with Chekhov the gift for comic recitation, which both could do with inimitable effect. Both of them could satirize people; they could, in fact, practise the art of living mime. Katherine at one time even used to earn money by it. A sharp sense of people's presence mingled with her intense search for beauty and for meaning. It is indeed a curious reflection that she had within her something of the detached sense of the human comedy that went to the make-up of Jane Austen or the young Fanny Burney. Yet

[7] Katherine Mansfield, *Journal*, 31 May 1919.

M

she had to combine this with an intense poetic vision and hysterical changes of feeling of which they knew little. We see this combined sense of the illuminated moment and the true storywriter's eye for people repeatedly in her journal. While the potential story for Katherine lies in the intense experience of the moment, the present instant also contains the past, and Anthony Alpers and others have shown how these subtle variations of time level, or interchanges of past memory and hope for the future, give depth to the brilliant present moment of her stories.

Katherine Mansfield on the whole uses even less direct and informative narrative than Chekhov. He was less troubled by his own failings and foibles of personality, and the conscience at work in his stories is more simply an artistic conscience, while Katherine's artistic conscience is mingled with a moral and then with an increasingly religious feeling for total self-abnegation; so that it becomes an urge, even deeper than her aesthetic urge, to remove herself completely from the page. In her journal she prays for the needed modesty, for the right state of mind (23 July 1921). She struggles for 'the deepest truth' and the avoidance of 'trickery'. She talks of the need for self-effacement and says of a character that she cannot tell the truth about her 'unless I am free to enter into her life without self-consciousness'. She refers to Blake—'the artist becomes the priest of the Everlasting'.

Her notes on a story called 'A Weak Heart' that she never succeeded in finishing are of especial interest, because they show how she moves in one breath from the original flash of perception to the consideration of a time-technique, and at once to a prayer for her own act of self-effacement. These stages are all linked together. The original note is:

A weak heart. Roddie on his bike in the evening, with his hands in his pockets *doing marvels* by that dark tree at the end of May Street.

Later comes the entry in her journal (21 November 1921):

To-day I began to write seriously The Weak Heart—a story which fascinates me deeply. What I feel it needs so peculiarly is a very subtle variation of tense from the present to the past and back again—and softness and lightness, and the feeling that all is in bud, with a play of humour over the character of Roddie. And the feeling of the Thorndon Baths, the wet moist oozy—no, I know how it must be done.

May I be found worthy to do it! Lord make me crystal clear for Thy light to shine through.

We see the vision, the technique, and the prayer combined. It is in this mood that she becomes the most intense practitioner of the technique by which the story reveals itself—the mime form: but a mime in which the characters are suffused with light from within. All the information, the narrative flow, is contained in the words spoken and the scene as it appears in the eyes of the characters. The use of interior vision is brilliantly externalized in imagery, so that when we enter into somebody's thoughts and feelings we do not leave the world of sensation. In this way she accomplishes what Virginia Woolf accomplished later, but she does it in far less space. If Virginia Woolf had written 'At the Bay', it might well have become the length of *To the Lighthouse*.

III

It is well known that Katherine Mansfield was in the last months of her life moving towards a state of mind that suggests a religious conversion. Some think this might, in the long run, have brought about the final stabilization of her personality and her artistic gifts. Others regret her associations in her last illness with Gurdjieff and his suggestions of an esoteric knowledge. Middleton Murry, writing as he did out of an emotion of deep love and loss, speaks of his wife as if she were approaching some other-worldly state, and as if a further vision was transforming her work. Katherine Anne Porter, herself a renowned writer of short stories, comments that Murry confuses religious longings with artistic performance, as indeed many people have done. She thinks that Katherine Mansfield was in danger of moving away from an art which she had slowly mastered to an aspiration which could only confuse her performance. The views of other short-story writers are naturally of interest, and Frank O'Connor, who is not over-sympathetic to Katherine Mansfield, finding her personality 'brassy' and some of her effects 'tactless', says, while appreciating 'At the Bay', that it is not so much a story as an act of reminiscent magic.[8] The author was intent on living again within herself her childhood days in her New Zealand home. This may be partly true, and entries in her own journal seem to bear it out.

(21 January 1922)
Grandma's birthday. Where is that photograph of my dear love, leaning against her husband's shoulder; it is she, my own grandma—young and lovely. That arm, that baby sleeve. Even that velvet ribbon. I must see them again.

This supports Frank O'Connor's view. But this passage comes from her journal, not from one of her stories: and 'At the Bay' does not move merely in the world of remembered childhood. It enters with great subtlety into adult life, into the passage of years; it is formed with an art that goes entirely beyond the consciousness of the small child Kezia, who, if anybody does, plays the minor part that Katherine herself would have played.

It is a rewarding perception of the process of authorship to realize that if we are talking of fact, Kezia was the 'I', and to realize that the story could not possibly have been narrated in the first person by Kezia or by anybody else within the story. We must treat 'At the Bay' as a work of fiction and not as a reminiscence. Any exercise of the techniques of assuring the reader that 'this all really happened' would be a gross intrusion on the reality of the fiction.

Moreover, Katherine Mansfield did not bring this particular creative mood only to 'At the Bay' or 'Prelude'. Others of her mature stories have the same quality of enshrining a vital experience, so that we become aware not so much of a reported story as an apparition of the event itself.

V. S. Pritchett comments that the whole scene and all the characters in 'At the Bay' exist in a kind of vacuum. There is no country, no society, in which they move, or to which they are joined. In Chekhov's 'The Steppe' he says, 'the condition of Russia' is the background, the perspective, 'the silent character'.[9] Anthony Alpers agrees with Pritchett, but he says the

---

[8] O'Connor, *The Lonely Voice*, pp. 140–1.

[9] V. S. Pritchett, 'Katherine Mansfield', *New Statesman* (2 February 1946), quoted from Alpers, p. 321.

absence of social background is indeed the truth. 'The silent character was the stillness of the bush, the disdain of the lofty islands for their huddled little pockets of colonial intruders, the silence of the vast sea desert that encircled them.' Is not this suggestion of 'the dark backward and abysm of time', a recurrent element in Katherine Mansfield's art? It is probable that she had her eye on 'The Steppe' when she created the silence and empti- ness of the opening pages of 'At the Bay'. By stripping the stage bare of all social implications, she establishes the impersonality of the viewpoint, and captures that dawn-like brilliance which hovers about her work.

Very early morning. The sun was not yet risen, and the whole of Crescent Bay was hidden under a white sea mist. The big bush-covered hills at the back were smothered. You could not see where they ended, and the paddocks and the bungalows began. . . .
     Ah—Aah sounded the sleepy sea. And from the bush there came the sound of little streams flowing, quickly, lightly slipping between the smooth stones, gushing into ferny basins, and out again; and there was the splashing of big drops as large leaves, and something else—what was it?—a faint stirring and shaking, the snapping of a twig and then such silence that it seemed someone was listening.
     Round the corner of Crescent Bay between the piled-up masses of broken rock, a flock of sheep came pattering. They were huddled together, a small tossing woolly mass, and their thin stick-like legs trotted along quickly as if the cold and the quiet had frightened them. . . .

Gradually spots of light are seen in the mist; a large tree appears, 'a shock haired giant'.

The sun was rising. It was marvellous how quickly the mist thinned, shed away, dissolved from the shallow plain, rolled up from the bush and was gone as if in a hurry to escape; big twists and curls jostled and shouldered each other as the silvery beams broadened. The far away sky—a bright pure blue—was reflected in the puddles.

The morning becomes brilliant. The 'first inhabitant appears'— a cat, not a human being. The sheep, followed by the shepherd and his dog, pass out of the picture on the other side of the bay.

All is silent again; and thus the stage is set for the first character in the story to run across the beach and plunge into the sea.

A creative, poetic mind of the 1920s moving towards religious experience reminds one inevitably of T. S. Eliot. I do not think Eliot was greatly given to the analysis of short stories, but in *After Strange Gods* he has an interesting passage on 'Bliss', James Joyce's 'The Dead', and D. H. Lawrence's 'The Shadow in The Rose Garden'. He chooses them as three modern stories 'of very great merit', and comments on 'the perfect handling of the minimum material' in 'Bliss'. His purpose, however, is a kind of heresy hunt, partially humorous at times, and he looks at these three stories in order to study their relation to orthodox and traditional moral sensibility, as apart from the exploitation of 'individuality' in moral notions. He says of 'Bliss' that the 'moral implication is negligible', and 'the centre of interest is in the wife's feeling'. Here I must differ. It seems to me that the moral meaning of 'Bliss', the parable, so to speak, is completely at one with the story itself. The images of the story bring out all the implications.

As a contributor of short stories to *The Criterion*, I occasionally exchanged views about short-story writers with T. S. Eliot. On one occasion I expressed my enthusiasm for Katherine Mansfield and he said he did not find her stories entirely pleasing. There was in them, he felt, an element that was not necessarily or even properly a part of the fiction writer's art. Her aesthetic appeal was 'not a pure aesthetic'. I remember this phrase particularly. He detected those overtones of a search for another level of experience.

I have often considered this opinion, which was given quite conversationally. Even if her stories are on analysis thought to be a by-product of a religious quest, or were intermingled with a form of prayer, this is not necessarily an adverse criticism of the result. When she is at her best her own agitated quest is absorbed into her art. Eliot was at this period concerned with poetry and criticism rather than with his later work as a dramatist. It was not until years afterwards that he himself tried to depict in a mimetic form a feminine spirit with a further level of vision; and it is re-

markable how close Celia Coplestone in *The Cocktail Party*
comes at times to Katherine Mansfield.

> You see I think I really had a vision of something
> Though I don't know what it is. I don't want to forget it.
> I want to live with it.

Or when Celia is hoping for intimate conversation she says:

> If there had happened to be anyone with you,
> I was going to say I'd come back for my umbrella.

This catches Katherine Mansfield's tone of voice almost exactly:
in fact this slight sounding remark is a comment on Katherine
Mansfield's art. Celia Coplestone, like Katherine, knew 'The
desolation of solitude in the phantasmal world', and Harcourt
Reilly says of her:

> I'd say she suffered more, because more conscious
> Than the rest of us. She paid the highest price. . . .

Celia, like Katherine Mansfield, movingly searches her doubts
and fears about the truths of her own experience and the sincerity
of her own personality.

> I have thought at moments that the ecstasy is real
> Although those who experience it may have no reality,
> For what happened is remembered like a dream
> In which one is exalted by intensity of loving
> In the spirit, a vibration of delight
> Without desire, for desire is fulfilled
> In the delight of loving. A state one
> Does not know when awake. But what, or whom I loved,
> Or what in me was loving I do not know.
> And if that is all meaningless, I want to be cured
> Of a craving for something I cannot find,
> And of the shame of never finding it.

This seems to me very near Katherine Mansfield indeed; and
recalls yet once again the 'Soul's yearning' and the image of the
exile in the waste land of the world, inherited from those strangely
intimate moments of the Anglo-Saxon poets.

XV

The Twenties and Thirties

I

. . . the least essential element of all is the actual story or anecdote on which the tale hangs . . . an anecdote is not a story if that is all the story contains. In fact, it is an interesting matter to consider just how much anecdote even a good story can stand without appearing artificial.

This quotation comes from Sean O'Faolain's book *The Short Story*, and linked with Harry Levins's comments on the element of 'epiphany' in James Joyce, it gives an impression of the general feeling for the art that was shared by the new generation of writers after the First World War.

Amid the most encumbered circumstances, it suddenly happens that the veil is lifted, the burthen of the mystery laid bare, and the ultimate secret of things made manifest.[1]

This quotation naturally describes the experience of the author rather than the power of any one short story. It is the welling up of such moments amid the bustle of life that is the point— moments of insight, seen as stories. As Mr. Levin points out, *Dubliners* is a collection of the author's 'epiphanies'.

Katherine Mansfield was, as we have seen, not only an uncertain performer but a dangerous model to follow. While she herself found it very hard to achieve her own best level, her imitators have found it impossible. Her work has suffered from bad imitations, but it has suffered even more from adroit imitations. People who are accustomed by now to half a century of Chekhov translations, and discussions of Katherine Mansfield,

[1] Harry Levin, *James Joyce: a critical introduction* (Faber & Faber, 1960), p. 37.

may wonder why she was so influential. The answer is that she put a match to a fire that was ready to blaze. Other writers with different gifts had been developing a similar feeling for the short story. Joyce, Coppard, and Lawrence in some ways preceded Katherine Mansfield, and it would be interesting if space allowed to take a close look at the exact dates of short stories in literary magazines in the ten years before *Bliss* appeared.

The reprint of James Joyce's *Dubliners* followed rapidly after the publication of *Bliss*. Coppard was already in the field. Then came Elizabeth Bowen, Liam O'Flaherty, H. E. Bates, Sean O'Faolain, V. S. Pritchett, and others, a whole group of story-writers who can be thought of not so much as coming after Katherine Mansfield but with her. Elizabeth Bowen speaks for many other people when she refers to Katherine Mansfield with a feeling of personal sadness as 'our lost contemporary'.

The difference between almost any short story of the writers who shared these influences, and the kind of remarkable event or strong action story put across by a self-important narrator, can be sensed in a paragraph, almost in a sentence. The stories are not so much narrated as revealed. The curtain rises and the scene acts itself out. Comments from outside the scene would be felt as an intrusion. Generalizations of any kind are dangerous, and are open to many qualifications. Liam O'Flaherty certainly gives us strong action. H. E. Bates at times introduces an 'I' as a tactful narrator who does not obtrude himself. Elizabeth Bowen gives comments that appear to come from her own penetrating wit rather than anyone inside the story, and her own remarkable gift for capturing the atmosphere of houses is unmistakable. Flaubert's ultimate ideal of banishing all trace of the author from the page can be applied too rigidly.

Katherine Mansfield and these others were creating in English a new way of treating the short story, and we may call it, for want of a better term, 'the Chekhov kind of short story'. The Chekhov kind of short story is not merely one kind among many. The phrase stands for a complete attitude towards the modest art which after centuries of development has, for a period at least, swept the field. J. B. Priestley, who is not given to praising the attenuated or over-refined, sums up Chekhov as 'a master of the type of story now universally accepted'.[2]

Leading American critics and story-writers acknowledge the same influence, and it is by no means confined to the European or Western world. Ian Morris, in his Introduction to *Modern Japanese Short Stories*, considers that the influence of the Western short story, and particularly of the French and Russians, for a time dominated the Japanese short-story writers, overwhelming traditional forms that had continued for centuries; and that a period of close imitation followed, after which the influence was more completely absorbed, and the Japanese spirit began to express itself again through the form of modern short stories.

II

In the long run, James Joyce's one book of short stories, *Dubliners*, has very likely had more influence than the work of Katherine Mansfield, although a widespread knowledge of his stories came more slowly. But it is hard to separate the influence of *Dubliners* from the general fame and influence of Joyce. All the stories deal with life in Dublin in the early years of the century: they tell us of family and private affairs; men in their jobs and their pubs, character sketches of priests and citizens, with certain touches of low life and intrusions of unpleasant people. We move, in fact, in the same Dublin scenes as those in *Ulysses*. Within this world James Joyce has a far broader range than Katherine Mansfield, makes himself more of a mirror and less of an intense microscope. *Dubliners* is early work for Joyce, but he shows himself a conscious master of the short-story form. The self-revelation that is the main theme of *Portrait of the Artist as a Young Man* is absent from *Dubliners*.

He eliminates also, or keeps very much under control, his wonderful gift for emotive and elegiac prose. In some of the best stories the magician of words and images is seen only in an art which conceals art. It is as if Shakespeare had begun with twenty homespun sketches instead of with *Venus and Adonis*. The final story in *Dubliners*—'The Dead'—has been greatly admired and

<hr/>

[2] J. B. Priestley, *Literature and Western Man* (Heinemann, 1962).

its closing pages much analysed and quoted. In this story, as is appropriate to the educated and emotional central character, Joyce does allow himself high colour and imagery. One might, however, choose 'Counterparts' as the outstanding example of his art. In this story we follow the afternoon and evening of Farrington—a burly strong man, angry and confined in a clerical job, at which he is lazy and inefficient. Farrington is rebuked at his work. He goes out drinking, and enters into a trial of strength with another strong fellow in a public house. He loses, takes it in bad part, goes home to find his house dark and cold, and the fire out. Then he gives vent to all his rage and misery by beating his small son. This and other stories in *Dubliners* are told very simply. The descriptions are few but sure. It is the depth of human insight that creates the situations and in the end achieves the effects, so that one understands and even feels for the wretched Farrington in his stupid rage, as well as for the terrified child. Probably James Joyce is more nearly the counterpart of Chekhov in English than Katherine Mansfield.

The complete simplicity of manner seems to have come so naturally to Joyce as the right style for his stories that it is a surprise to learn that it was most carefully considered. Once again one is reminded that the natural is hard to achieve and that simple scenes of life, that are mysteriously turned into living short stories, are not mere snapshots.

Joyce wrote of *Dubliners*, 'I have written it for the most part in a style of scrupulous meanness, and with the conviction that he is a very bold man who dares to alter in the presentment, still more to deform, whatever he has seen and heard.'[3] Here we meet again the Chekhovian passion to see the truth, the Chekhovian instinct to reveal it by dwelling briefly but with penetrating clarity on individual human beings, one or two in each story.

We may be surprised also to learn of the moral feeling that lay behind *Dubliners*: 'My intention was to write a chapter of the moral history of my country, and I chose Dublin because the city seemed to me the centre of paralysis.'[4] Chekhov also was moved to expose the hopeless banality of life in provincial

[3] James Joyce, *Letters*, ed. Ellmann (Faber & Faber, 1966).   [4] Ibid.

Russian towns. 'Banality,' he said, 'is the great enemy',[5] and the banality of which he spoke may be compared to the 'paralysis' of which Joyce was conscious. Fortunately for the result, however, the artist in Joyce dominated any urge to expound except by creation. His people are not wholly drab; many of them have intimations of joy glimmering through the drabness. It is Joyce's understanding of their half-choked realizations that gives them depth.

In technique there is a considerable progression in the course of *Dubliners*. A number of stories are narrated, in the subdued and limited language chosen by Joyce, and are to some extent explained; yet they move towards an inward meditation, still expressed within the limited terms of the character's own language. In 'A Painful Case', James Duffy, a middle-aged bachelor, who is a bank clerk, forms a friendship with a married woman, Mrs. Sinico. He realizes that Mrs. Sinico is becoming too fond of him, and he cautiously ends the friendship. She returns his harmless gifts of books and music. Four years later he reads in a newspaper that she has been killed while crossing in front of a train. At the inquest it is revealed that she had been drinking heavily in spite of remonstrances from her husband and grown-up daughter. Duffy is deeply disturbed at the thought that he may have been implicated in her death; and then feels a mood of egotistical disgust that he could ever have been connected with anybody so squalid.

Technically this story is of considerable interest, because one feels that in the course of it Joyce is moving not so much towards a more perfectly realized method of writing a short story but towards *Ulysses*. The chilly, well-arranged nature of Duffy's personality is conveyed at the beginning with an exact account of his room and his furniture, a catalogue of symbols which has its ultimate expression in the question and answer chapter in *Ulysses*. When Duffy's thoughts move into an interior meditation, his vague fears are at first somewhat over-explained in abstract terms, but are then changed into haunting images of scene and sound.

[5] See *Notebooks of Chekhov*, pp. 104–6.

He looked down the slope and, at the base, in the shadow of the wall of the Park, he saw some human figures lying. Those venal and furtive loves filled him with despair. He gnawed the rectitude of his life; he felt he had been outcast from life's feast. One human being had seemed to love him and he had denied her life and happiness: he had sentenced her to ignominy, a death of shame. He knew that the prostrate creatures down by the wall were watching him and wished him gone. No one wanted him; he was outcast from life's feast. He turned his eyes to the grey gleaming river, winding along towards Dublin. Beyond the river he saw a goods train winding out of Kingsbridge station, like a worm with a fiery head winding through the darkness, obstinately and laboriously. It passed slowly out of sight; but still he heard in his ears the laborious drone of the engine reiterating the syllables of her name.

Small wonder that when Leopold Bloom goes to a funeral he recalls the funeral of Mrs. Sinico.

Joyce moves other stories away from the muffled effect of the narration used in 'A Painful Case'. 'Counterparts', with the hopeless and unhappy evening of Farrington, certainly gains from being almost completely realized in the mime or dramatic form, with little intervention from the author. It is also a perfect example of the story of a single scene—a portrait in depth yet within the compass of all that can be meant by 'short'. 'A Mother' is a story more light-hearted in manner, yet almost equally drear in its effect. Mrs. Kearney stands so fearsomely on her own dignity and her daughter's 'rights' that she ruins her chance of appearing to advantage in 'The Grand Concert'. In 'Grace' and 'Ivy Day in the Committee Room' the fustian of the conversation is, like Mrs. Kearney, approaching caricature. Joyce told his brother Stanislaus that in writing 'Grace', which opens with Tom Kernan falling down the lavatory stairs in a public house, he had in mind Dante's Inferno, Purgatory, and Paradise. Arguments with the theological instruction of his youth were always in Joyce's thoughts, and may colour his art at many points: but such knowledge of the workings of his mind adds nothing to the effectiveness of a short story.

In 'The Dead' we see Joyce beginning to move away from the short story to a more elaborate technique, towards a technique that needs more space. Yet it is still a genuine short story, once again, a single scene. 'There are moods,' says Rhys Davies in his Foreword to *Collected Short Stories*, in the words of a true short-story addict, when 'Joyce's masterly tale "The Dead" makes *Ulysses* seem like an obstreperous curiosity.'

Finally, there is one more story that Joyce wrote after 'The Dead'. He thought of calling it 'Mr. Hunter's Day'. It is not included in *Dubliners*, for by the time Joyce had finished with it, 'Mr. Hunter's Day' had turned into *Ulysses*. And here, one might say, is the broth of a short story indeed. For curiously enough, just as Kipling and Chekhov never saw events and plots in the broad novelist's way, Joyce did not either. *Ulysses*, in fact, resembles the tallest midget in the world. It is the longest short story ever written; a short story of one day in which every implication and nuance is followed up, realized, and achieved.

Elizabeth Bowen, whose first book of stories was published in 1923, does not, like Joyce, practise a conscious meanness of style. She is for the most part writing about more sophisticated people, yet she uses her own brilliance of observation, her own arresting imagery, to bring scenes and people to life. The two unmarried sisters, for instance, in the 'Easter Egg Party':

Eunice and Isabelle Evers were both just over fifty: their unperplexed lives showed in their faces, lined only by humour, and in their frank, high foreheads. They were Amazons in homespuns, Amazons, without a touch of deprivation or pathos; their lives had been one long vigorous walk. Like successful nuns, they both had a slightly married air.

This suggests a certain aloofness on the part of the author, a standing apart from her characters. She is not afraid, as Katherine Mansfield was, of saying 'something clever'. The 'Easter Egg Party' tells the story of the quite unsuccessful attempt of the two country spinsters to assuage the boredom and also the distress of a town-dwelling girl of eleven who they think has been through some 'unspeakable' experience. In the fiasco of Hermione's visit both points of view are seen with understanding. The Misses Evans are really distressed on Hermione's account; Hermione wants simply to go home, and, missing every conceivable point about their efforts to be kind to her, says, 'Couldn't you get some other girl to stay with you?'

The brilliantly lighted sets and the air of light banter does not pass into sarcasm or rebuke of her characters. Elizabeth Bowen is capable of saying something clever that is also something friendly. That she can truly share her characters' emotions is shown in the small, single-scene story called 'Tears Idle Tears', in which a boy of seven shames his very brave and soignée widowed mother by weeping hopelessly in Regent's Park.

Frederick stumbled along beside her, too miserable to notice. His mother seldom openly punished him, but often revenged herself on him in small ways. He could feel just how this was. His own incontinence in the matter of tears was as shocking to him, as bowing-down, as annulling, as it could be to her.

He never knew what happened—a cold black pit with no bottom opened inside himself; a red-hot bellwire jagged up through him from the pit of his frozen belly to the caves of his eyes. Then the hot gummy rush of tears, the convulsion of his features, the terrible square grin he felt his mouth take all made him his own shameful and squalid enemy.

The mother walks on in front, disowning her awful child, and he is braced up by a complete stranger, shabby in contrast to his mother and quite practical: she treats his outburst in a most matter-of-fact way, and says she has a young brother who has just the same trouble.

If this small story has a flaw it is to be found in the suggested explanation of the boy's hysteria, making him a prime object for later deep analysis. That kind of thing belongs very much to the psycho-analytical fashion of the twenties and thirties, and the mother, the child, and the stranger are all the story needs, without the embedded Freudian footnote.

In her sensitivity to colours, sounds, and impressions, Elizabeth Bowen challenges comparison with Katherine Mansfield. On the other hand, her own emotions are considerably more balanced than those of Katherine Mansfield. Even when she was young, she had as an author far more sophistication. She often writes about family groups and homes in which complicated situations may have arisen. She has a unique gift for catching the atmosphere of houses as if they were characters in the story. Outwardly the people in these houses are serene and calm, but they move towards outbreaks. She likes to show the civilized surface with the tensions underneath, approaching a nervous breakdown; yet in the end that crisis may never reach the point of an outbreak. It may seem a strange comparison to mention the long-winded Henry James at this point, but if one could distil out of 'The Aspern Papers' or 'The Real Thing' some elixir in a few pages, one would find the kind of situation that Elizabeth Bowen brilliantly condenses. In fact she herself refers to the in-fluence of Henry James and at times her art moves towards the over-contrived 'situation' or towards spooks, as James's did also.

Here is the close of 'Joining Charles', the title story from Miss Bowen's second volume of short stories. Louise, the wife of Charles, is staying with her husband's mother and sisters in the family house. She is going to join Charles in Lyons, and the whole surface of the story is taken up with the chilly, nerve-stretched atmosphere of early rising and preparing for departure. Louise is petite and dainty and seems rather childish, surrounded by her larger, more boisterous sisters-in-law, and her efficient mother-in-law. They are kind to Louise, anxiously trying to break her precise reserve, yet never approaching her directly.

Out in the dark hall Mother was bending over the pile of boxes, reading and re-reading the labels upside down and from all aspects. She often said that labels could not be printed clearly enough. As Louise hurried past she stood up, reached out an arm and caught hold of her. Only a little light came down from the staircase window: they could hardly see each other. They stood like two figures in a picture, without under-standing, created to face one another.

'Louise,' whispered Mother, 'if things should be difficult—Marriage isn't easy. If you should be disappointed—I know, I feel—you do understand? If Charles——'

'Charles?'

'I do love you, I do. You would tell me?'

But Louise, kissing her coldly and gently, said: 'Yes, I know. But there isn't, really, Mother, anything to tell.'

Throughout this story we see the subtlety and feeling for tentative communication typical of James, crystallized in a way that he never approached.

In strong contrast to Elizabeth Bowen is another Irish writer, Liam O'Flaherty. O'Flaherty's stories deal with the Irish peasantry, and by nature he takes the plain themes of peasant life and writes about them with a vigour and clarity that seem to clothe the simplest happening with poetry. His stories are rough and even brutal at times, but that is not an important aspect of his work. He is extremely good at writing about children, animals, and men caught up in exciting action. One could take as a single example 'Three Lambs', which deals with a small boy who was the sole observer of a ewe giving birth to her lambs. The boy's utter joy in seeing the new life, in helping the lambs in their first minutes by cleaning them with tufts of grass, and putting their mouths to the ewe's teats, turns the straightforward prose into a rhapsody of happiness. The emotion is conveyed without any obvious lyricism. It is simply there. O'Flaherty shares with Bates and Coppard an atmosphere of daylight wonder, almost as if we had entered the world of magic folk-tales; but the magic consists simply in the fact of existence.

O'Flaherty has, in fact, the innocent eye, and the gift of writing stories that are absolutely without comment on the ways of men and God. Frank O'Connor, in *The Lonely Voice*, makes an interesting comparison between O'Flaherty's story 'Going into Exile' and George Moore's 'Home-sickness'. Moore connects the emigration with a view of its cause, boredom with religious authoritarianism. 'O'Flaherty,' says O'Connor, 'could ignore everything except the nature of exile itself...'

The stories of H. E. Bates, also, began to appear in the earlier years of the 1920s. His art, like that of Elizabeth Bowen, may appear slight at first sight, yet perfected. From his earliest stories we see that natural, unforced clarity that he has maintained for many years. Bates wrote from the first about English country people, the cottagers, the holders of small farms, the lesser shopkeepers. One feels on every page an intense sympathy with their feelings, their toil, their varied characters, their success or failure.

N

The author knows what country work means; yet he is alive to country joys.

Centuries ago the medieval parish priests in their sermons gave endless passing glimpses of the country people in their daily life, glimpses that were no sooner seen than withdrawn. Bates is an artist who could turn the lives of their twentieth-century descendants into stories, without seeking for religious apologues, without the farce of the medieval fabliaux, without the plots of the novelle, without the comment of the urbane essayists; in fact, pure stories. Yet what seems so natural took centuries to produce.

Bates's early stories are revealed in a clear visual setting. There are no tricks of style, no elaboration, yet we seem to be living in the tangible yet lyrical world of some of Shakespeare's songs. It is fortunate that Bates's childhood carries him back to the early years of this century. Many corners of England still wore an age-old aspect, and village ways had not changed greatly for generations. In 'The Gleaner', Bates's little story of the old woman gleaning alone, he tells us that she was the last of her kind—the last relic of times when whole families, whole villages, gleaned together.

Her fingers are rustling like quick mice over the stubble, and the red wheat ears are rustling together in her hands before she has taken another step forward. There is no time for looking or listening or resting. To glean, to fill her sack, to travel over that field before the light is lost; she has no other purpose than that and could understand none. . . .

But later, in the heat of the afternoon, with her sack filling up, and the sun-heat and bright light playing unbrokenly upon her, she begins unconsciously to move more slowly, a little tired, like a child that has played too long. She will not cover the field, she moves there, always solitary, up and down the stubble, empty except for herself and a rook or two, she begins to look smaller and the field larger and larger about her. . . .

At last she straightens her back. It is her first conscious sign of weariness. She justifies it by looking into the sky and over the autumn-coloured land sloping away to the town; briefly she takes in the whole soft-lighted world, the effulgence of the wine-yellow light on the trees and the dove-coloured roofs below and a straggling of rooks lifting heavily off the stubble and settling further on again.

If we want to see how rapidly the short story has developed in a generation we might compare this with a passage from 'The Foolish Virgin', a story by G. R. Gissing, who also had an interest in social strata and the way in which people scratched a living.

She had enjoyed a country breeding; something of liberal education assisted her natural intelligence: thanks to a good mother she discharged with ability and content the prime domestic duties. But physically she was not inexhaustible, and the laborious anxious years taxed her health. A woman of the ignorant class may keep house, and bring up a family, with her own hands: she has to deal only with the simplest demands of life; . . .

It is remarkable how much of this kind of social discussion Bates puts into his purely visual pictures. He does not analyse the problems of society; yet it is easy to see where his interest lies. In his earlier stories the squire, the rector, and the gentry go by default. They are hardly there. Sometimes he depicts a great house empty and decaying, inhabited, perhaps, by a dwindling and neurotic family. In his novels he gives a wider view of the construction of society, but in his short stories he keeps to individuals.

No story reveals more simply or clearly his own social sympathies than one he wrote when he was in the R.A.F., using the pseudonym of Flying Officer X, called 'The Greatest People in the World'. It tells of a young bomber pilot who had been inspired as a boy by the phrase of the title which a lecturer at school had used in describing those who flew aeroplanes. His simple, hardworking parents make great sacrifices, and in due course he is trained as a pilot.

His father was a hedger and ditcher with a fancy for leaving little tufts of hawthorn unclipped above the line of the hedge. These tufts would grow into little ornamental balls, and later were clipped, gradually, summer by summer, into the shape of birds. His father hoped, Lawson would explain to me, that bullfinches would use them for nesting places. . . . I gathered too that his mother cleaned at the local rectory and that she worked in the fields, harvesting and haymaking and pea-picking and cabbage planting, whenever she had the chance or the time. . . . And somehow, out of this, they bought him an education.

Later, Lawson's parents are killed in their cottage in an air raid, and flying in low to land one day, Lawson himself sees an old couple working in the fields, who bring the memory of his parents vividly to him 'as if they were the same people, the same simple people, the same humble, faithful, eternal people'.

Bates has continued writing stories ever since the 1920s. His wartime experiences and later years have taken him farther afield, and we see his gifts applied to scenes in the East or in European countries. At times we see him in the Kipling country among English people living in India; but England itself was also very much the Kipling country, should one wish to make a direct comparison between these two short-story writers, who are often diametrically opposed in their artistic aims and social values.

A. E. Coppard wrote some of the finest short stories of the 1920s. They are also some of the most characteristic stories of the period, capturing the unmistakable freshness that comes from seeing the new approach, of realizing how to write down stories that are penetrating yet simple in appearance. Coppard did not do this without premeditation. Although the impulse came to him naturally, he was, by the time he began to write, a thoughtful and, in the good sense, a self-conscious artist.

Coppard's situation as an author is as interesting as the results he achieved. To begin with, he was far older than the writers of the 1920s with whom he is often associated. He was born in 1878, seven years before Lawrence, twenty-seven years before H. E. Bates. Though he could write with great simplicity, he often had in his mind models of Victorian richness, which attracted him as a young man. One cannot, for instance, imagine H. E. Bates writing, 'Time was as the sephyr in an ilex, resting in my hands like a tress of golden hair.'[6] One even feels Walter Pater might be at work in the background.

Coppard took a long time to get going, to bring his individual gift to bear on creative writing. The reason for this was that he was born into a very needy home. His father was a tailor, who died when his children were very young. Coppard was delicate, and had little formal schooling of any kind. He was almost

---

[6] A. E. Coppard, *It's Me, O Lord!* (Methuen, 1957), p. 237.

entirely self-educated, and he describes the process modestly as 'The efforts of a bawdy uneducated larrikin to lift himself, as it were, by his own boot straps to a place wherein he could recognise and worship fine expression in art, literature, and music.'

Coppard read the great works of English poetry. One may ask how many well-educated people have read and pondered, as he did, on *The Canterbury Tales*, *The Faerie Queene*, *Hudibras*, and *The Excursion*. These works were appreciated by a sure yet quite untutored taste. Then fortune gave Coppard's life an unexpected turn. He went to Oxford in 1908 at the age of thirty, not as an undergraduate but as a clerk in an iron works. He began to meet regularly, and on terms of increasing friendship, dons and undergraduates, men older and younger than himself, who were educated in the heritage of culture and recognized that Coppard had received it by nature.

Unlike D. H. Lawrence, Coppard did not feel a strong revulsion against the 'dying' world of 'upper class culture'. He did not feel resentment, although he showed a rueful sadness that when the talk ran on all the latest French authors he could not participate. However, his mind was completely his own. He not only concentrated on English literature, but he had a strong feeling for a culture in English country life that had continued for generations among people who could not necessarily read or write at all. Thus there are two strands in his art, a penetration into the depths of unlettered minds, and an understanding of the poetic literature that surrounded them, and to which, through generations, they had themselves unknowingly contributed.

Gradually he started to write. He began with poetry; then realized an especial call to the short story. He said he could never be worried with the complexities of the novel. He admired especially the 'great Russians' and Hardy's *Life's Little Ironies*. Yet he knew clearly that he was aiming at something different.

I already envisaged the Short Story as a work of literary perfection, supreme though small, a phoenix, a paragon. . . . I felt that it was my métier, and that I could give it a significant setting, gold maybe, and adorn it with gems, a creation to be treasured.[7]

[7] Coppard, *It's Me, O Lord!*

He did not begin writing stories till he was nearly forty. While he wrote with the enthusiasm of a novitiate, he himself was a man of matured thought and endurance. He draws a direct line, as it were, from Hardy to the short stories of the 1920s and 1930s. In a sense he is first in the field, because *Adam and Eve and Pinch Me* was published in 1921, before *Bliss*, before the reissue of *Dubliners*, and before the first books of Elizabeth Bowen or H. E. Bates.

Coppard has two veins. One is highly fantastic; scenes put before the reader with a vivid poetic naturalism are invaded by faun-like presences and magical events. 'Adam and Eve and Pinch Me', the title story of his first book, is such a story and it caught the eye of many critics. On the other hand, Coppard could from the very beginning move on a plane that was perfectly simple and natural on the surface. In such fine stories as 'The Higgler', 'The Water Cress Girl', and 'The Field of Mustard', his experience of humanity, his singular yet poetic eye are fused into a profound art. In 'The Higgler' we can see the kinship with Hardy clearly. The Higgler, who goes from place to place buying and selling whatever comes to hand, is portrayed with a practical understanding of how small country affairs can be made to prosper. His character is seen in his work, enterprising yet careful, solitary yet gregarious. The story is a love story, or one might rather say a mating story, and is a small tragedy of misunderstanding. The girl is far too shy to let her feelings be seen by the Higgler on his brief visits. Her mother tries in all earnestness to explain the situation, but her middle-aged approach strikes him as some kind of a trading proposition, and higgling being the nature of his life, he is far too cautious. He tries too hard to see if he is being got at, and in the end marries an empty-headed, selfish girl who is completely penniless.

'The Water Cress Girl' has in it an illegitimate baby, an incident of vitriol throwing, and a great deal of love and tenderness. Here Coppard shows his penetration of strange crudities and acts of violence which break out and are suddenly dissipated again into gentleness, the complex anger of the apparently simple heart. The atmosphere of this story is utterly different from the predetermined and unrelieved brutality of the characters in Arthur Morison's *Tales of Mean Streets*.

Frank O'Connor has high praise for Coppard, and says that he knew Chekhov and Maupassant intimately without being unduly influenced by their methods. Coppard, in fact, was completely himself. The disadvantage, the weaker side, of his work is that he strikes his best level all too seldom. His self-conscious fantasies and deliberate absurdities, and at times violence, are of far less account than his realistic stories. It is not often that the complexities of his gifts are fused together into the pure gold that he sought; and increasingly he became as he grew older an unsuccessful alchemist. Many of the best short-story writers produce far too many stories—and write some of their finest stories in their early work. No one exemplifies this rarity of achievement more regrettably than Coppard. No one surpasses his best level.

III

While these, and a number of other short-story writers who belonged to the same generation, cannot be called a group, they were using the short story in a similar way. They observed each other's work. E. J. O'Brien, who edited *The Best Short Stories of the Year* in America as well as in England, was a great influence on younger writers all through the 1920s and 1930s, and all living short-story writers owe him a debt. He was usually cautious about expressing written views, but his short Prefaces to his various volumes were penetrating, and the quality he looked for was 'organic life', or 'organic form'. In conversation he would refuse to define this further except by saying, 'A tree has organic life and shape, and that's all there is to it.' Such a remark is a challenge to the theorist, but satisfying in showing a trend. It reminds us once again that the Greeks regarded 'imitation' as a part of poetry: and for generations Greek scholars have praised that charming poetic mime, the fifteenth idyll of Theocritus, for having much the same qualities as these modern short stories.

Copyright problems probably kept the work of some of the

long-established masters, such as Kipling, out of E. J. O'Brien's collections, because the reproduction fee was small. This over-emphasized a distinction between 'commercial' short stories and those sought for by O'Brien. It was a pity that at this date there was not more of a mixture of the old and new between hard covers. *The Best Short Stories of the Year* was sometimes criticized for having a presumptuous title, and for over-indulging in stories which were merely minor explorations of mood and scene. However, O'Brien subjected himself to a wholesome cross-check on his own taste: all the stories he used had already been accepted and published elsewhere, and he took them from far and wide. Between the two wars there were good opportunities in England for short stories of the more original and interesting kinds. *The Criterion*, edited by T. S. Eliot, *The London Mercury*, edited by J. C. Squire, and afterwards by R. A. Scott-James, *The Adelphi*, edited by Middleton Murry, and later by Richard Rees; these and other monthlies and quarterlies were all taking short stories and providing in themselves a variety of critical selection. Moreover, national dailies and Sunday papers would sometimes clear a whole page for a new short story with illustrations. There were also well-known and influential anthologies, such as *The Faber Book of Modern Stories*, with a Preface by Elizabeth Bowen. O'Brien also edited some selections drawn from his annual publications. These in themselves tell the story of his own judgement.

Such anthologies give a view of the leading short-story writers of the period. They include the writers already discussed: others, such as V. S. Pritchett and Frank O'Connor, who have since become famous names as short-story writers; others, again, such as Aldous Huxley, Sir Osbert Sitwell, or Dylan Thomas, have written memorable short stories, though their best work is in other fields. Leslie Halward, Malachi Whitaker, Norah Hoult, H. A. Manhood, Fred Urquhart, Rhys Davies, William Plomer are all short-story specialists whose contribution to the short story belongs partly to these years but has continued since. These and still others deserve space which it is not possible to give.

To mention names or omit them is invidious, but one must certainly refer to the extremely interesting group of Welsh writers following Caradoc Evans who brought a very particular kind of Celtic life and vision to short stories, and some of whose best work is to be seen in the *Welsh Review* of those years.

Good stories were written by authors who do not seem to have absorbed the more modern influences, but who can by no means be associated with tough yarns or self-conscious narrators. Constance Holme is such a writer. She writes mainly of homely country scenes, yet with traces of the old-fashioned air of one who, like Mary Russell Mitford, observes quaint doings from a slight distance. 'Train up a Child' is an excellent story told by old Mrs. Ellwood, who talks with a very broad accent. She describes to the listening 'I' how a vindictive old farmer allowed a dangerous bull to graze in a field which she had to cross on her way to school.

'But surely you told the teacher?' I enquired. 'Or the police or somebody? You didn't just let him get away with it?' Mrs. Ellwood did look at me then, and almost pityingly. The contempt of the dweller in wild places for his softer and more protected fellow showed for a moment in her eyes.

These comments of the narrator, the interviewer, as it were, are fussy. She is over-explaining Mrs. Ellwood; but the end is left to Mrs. Ellwood herself, and it is perfect. The bull, it seems, quietened down. Or perhaps, as 'I' suggests, it was quiet all the time. ' "Well," said Mrs. Ellwood. . . . "There's quiet and quiet. It killed its owner, t'next week." ' The use of the narrator in this story is in fact a very nice point. It could be argued that by her own attitude in presenting Mrs. Ellwood as a 'character' the author is preparing for, and enhancing, the grim truth of the ending. Yet one is left with a slight feeling that the author is really showing how her protegée had to have the last word, and by establishing herself as a collector of personalities, she is throwing some doubt on Mrs. Ellwood. The true bite of this story surely consists in the experience of the child seen at first hand through her own eyes.

In direct contrast is Constance Holme's perfectly realized story 'The Last Inch'. Without introducing any narrator it tells how Lauder, the leading horse of a timber team, although under-sized for a timber horse, and an excitable nervous creature, had just that extra degree of intelligence and perfect grasp of his work to save a human life. It is a story that is at once simple and extremely exciting. Bates or Coppard might have done it differently, but they could not have brought it off more truthfully.

IV

We have been looking at writers who show the new characteristics of the 1920s and 1930s. In the same period Kipling was producing many of the best-known and most discussed stories of his later years. Some have thought, like Mr. Alpers, that the new and creative element of his work was far behind him by this time, but certainly his influence was still alive. And it was his form of story just as much as his subject matter that the younger writers wanted to avoid.

It is largely the protagonists of the strong plot and straightforward narration who are apt to claim that what they represent is traditional and popular, and really 'wanted by the reader'. The contrast is often overworked, and has given rise to some boring arguments about the principles of 'a good short story' in the abstract. Stories become artificially divided into two opposed groups, those 'with a plot' and those without.

The success of the big circulation magazines was responsible for emphasizing these arguments, and the complete difference between a working editorial policy and serious literary criticism was often overlooked. The Americans have probably suffered more than Europeans from this kind of rule-of-thumb discussion, and no one has dealt with it more effectively than Katherine Anne Porter in her essay 'No plot, my dear, no story', a piece of criticism which fully bears out the quotation from Sean O'Faolain's book given at the beginning of this chapter. Miss Porter writes:

Now listen carefully: except in emergencies, when you are trying to manufacture a quick trick and make some easy money, you don't really need a plot. If you have one, all well and good, if you know what it means and what to do with it. If you are aiming to take up the writing *trade*, you need a very different equipment from that which you will need for the *art*, or even just the *profession* of writing.[8]

Meanwhile, in the period between the wars, three authors of world-wide fame were in their individual ways making major contributions to the short story, which we will consider in the next chapter. They were Somerset Maugham, D. H. Lawrence, and Walter de la Mare. To these can be added a fourth, T. F. Powys, an individualist if ever there was one, though less well known and of lesser stature than the others.

[8] K. A. Porter, essay in *The Days Before* (Secker and Warburg, 1953), p. 133.

XVI

Four Individualists: Maugham, Lawrence, de la Mare, T. F. Powys

Of the four authors discussed in this chapter, it is appropriate to take Somerset Maugham as the leading exponent of a certain approach to short-story writing. In addition to being a practitioner of the short story of almost unrivalled success and fame, he was a pre-eminent controversialist on the art of the short story. Somerset Maugham chose very deliberately to expound and to ally himself with certain methods and views, so we can well consider his opinions about short-story writing before the stories themselves. He is probably the leading influence on the last thirty years to stand against the Russian models.

Somerset Maugham practised what he preached. Yet it would be more to the point to say he preached what he first practised. He preached the kind of short story that he found he could write. At first he seems to have been very much drawn to Chekhov. Later he complains that 'if you try to tell one of his stories you will find there is nothing to tell'. The emphasis is on the word *tell*, as opposed to *write*. Somerset Maugham made himself the great exponent of the story that can be *told*—or can seem through the medium of print to be *told*.

In *A Writer's Notebook* Maugham tells us that he was on a secret mission to Russia in 1917: this helped him to know the work of several Russian authors and 'in Chekhov I found a spirit greatly to my liking'. After a comparison with Dostoevsky he continues with the passage already quoted on page 5:

But with Chekhov you do not seem to be reading stories at all. There is no obvious cleverness in them, and you might think that anyone could write them, but for the fact that nobody does. The author has had an emotion, and he is able to put it into words, then you receive it in your turn. You become his collaborator.

Somerset Maugham was never the man to follow fashionable literary opinions. In fact, this was written before there was any noticeable fashion for Chekhov's stories in England. Maugham gives a spontaneous reaction to Chekhov, and he expresses it in the usual terms of those who are moved by Chekhov naturally.

In 1939 he still writes admiringly of Chekhov in his Introduction to *Tellers of Tales*, an anthology of a hundred nineteenth- and twentieth-century stories.

And so Chekhov gets the effect that is the most impressive that a writer of fiction can achieve: he fills you with an overwhelming sense of the mystery of life. That is the sense, terrifying yet imposing, that lies at the bottom of our activities, that lurks at the back of all our thoughts, the most trivial as well as the most subtle: and to my mind it is by this power that Chekhov is unique. It is this power that gives point to the stories that otherwise seem pointless.

And he adds that when Chekhov's stories succeed, 'they give you a sense of reality which de Maupassant even at his best cannot do'.

We see that Somerset Maugham's first feeling for Chekhov was expressed before he himself became famous as a short-story writer, or had even written many short stories. When he came to it he found that his own gift did not encompass the Chekhov kind of story. Gradually he came to decry it. Possibly, severe criticism of his own work goaded him to a kind of in-fighting with his critics, which included side-attacks on other short-story writers. Thus Somerset Maugham has in due course become the great modern exponent of the art of the literary narrated story. Though he does not always use a personal narrator, his characteristic method is to tell the reader the story himself, in the first person, simulating in print an easy spoken style, and deliberately using plenty of those verbal clichés which must tend towards clichés of scene and character. This is how he talks of his own method:

The reader will notice that many of my stories are written in the first person singular. That is a literary convention, which is as old as the hills. It was used by Petronius Arbiter in the Satyricon, and by many of the story tellers in the Thousand and One Nights. Its object is of course to achieve credibility, for when someone tells you what he states happened to himself you are more likely to believe that he is telling the truth, than when he tells you what happened to somebody else. It has beside the merit, from the story-teller's point of view, that he need only tell you what he knows for a fact, and can leave to your imagination what he doesn't or couldn't know.[1]

He goes on to say that some of the older writers of fiction who wrote in the first person 'were very careless'. They narrate conversations and incidents that they could not have witnessed: 'Thus they lose the great advantage of verisimilitude which writing in the first person singular offers.'

This passage is interesting for its frankness. *Credibility* and *verisimilitude* are the key words. The object is to aim at credibility, even if the story is incredible, as in *The Thousand and One Nights*; to achieve verisimilitude, which is sometimes defined as 'the mere appearance of truth', and has even been called 'the enemy of truth'. It is to a story what *trompe l'oeil* is to a painting. In the Ashenden stories Somerset Maugham plays a further amusing trick as if the *trompe l'oeil* artist had pretended to frame the whole picture in a mirror. Here Ashenden, not 'I', is the observer; but we know all the time that Ashenden is really Somerset Maugham relating pieces of what appear to be autobiography, thus the 'he' gains the added effectiveness of an 'I'.

Somerset Maugham, however, goes on further to tell us that the 'I' is partly fiction. If the author makes the I of the story 'a little quicker on the uptake, a little more level-headed, a little shrewder, a little braver, a little more ingenious, a little wittier, a little wiser, than he, the writer, really is, the reader must show indulgence.'[2] Certainly Somerset Maugham has received plenty of this indulgence. There is no need for him to complain, as he does, 'It is

[1] W. Somerset Maugham, *Complete Short Stories* (Heinemann, 1951), vol. II, Preface.
[2] Ibid.

a misfortune for me that the telling of a story just for the sake of the story is not an activity that is in favour with the intelligentsia.'[3] Yet it is only for a good yarn that he asks indulgence. According to himself, he does not aim to go deeper. When he analyses the basic incredibility of Maupassant's story 'The Necklace', he says that very few readers, once they are caught by the interest of the story, will pause sufficiently to see through it ; I think many readers of 'The Necklace' would disagree.

In this kind of theorizing, as well as in his practice, Somerset Maugham shifts the whole emphasis of craftsmanship away from the point of 'single effect' to that other basic question of 'Who is the narrator?' In his address to the Royal Society of Literature he made a pronouncement that has been almost as much quoted as Poe's famous words about unity of effect. He says of his own type of story: 'One thing you will notice about it is that you can tell it over the dinner table or in a ship's smoking room and it will hold the attention of listeners.'[4]

Chekhov, on the other hand, he considers, 'had no talent for telling the sort of story you can tell across the dinner table and we know he did not want to'.

Nevertheless, Maugham remains the supreme craftsman and sometimes artist of his own method. In claiming merely verisimilitude he underrates some of his own results. Unlike the persona of Kipling, the narrating 'I' of Maugham is objective. He keeps his head, when all about him his characters are losing theirs. He does not like schemes of ideas any more than Chekhov does. One feels a fastidious mind, a balanced philosophy in the background, but he is strictly against preaching.

The whole problem with Maugham is to abstract the deeper creative insight from the marvellously successful professional entertainer. Certainly there is no doubt about the skill, the assured tone of voice of the entertainer. He has the confidence, or can play the *blagueur* sufficiently to begin a story with a disavowal of its probability, as in 'The Kite':

[3] W. Somerset Maughan, *Creatures of Circumstance* (Heinemann, 1947), Introduction.

[4] Maugham, *Essays by Divers Hands* (O.U.P., 1950), p. 125 .

I know this is an odd story. I don't understand it myself and if I set it down in black and white it is only with a faint hope that when I have written it I may get a clearer view of it, or rather with the hope that some reader, better acquainted with human nature than I am, may offer me an explanation that will make it comprehensible to me.

How interesting he can be when he is describing human beings, as in this example from 'The Consul':

He was a man of singular appearance. His body was small and frail and when he walked he gave the idea of a dead leaf dancing before the wind; and then there was something extraordinarily odd in the small Tyrolese hat, with a cock's feather in it, very old and shabby, which he wore perched rakishly on the side of his large head. He was exceedingly bald. You saw that his eyes, blue and pale, were weak behind the spectacles, and a drooping ragged dingy moustache did not hide the peevishness of his mouth.

If we turn from Somerset Maugham's theory to his practice we find that in his famous sentence about telling his stories after dinner he himself had really said the first and last word about his own art. He exemplifies to the full the advantages and the limitations of his chosen method. He carefully defines a group audience in rather a blunted frame of mind, which wants to be told something odd or striking, but is not ready to be upset or to enter into subtleties. Therefore he chooses a blunted kind of language, which is the very opposite of Katherine Mansfield's; and where Joyce aimed for a 'scrupulous meanness' because it was integral with his characters, Somerset Maugham becomes the conscious artist of the cliché, because it suits the narrator.

Thus you will find the narrator telling you that a man 'was grey with anguish'; that he 'forced a laugh to his shaking lips'; he 'crumpled into a chair'; 'his eyes blazed with passion', and 'his voice was rasping'; later 'he shivered as though of an ague'. These phases all come from one story, 'Lord Mountdrago', a story of uncanny experiences, in which a worldly and successful man dreams of horrible things which then happen in real life. Finally:

'With some kind of a spiritual sense he seemed to envisage a bleak, horrible void. The dark night of the soul engulfed him, and he felt a strange primeval terror of he knew not what.'

It is remarkable how closely this approaches Frank Sullivan's comic series 'The Cliché Expert'; it is also extremely infectious, and it is all too easy to write down after 'perusing' 'Lord Mount-drago' that Maugham 'for once ventured into the realms of the uncanny'; that 'he eschewed literary refinements', and that when 'taken to task', he 'waxed wrath with the critics'.

Looking at the stories themselves, we find that Maugham consistently reveals the broader patterns that usually go with a ready-made kind of language. If the famous 'Rain' is taken as a typical Maugham story, showing the movement of prim-looking lives to a ghastly tragedy of self-condemnation and suicide, one is compelled to say it is coarse-cut and over-simplified. Some might argue that it is none the worse for that. Life is crude. Yet the crudities of life do not lie in broad generalities of character drawing. In 'Rain' we meet a self-controlled missionary, and his tight-laced wife, who says it is 'so hard to give the natives a sense of sin', and a genial prostitute. They are herded together by circumstances and confined to the same small island by quarantine. The outcome is obvious. The minister falls for the temptations of the prostitute, and cuts his throat in an agony of remorse. Sadie Thompson, the prostitute, having seduced the preacher, blames what has happened on to the fact that 'all men are pigs'.

Maupassant's 'Boule de Suif' is a more subtle and a far more cynical story than 'Rain'. Maugham's criticism of rigid missionaries is so blatant that it loses point; in Maupassant's story the behaviour of the coach-load of human beings towards Boule de Suif, and their different kinds of selfishness, cuts deeper, leaves more bitterness behind it, than the affair of Sadie Thompson and the Reverend David. It is also more believable. In 'Boule de Suif' virtue is triumphant in its own degrading way, but Boule de Suif herself, who is far more vulnerable than Sadie Thompson, is forced to act against her own honourably cherished principles of patriotism. 'Rain', on the other hand, is more crudely dramatic; its climax is a blow with a mallet and its situation is summed up in one violent, bloody deed.

Somerset Maugham often deals with intensely theatrical events and effects, in his subdued tone of voice. 'Before the Party' is

o

another famous story which seems designed to shatter moral complacency. Here, a very ordinary and proper-seeming family are about to set out for a garden party, at which they are to meet a bishop. Their very desire to appear at their conventional best on this occasion breaks through the reserve of the widowed daughter, who has newly returned from the East. In a mood between hysteria and controlled bitterness she chooses this moment to reveal that her marriage was a sordid tragedy, and her husband a repulsive drunkard, whom she herself shot. She has been living with this secret, and now the family must share it. They move off rather late and only in slight outward disarray to meet the bishop, who has himself been in the Far East and who may have heard some local version of this story. One almost wants to clap at the end.

It is this 'seeing through', this underlying theme that truth may be totally different from outward appearances, that produces the typical Maugham situations; but the sense of disillusion begins to become stereotyped, so that one is soon drilled into looking for the situation within the situation. A less violent, more intimate disclosure is made in 'The Door of Opportunity', one of Somerset Maugham's finest stories. Here we see a married couple happily returned from the East, about to settle into their London hotel for their first night in London. It is at this point that the wife is compelled to tell her husband that she has long since decided to leave him. His exhibition of caution, amounting to cowardice, on the occasion of a dangerous riot had disgusted her to the point of accumulating hatred. She sees this cowardice linked with self-approbation flooding his whole personality, making his outward complacency unbearable. This surely is a story which penetrates beyond the dramatic event itself into the recesses of individual life. It is the husband's complacency and then suffering that is the point of the story, not the dramatic scene of the riot. Interestingly enough it has no narrating 'I' and is told in dramatic form.

Other stories, such as 'The Lion's Skin', show further variations on this theme of pretence and reality. These revelations do not always lead to tragedy or violence. In a number of stories the twists are farcical, especially when Maugham is dealing with pretentious literary highbrows. Occasionally the stories have a gentle and pervasive humour, as in 'The Colonel's Lady', the story of a very quiet, unobtrusive woman somewhat neglected by her likeable but obtuse husband. She makes a great success, the nature of which her husband never grasps, with a volume of amorous poetry.

Yet as Somerset Maugham moves farther away from the dramatic event, he moves farther away from his own best vein. He himself says in the Preface to volume III of his short stories that it is hard to write stories about 'good decent normal people. . . . I respect, I even admire such people, but they are not the sort of people I can write stories about.' How, in fact, does Somerset Maugham's art appear, when he approaches a quiet theme which has no strong drama? At times he writes a story that needs a more emotional, a more penetrating vision than he ever brings to bear. 'The Colonel's Lady' is such a story. Writing conversationally about an odd situation, he tells us almost nothing about its deeper truth. Another story of implications and overtones is 'The Treasure', which is characteristic of Maugham in its manner, but quite inimical to his own skill in its essence. Richard Harenger is a very polished Londoner, and he has a perfect treasure of a servant who runs his flat, presses his clothes, and understands his wine and dinner parties to perfection. Surprisingly enough, this admirable butler and valet is a young woman, not beautiful but presentable. For years they continue in perfect harmony—a relationship of pleasant but quite formal efficiency.

One evening, however, he decides on the spur of the moment to take her to dinner in a restaurant. The evening passes very well. When they return to the flat, with an impulse utterly unforeseen, he embraces her with physical ardour. She responds. They go to bed together.

Next morning when he wakes up alone in his room he is horrified. How can he treat her now? How will she treat him? Then she enters the bedroom neat and formal, in her morning dress, hands him his tea as usual, makes her remarks about the weather as usual.

With her slow quiet movements, unruffled, she left the room. Her face bore that rather serious, deferential, vacuous look it always bore. What had happened, might have been a dream. Nothing in Pritchard's demeanour suggested that she had the smallest recollection of the night before. He gave a sigh of relief. It was going to be all right. She need not go, she need not go. Pritchard was the perfect parlourmaid.

I first read this story in 1929 and it has lingered. Yet it has always lingered with a sense of blank disbelief. It sums up the sensation that Somerset Maugham's art at such moments simply stops short. What he produces is little more than a smart ending to a revue sketch.

There must have been repercussions of feeling, of behaviour. Yet curiously enough Somerset Maugham felt drawn to this story, which is really a situation for Chekhov or Joyce or Katherine Mansfield; or with its mixture of class consciousness and sex, of animal impulse mingled with deeper human feelings, a theme for that other great novelist and short-story writer D. H. Lawrence. It is, in fact, a horse that might well have bolted with Lawrence, while Maugham could hardly make it trot.

II

As a man and a writer, Lawrence is a complete contrast to Maugham. That he was an extraordinary genius goes without saying. His personality is one of great power and at times amazing brilliance. While the range of his view over society became wide, his interest in human beings remained intense rather than broad: it was focused on themes and feelings that sprang from the intensity of his own experience. Though his short stories deal with many different people, his interest is concentrated on certain depths of personality. In his novel *Kangaroo*, for instance, he talks of a need 'to refer the sensual passion to the great dark God, the icthyphallic of the first dark religions'.

Lawrence is known primarily as a novelist, but he is famous also as the writer of theoretical books that study the half-realized and dream-like layers of consciousness. Poems and short stories add to his achievement. His short stories may not form a very large part of his output, yet, as Dr. Leavis has pointed out, if he had produced nothing but these stories they would have brought him recognition as a writer of great and distinctive power.[5] H. E. Bates feels that Lawrence is a better short-story writer than a novelist.[6] His essential vision is contained in his stories to a degree that has been overlooked, and he is at his own best when the limitations of the short-story form force some shape and brevity on him, and make him concentrate on the story itself, rather than on his theoretical notions or his passionate floods of words.

People who know Lawrence by one or two novels only, who think of him as Paul Morel in *Sons and Lovers*, can have no idea of the number of scenes and people that he creates, the sheer range of his stories which, like those of Maugham, fill three volumes. From the very first they show Lawrence's visual radiance, which makes the scenes spring to life. Ford Madox Hueffer knew that he had discovered an original genius after reading the opening paragraph of 'Odour of Chrysanthemums'. He might have responded with equal certainty to the opening words of 'Fannie and Annie':

Flame-lurid his face as he turned among the throng of flame-lit and dark faces upon the platform. In the light of the furnace she caught sight of his drifting countenance, like a piece of floating fire. And the nostalgia, the doom of home-coming went through her veins like a drug. His eternal face, flame-lit now! The pulse and darkness of the red fire from the furnace towers in the sky, lighting the desultory, industrial crowd on the wayside station, lit him, and went out. . . .

This story goes on to tell of a man's choice between two girls: one serious, hard-working, and efficient who has been away in service with well-known and wealthy people; and the other a more sensual, flamboyant girl who has not been restrained by thoughts of respectability. It is a typical Lawrence theme; some of the best of Lawrence's earlier stories deal with the life of the small colliery towns in which he grew up, and with his own violent feelings; feelings about sex and love, family relationships, jobs, and social surroundings, all of which seethed together in one blast furnace

---

[5] F. R. Leavis, *D. H. Lawrence, Novelist* (Chatto & Windus, 1955).
[6] H. E. Bates, *The Modern Short Story* (Nelson, 1941).

inside Lawrence's spirit. It is hard to distinguish thoughts from feelings. He seems to think with his feelings and feel with his brains.

Some of the early stories may be described as miniatures from the world of *Sons and Lovers*, truly focused in short-story form. Some have a refreshing light-heartedness. This gayer element appears also in *Sons and Lovers*, though the general tone of this great novel, as of the stories, is profoundly serious. 'Strike Pay', for instance, is an unpretentious, very human comedy. A group of colliers draw their strike pay and decide to take a nine-mile walk, see a football match, have a beer and cheese lunch at a pub, and walk home again. They lark about, and find some horses which they ride bareback. There are some jokes and some bickering. One of the younger men, Ephraim, has the bad luck to lose his strike pay, returns home late, and is then violently abused by a very unpleasant mother-in-law.

Kindly order me about, do. Oh, it makes him big, the strike does. See him land home after being out on the spree for hours, and give his orders, my sirs! Oh, strike sets the men up, it does. Nothing have they to do but guzzle and gallivant to Nottingham. Their wives'll keep them, oh yes. So long as they get something to eat at home, what more do they want! . . . Let tradesmen go—what do they matter! Let rent go. Let children get what they can catch. Only the man will see *he's* all right. But not here, though!

Ephraim is goaded into answering his mother-in-law rudely.

'Maud!' said the mother-in-law, cold and stately. 'If you gi'e him any tea after that, you're a trollops.' Whereupon she sailed out to her other daughters.

Maud quietly got the tea ready.

'Shall y'ave your dinner warmed up?' she asked.

'Ay.'

She attended to him. Not that she was really meek. But—he was *her* man, not her mother's.

Wives, daughters, mothers, husbands; though lightly touched on in 'Strike Pay', these provide the typical Lawrence characters. He explores such themes again with more depth in 'Odour of

Chrysanthemums'. Here, also, Elizabeth, the wife, is waiting for her husband to come in. She is furious with him because lately he has taken to drinking heavily in the pub instead of coming home, which she looks on not only as deplorable in itself but as socially degrading. However, this time there has been a swift, unexpected accident at the mine and other men bring him home dead. There follows a most moving scene in which Elizabeth and her mother-in-law wash and lay out the body together. The play of Elizabeth's feelings, partly love and partly hate, partly relief, partly horror of death, are far more intense and complicated than the simple grief of the old woman. This is the true vein of Lawrence's insight, and in this mood he searches the heart.

Others of Lawrence's stories dwell for long paragraphs on wild emotion, and the central character becomes overwhelmed in a vague prose rhapsody. This kind of writing can both rise and sink, and we see people under the compulsion of chaotic passion, hating, loving, gnashing at each other.

In 'The Prussian Officer', for instance, which contains a sadistic and homosexual assault, a frenzied revenge, and a delirious death, both the story and the character in the story are swallowed up in a long-drawn welter of feverish, formless nightmare. In these moods Lawrence must be experienced rather than judged. Ordinary standards of literary form and control do not apply. He is desperately anxious to pour out his private revelations.

'The Man Who Loved Islands' has the same intensity. In this story, which was discussed in chapter III, the central character, a man who tried to withdraw from all human beings, is gradually isolated and left struggling with the elements, waves, snow, thunder, and gales, which utterly cow and overwhelm him. Here, however, the imagery of rhapsodic utterance and the crashings of the descriptive prose are fused into a potent unity. The story is one of Lawrence's masterpieces. Maybe it has a message: a message within the canon of the Lawrence teaching. If one cares to extract the message from the story, it is presumably that to withdraw into private worlds is a kind of suicide.

In projecting his own range of human emotions, Lawrence is

unsurpassed. He has a power of expressing the interchanges of many feelings of love and hate, vibrations in the air, one might call them, that pass between people and affect them deeply; as Dr. Leavis says, 'a drama of the inexplicit and almost inexpressible in human intercourse'. Lawrence can convey the physical presence of people and can set them in the particular scenery of their family surroundings with a depth and strength, and at times a brevity, that are entirely his own.

He does this again and again. Yet unfortunately he is all too apt to leave the inexplicit for the direct exposition and to use his stories as lectures. Lawrence, like Kipling, thought of himself as a man with a message. He wanted to reinspire humanity in large wholesale terms. In a letter to Lady Cynthia Asquith he discusses a new magazine and says ,'I am going to do the preaching—sort of philosophy—beliefs by which one can reconstruct the world— Katherine Mansfield will do her little satirical sketches.' In another letter he tells Katherine Mansfield that he thinks little of Chekhov, whom he refers to as a 'Willie wet leg'. He wants to go behind personality and character to some larger force.

It is often overlooked that Lawrence has stories in moods that are much cooler, more collected, more quietly presented. In his later stories, we find him writing caustically observed social satires, in which he throws his penetrating rays on the lives of educated people, civil servants, wealthy widows, successful authors, the kind of people whom he met as he grew older. 'Blue Birds' is such a story, which describes how an established yet shallow author, whose wants are perfectly supplied by an adoring secretary, housemaid, and cook, is punctured by his wife. Lawrence sees the wife as a she-wolf prowling. She cannot bear her husband's shallow success and his self-satisfaction built up of trivial clichés, so she politely rends both him and the adoring secretary. This is a story that seems to have been produced by a happy collaboration with the art of Somerset Maugham. The story is well shaped and controlled. It reflects the world of Maugham and it is a Maugham situation; but the similes and the glimpses of psychic depth come from Lawrence: a strangely effective combination.

Lawrence thus seems to achieve short-story form at times with studied skill, at times by sheer chance; at other times one feels he is simply not interested in the form of the story. He is content to move at a nineteenth-century tempo to cover long years with an informative synopsis, to break off, to argue, to propound. To his ardent admirers the question 'What did Lawrence add historically to the art of the short story?' must seem beside the point. He added the power to put his own amazing gift into short-story form. Yet if we think of dates, and recall that the whole volume of *The Prussian Officer* was published in 1914, we may see that he did at times make a very remarkable contribution to the form as well as to the substance of short stories; and at times the discipline of the short-story form is a very great help to him.

His especial genius is seen in displaying close personal and family relations in depth. His famous interest both in sex and in class is seen again in the way these forces affect individuals. He is intensely aware of animals and the natural world; but this interest also is an organic part of his view of men and women. These poetic insights are expressed brilliantly in his stories.

There is not room to enter here into the labyrinth of argument about the nature of Lawrence's teaching. It has been judged inspiring, revolting, or merely confusing. It is nowhere brought to a clearer point than in that most beautifully written of Lawrence's shorter prose works *The Man who Died*. This long short story tells us that Christ is revived after the Crucifixion and slowly returns to health; then as the crowning point of His resurrection he has sexual intercourse with a priestess of Isis. 'You are Osiris,' she says to him. Lawrence makes his point perfectly explicit, and the scene in which the priestess brings His scarred weakened body to life is one of the most tender passages he ever wrote on his own chosen theme. It is an attempt to identify sexual joy with the poetic essence of the created world. It is a far more complete and outspoken revision of Christian teaching than the equivocal words about baptism given to St. Peter by Kipling, in 'The Church that was at Antioch'.

III

Walter de la Mare is a poet who, throughout the first fifty years of the twentieth century, continued to express his haunting and dream-like vision, following his own intimations, largely unaffected by the major changes in poetic style and outlook. This vision of waking dreams, of strange, still moments, of a journey towards a mystery that is always just beyond reach, he conveys also in his short stories. As unaffected as his poetry by changes of fashion, they are unique and perfectly formed to express their creator's experience.

It would be a pleasure to write a fuller examination, but here there is space only to suggest that anybody who is interested in the art of the short story should know some of de la Mare's. To convey so rare a poetry in the form of the prose short story is unexpected. A few stories only have an obvious element of fantasy, and though they are pervaded by changing levels of consciousness, his stories frequently move through an outer world of natural events. They are neither contrived allegories nor ghost stories, though they do at times seem to be voices whispering in sleep.

T. F. Powys is another writer who is better known for his longer works, but who has succeeded in conveying the essence of his unique creative gifts in short stories. His vision is at once mystical yet very earthy. The son of a Church of England clergyman, Powys chose a life of seclusion and poverty in a Dorsetshire village, and his writing is the true outcome of cottage meditation. He sees life in death, light in darkness, and the presence of God in everything. At his best a page of Powys provides a marble surface on which passages of D. H. Lawrence and even Blake may be rung to test their note.

His people tend to move in an allegorical or theophanic field of extreme simplicity, so that at times one seems to be conversing with hedgehogs and badgers on transcendental themes. His short stories are sometimes at their best when they are fables, though too often he can descend into mere whimsy. One of the best and most characteristic is 'Mr. Pim and the Holy Crumb', which, though it has much of the fable in it, takes place on a natural

plane. Mr. Pim is a rabbit trapper and a ploughman and has become in his later years a church clerk. One day near the altar he
finds a minute crumb of consecrated bread. In this consecrated
crumb he sees quite literally God Himself, and talks to the crumb
with a slightly awed familiarity, deciding that he would sooner be
allowed to rest in his grave than rise again. His meditations are
brought to an end when a mouse appears, and undisturbed by
him, eats the Holy crumb—the mouse being thus seen and known
to contain all that is miraculous. The story is both humorous and
serious at the same time

In their several and interesting ways these four authors each
made a distinctive contribution to the short story: Maugham by
the immense prestige and success of his stories, and his controversial insistence on the merits of his own man-of-the-world form
of narration; Lawrence by his power to fuse his own intensely
personal feelings into fine short stories; de la Mare by pursuing
the haunting vision of his poetry also in the form of stories; and
Powys by being one of the very few modern writers who could—
however precariously he may succeed—create fables of sticks and
stones and animals in converse with human beings.

XVII

Moods after Two World Wars

I

The writers who were discussed in chapter XV were not a coherent group in the sense that they had ever written a manifesto or
consciously clubbed their ideas together. However, some of them
did feel that they had not merely written a number of stories, but
had made a contribution to the art of the short story. Some hoped
that their own path-finding would help the following generation of
writers.

Elizabeth Bowen wrote in 1945, in an article in the May number
of *Britain To-day*:

The short storyist shares—or should share to an extent—the faculties
of the poet: he can render the significance of the small event. He can
take for the theme of his story a face glimpsed in the street, an unexplained incident, a snatch of talk overheard on bus or train. . . .
Wartime London, blitzed, cosmopolitan, electric with expectation now
teems, I feel, with untold but tellable stories, glitters with scenes that
cry aloud for the pen.

Bates' book *The Modern Short Story* expressed similar views, and
referred to the outstanding achievement of writers on both sides
of the Atlantic in the 1920s and 1930s 'giving the short story a
greater distinction than it had ever known before'. In May 1962,
however, Bates wrote in the *Bookman* that his expectations and
hopes had not been fulfilled.

Prophecy like lending money to friends is a mug's game, but when I
prophesied in *The Modern Short Story* in 1941, that the inevitable dis-
trust and dislocation of war's aftermath would lead new writers to find
in the short story the essential medium for what they had to say I felt
certain I was right: time has proved me wrong.

If one turns to modern reviews of books of short stories one meets repeatedly a kind of query placed against the whole approach of the 1920s, the feeling that this kind of story is exhausted. Here is such a review, of Nadine Gordimer's *Not for Publication*, by Hilary Corke:

Every story has a clear theme, beautifully worked out: and it is surely to the good that one cannot extract a motif common to them, unless it be that we are all human, and deserve a hearing. And yet . . . does one close the book with a slight sensation of indigestion, and of the smell of death that goes with it? Because a reviewer has to break his own excellent rule of never reading more than one short story a day? Or because the whole form is dying, and one catches the whiff? . . . Why is it dying? Is it not just *because* the art is practically one with the craft. That one can write a perfect short story. (What on earth would a perfect novel look like?) That this art/craft can be taught like tennis?[1]

This seems unfair to writers who would never have supposed for a moment that there was such a thing as a 'perfect short story' or that anyone could be taught what comes from natural gifts. 'Gallant war horses of the form,' says Hilary Corke, 'having sold their eighty stories annually for three decades sired treatises entitled "The art of the short story" or for that matter, "The craft of the short story".' But if any war horse could really sell 2,400 stories, his advice on writing magazine stories would certainly be worth hearing, though it might have little to do with the art of the short story.

Alan Coren, writing a review of stories from the *London Magazine* in *Punch* (26 August 1964), presents another view:

The English literary magazine has never provided a forum for the short story. Whether this is a contributory cause to the general critical contempt in which the genre is held in this country, or whether it is merely a result of it is difficult to assess: what is undeniable is that during the heyday of the form in America between the two wars, English periodicals were concerned almost exclusively with the publication and criticism of poetry.

This, he says, not only had the effect of stimulating both poetry and readers of poetry, but it froze out the short story, and 'what

[1] From the *Listener*, 10 June 1965.

overtones of dilettantism, of superfluous also-running that title (of short-story writer) carries in England'. However, when we turn to the views of the younger generation of American short-story writers, in the next chapter, we shall see that the names of the English writers of the 1920s often crop up as leading influences.

In the last twenty years there has unquestionably been a movement away from the particular impulse of the 1920s. 'Satire', 'commitment', and 'social criticism' became vogue words for a time, and as conscious aims in a writer's mind they obviously act against the conception of poetic mimesis. There have been a number of influences at work, the views of some leading writers among them. Aldous Huxley, for instance, practised the novel *à thèse* in his own brilliant and very effective way; and he also wrote brilliant short stories, which naturally exemplify his general feeling for the art of fiction. Mr. Propter, in *After Many a Summer*, is often taken as a mouthpiece for Huxley's own views, and Propter has expressed complete boredom with the naturalistic novel: 'the wearisomeness to an adult mind of all these merely descriptive plays and novels, which critics expected one to admire. All the innumerable, interminable anecdotes and romances and character-studies, but no general theory of anecdotes, no explanatory hypothesis of romance and character.'[2] This gives an excellent view of the old utilitarian argument against fiction, and the feeling that fiction would really be better if it were fact, or a sociological argument. Perhaps the greatest of all literary influences on the short story in the years following the Second World War has been the tremendous prestige of Somerset Maugham, both in his practice and in his critical opinions. In spite of the admiration of Chekhov that he repeatedly expresses, in the end his whole weight of opinion seems to move against Chekhov's art.

Behind such literary influences which have opposed the feeling of the 1920s for the short story, there have been the far more general arguments that writing, and in fact all the arts, ought to be allied with social protest: that the examination of individual

[2] Aldous Huxley, *After Many a Summer* (Chatto & Windus, 1939), pp. 225–6.

reality is not enough. Many younger writers burning to express their views have clamoured for commitment of all writers in some cause or another. It is inevitable that subjects such as the advance of scientific knowledge, the threat of nuclear war, the emergence of new nations, and the general speed of social change and turmoil should have been uppermost in people's minds.

In fact, dissatisfaction with the sheer helplessness of the individual has led at times to moods of despair which contrast painfully with the hopes held out by humanism, by the promises of social reformers, and the facile dismissal of 'old-fashioned' views of right and wrong. This despair may be deeply felt, or it may be a kind of fashionable despair—and we see it expressed plainly, sarcastically, humorously, or farcically. Possibly a new form of parable or brilliant satirical short story is possible, with all the outward sparkle of Beerbohm or Saki, and a more serious insight into social justice; yet in the past the man with an argument, the sermon writer, the essayist, the teacher have been all too apt to choke the life out of short stories.

The distinction between portraying individuals as examples of the social scene and creating individuals as they pass through the social scene may sound slight, but it is all the difference between sermonizing and creating a short story. As John Hawkesworth said in the eighteenth century, 'It is far harder to invent a story than to recollect topics of instruction'; and as H. E. Bates has maintained, 'the short story is a poetic form; it is no vehicle for messages'. In a session of the International Writers Conference which was especially devoted to the topic 'Is commitment necessary?', Mr. Kushwant Singh pointed out that political commitment was apt to be loudly proclaimed; but his own personal commitment as a writer was to four themes, 'truth, love, solitude and death'.[3]

If we look at the historical development that this book has attempted to trace, the unexpected depths and difficulties that lie behind this apparently simple art, it is this long perspective that we necessarily bring to bear. The social or documentary content of the day seems of less importance, compared with the deeper

[3] *The Times*, 23 August 1962.

insights that short-story writers have achieved in the past. The use made of an inherited art form becomes of greater interest. Many good journalists can write accounts of contemporary life. Behind the journalists, documents and statistics flourish as never before. But a million facts about teenagers taking drugs, or marriages breaking up, do not add up to one short story.

II

Since the end of the Second World War, the outlets for short stories have altered. In the main, they have steadily diminished. Popular magazines as well as literary magazines have been disappearing. It has become harder for any short story to appear in print. Reputations can no longer be built as Manhood's or Coppard's were, on short stories alone.

Bates pointed out in the article already mentioned that it is not true to say that people do not read books of short stories, because obviously they do read and cherish them over years. Yet it is true that a good many people who read fiction of various kinds simply do not like short stories. Thus, volumes of short stories have an audience that is small, even if it is appreciative; small in numbers compared with the large sales necessary for books nowadays to pay their way.

Although the magazine and book outlets have diminished, the short-story writer has found increased opportunity of broadcasting. Sound broadcasting has a special relationship to the short story—and various good comments have been written on the craft of radio stories, such as an article in the *Radio Times* of 4 May 1956 by James Langham, who was a most understanding producer of short stories of all types for the B.B.C. for many years.

In the earlier years of broadcasting there was a somewhat self-conscious theory on the part of radio producers that sound radio would lead to a revival of the 'old art of story-telling', and the intriguing anecdote with the cleverly assumed spontaneous manner was widely acclaimed. In the long run authors and B.B.C. men have learnt that the more visual and intimate stories can be told by broadcasting, but it remains true that typical Somerset Maugham stories, with a personal narrator, an easy talkative style, and a clearly pointed event, are naturally suited to radio as they stand.

Television producers have shown sympathy to the kind of story creation that does not necessarily depend on outward action and event. As a result, short plays have given an outlet to conceptions that might well have appeared as printed stories between the wars. Sometimes one still feels that the incidents would have been more tellingly and artistically conveyed as printed stories. This is a matter for speculation, but it is beyond argument that once a story has been created as a television play in the first place, it is not likely to appear in the form of a printed short story afterwards; and it is the literary creation, once it is given depth and visual effect on the printed page, that can be apprehended and re-read on countless future occasions.

Since the Second World War short stories have had also an interesting relationship to films, and some short stories have won outstanding fame by being used as the basis of films. On the whole it is the stronger situations, the more dramatic stories, such as those of Graham Greene or Somerset Maugham, that have appealed to the film makers. Graham Greene's 'The Fallen Idol' and 'The Third Man' both achieved success as films. These and others of his stories convey on a small scale his own view of unhappy humanity moving in a sinful world towards a painful climax. Less dramatically conceived short stories can also be turned into films. The Russians have shown this with their version of 'The Lady with a Dog'. However, this is the kind of film which, like the story itself, is dependent on atmosphere and on visual suggestion of internal stresses for its effect. In any case, the success of the film is only partially relevant to the success of the story on the printed page.

III

These are, however, influences that extend up to the present moment. Let us look at some writers whose work may be associated with the 1940s and the years immediately following the war; V. S. Pritchett, William Sansom, Mary Lavin, A. L. Barker, and Angus Wilson. Pritchett is the eldest of these four writers; in

P

fact, his work was already known in the 1930s, though he began to command recognition rather later. One of his best-known stories, 'The Saint', first appeared in 1940 in *Horizon*. In some ways Pritchett stands a little apart from the short-story writers of the 1920s and 1930s. His work is entirely individual, and seems frequently to be moving into the grotesque and the pungent, although in the end its general feeling is one of realism: comic, but not going beyond the odder events of common experience. *Odd* is perhaps the word for a good many of the people and incidents in Pritchett's stories—odd and yet extremely human. He has been compared to Dickens, and the comparison holds, if we can imagine *Sketches by Boz* written by a mature Dickens—a Dickens who had absorbed the influence of Maupassant and Flaubert, and had pruned the Dickensian style to short, swift sentences. A quotation from 'You make your own Life' illustrates his method:

'Take a seat. Just finishing,' said the barber. It was a lie. He wasn't anywhere near finishing. He had in fact just begun a shave. The customer was having everything. In a dead place like this you always had to wait. I was waiting for a train, now I had to wait for a hair-cut. . . .

I picked up a newspaper. A man had murdered an old woman, a clergyman's sister was caught stealing glasses in a shop, a man who had identified the body of his wife at an inquest on a drowning fatality met her three days later on the pier. Ten miles from this town the skeletons of men killed in a battle eight centuries ago had been dug up on the Downs. That was nearer. Still I put the paper down. I looked at the two men in the room.

One does not as a rule have the sense that Pritchett is deeply moved by the people in his stories. He observes, he is tart and shrewd in his character drawing; yet on the whole he is generally more on the side of sympathy and understanding rather than re-buke, as with the reminiscent middle-aged woman in 'Things As They Are', who passed out quite respectably while talking to her friends in a pub—a sadly comic event which had clearly happened before and was going to cease being comic before long: or with the disreputable old Welsh priest in 'The Voice', singing his hymns while buried under the bombed ruins of a church, keeping

his courage up by drinking whisky and by annoying his fellow
priest. This is one of the finest of Pritchett's stories, simply because it does seem to impart the deeper sense behind the odd
incident.

A collected edition of Pritchett's stories appeared in 1961, and
of William Sansom's in 1963 (with an Introduction by Elizabeth
Bowen), and they make an extremely interesting comparison.
Sansom's work began some ten years later than Pritchett's, and
his earliest stories appeared in *Horizon* and other magazines in the
early years of the war, when he was serving at the time of the
Blitz in the London Fire Service. Sansom has a far more elaborate
prose style than Pritchett and many other short-story writers. He
is a master of sensuous and atmospheric effects, an artist in working up the sounds, the scents, and the colours which surround his
characters. He writes paragraphs of rich description, which
Pritchett might cover in a sentence or a phrase. He makes a whole
story, for instance, out of the sheer *tour de force* of dwelling on the
agonizing seconds when the wall of a blazing five-storey building
falls towards a team of firemen; or again on the moment in which
a lion who has escaped from his cage faces a solitary man,
screened from view behind a bed of dahlias. In his early stories
the influence of Kafka and Rex Warner is plain, but he eliminated
a number of these stories from his collected edition, and his work
shows a movement away from the symbolic, and towards human
feeling.

Most of the stories in this volume are, as Elizabeth Bowen
points out, brilliant examples of atmosphere, often enough a
frightening atmosphere which may be resolved into comedy or
triviality, or may in the end turn out to fulfil the worst fears that
have been aroused. In 'Something terrible, Something lovely', for
instance, two little girls are obsessed with an apparently frightening secret, but all they do is to chalk a childish message on the
wall. In 'Various Temptations', on the other hand, the girl who
has already been terrified with stories of the 'Victoria Strangler'
does, in fact, make friends with the murderer himself. A number
of Sansom's stories depend on waiting for the ending. They are
suspense thrillers painted with an artist's brushwork; and though

this is not the most profound form of story, they can be compulsive reading. His best stories are those in which a more recognizable human interest lies at the centre of the tension, such as 'Waning Moon', when a foolish and then raging quarrel between a honeymoon couple nearly ends in a disaster. The steps by which the quarrel mounts and hysteria turns to terror are all too believable, and they do not spring merely from atmospheric writing.

In some of Sansom's humorous stories the slight exaggerations and arabesques come nearer to the feeling of Pritchett. One might compare the two priests in 'The Voice' with the two elderly men, landlord and lodger, in Sansom's 'A Last Word': Mr. Cadwaller and Mr. Horton are keen rivals in petty meanness.

Henry Cadwaller was a man of thrift, and the old gold letters lost from the fanlight of the original house had never been replaced, nor had half the black and white tiles on the steps, nor had the stained-glass lights to his hallway. These red and yellow and purple panes, patched nowadays with wood and cardboard, shed a more gothic gloom than ever: indeed, the whole house was patched, its large Victorian rooms were partitioned with papered three-ply—each lodger lay and stared at his own piece of ceiling frieze, coming from nowhere and disappearing with mad purpose. . . .

After Cadwaller has hastened his own death by denying himself warmth, Horton cuts flowers for the funeral from one of Cadwaller's own shrubs: but the final point is a verbal joke. As the author explains to the reader, what Horton has placed on the grave is *Rubus idaeus*, just the common raspberry.

Mary Lavin's first book of stories, *Tales from Bective Bridge*, appeared in 1942, and won the James Tait Black Memorial prize. Since then her volumes have appeared at regular intervals, and her stories have gained in depth and power. In the years since the war she has written one or two of the finest stories in the English language. Mary Lavin has no especial tendency towards the comic, the sarcastic, or the grotesque. She is a natural artist of the quietly realistic; natural on the surface, poetic in her perception. She makes no break with the general trend of short-story writing between the two wars, and continues with the tradition of her

Irish compatriots, adding to that inheritance which descends through George Moore and James Joyce.

At her best Mary Lavin seems to combine the qualities of other Irish writers—the penetration of Joyce, the colour of Elizabeth Bowen, the more primitive vision of Liam O'Flaherty. No finer story has appeared in fifty years than Mary Lavin's 'The Great Wave'. It enters into the feelings of island dwellers, simple and yet subtle, their lives remote and sea-bound in one sense, yet very near at hand in another; it describes the impact of the great wave, as it is seen through individual eyes, with a frightening visual clarity; and being presented as the reminiscences of an elderly bishop, it challenges and deserves comparison with Chekhov's famous story 'The Bishop'.

'The Great Wave' won the Katherine Mansfield Mentone award, and its fame is partly dependent on the description of a disaster of the elements. This kind of outward event is by no means typical of Mary Lavin's art. In its lower pitched drama 'The Will' is one of Mary Lavin's most moving stories. Here there is little dramatic action, little call for impressive writing. A middle-class Irish family have gathered at the death-bed of their dominant mother. One daughter, Lally, far poorer than the others, is excluded not only from her mother's will but also from her affection. She alone realizes that on her death-bed her mother died still feeling anger against her. And it is she alone of the family who, in a state of agonized anxiety, goes to the priest's house late at night insisting she must see him, pleading with him to say a Mass for her mother, a Mass that must be paid for out of her own small store of money.

'She was very bitter against me, all the time, and she died without forgiving me. I'm afraid for her soul.' . . . Humbly the priest in his stiff canonical robes piped with red, accepted the dictates of the draggled woman in front of him. 'I will do as you wish,' he said. 'Is there anything else troubling you?' 'The train! The train!' said Lally.[4]

Then Lally rushes off to catch a late train home and to scratch the money together as best she may.

[4] From *The Long Ago and Other Stories* (Michael Joseph, 1944).

A. L. Barker is another woman writer with a slight though distinctive output. Her volume of stories, *Innocents*, was published in 1947. Her art also developed from the writers of the twenties and thirties rather than representing a new post-war departure. She has a very penetrating gift of expression, especially for some of the more frightening experiences of children. To say that she is sensitive is not to say that she is unduly mild. At times she is very far from it, as in 'The Iconclasts', the story of a small boy who tries too hard to imitate the fanatical self-testing courage of war-time pilots. Simple in its terms, this story of children is more disturbing in its unhappy truth than the spooks of 'The Turn of the Screw'.

With Angus Wilson, we turn to a very different author, a very different vision. His first book of short stories, *The Wrong Set*, appeared in 1949 and with it a sharper cutting edge came to the short story in England. Angus Wilson is a satirist. It is for the exposure of weakness, of self-deception, and self-love that he is admired. He collects unpleasing specimens of humanity and impales them in his stories like curious beetles.

In *The Wrong Set* he turns a sarcastic eye on the hypocrisies and false values of certain middle-class people who feel themselves to be threatened by the disappearance of their privileges, and the onset of the Welfare State. In fact, he reveals many of his characters as almost nauseatingly unpleasant. In 'Union Reunion' the loud-voiced, outwardly cheery family repel us with their crude jokes, the gargantuan meals they eat, the wind they pass; with this behaviour and their stereotyped dominance towards the Africans, their obsessive selfishness, and their failure to help even each other in time of need, we seem to be at a family party of laughing hyenas.

In the title story of *The Wrong Set* Vi is more idiotic than sinful. No longer a girl, yet without the compensation of being a wife, she moves among of a seedy, needy set of people, who keep up an outward pretence of upper-class standards among the drinking-clubs of some Kensington hinterland. Vi is living in a bed-sitting room with a man to whom she often refers as 'my husband Major Cawston'. They are quarrelsome, pretentious, gin-drinking, and vacant. Vi feels some twinges of responsibility for a young nephew on whom she has been asked to keep a careful eye. When she meets his tedious but entirely sincere labour friends, and hears their perfectly ordinary views, she is shocked to her bedraggled yet superior-feeling core. After cadging a great many gins off an Italian club proprietor, who may well demand a *quid pro quo*, she decides to do her duty by her nephew, and lurching to the telephone, dictates a telegram to his mother: 'Terribly worried. James in wrong set.'

This is certainly funny. The wild inappropriateness of her judgement, the attempt to build up her own status, the owl-eyed drunken seriousness of conveying her report in a telegram are splendid strokes of the ridiculous. One feels, moreover, this could happen. This character could send such a telegram, and this makes a clever ending. Yet the inner meaning of the story is not so much the joke as the haunting question—What is Vi's fate? What does it feel like to be in her skin, rather than merely to poke fun at her? Yet to depict Vi, one must feel with her; and if one feels with her, one must know she needs help, protection, comfort. She is not truly a subject for scorn and sarcasm, any more than the clerk in Gogol's 'The Overcoat'.

However, whether we find Wilson's attitude too censorious or whether we believe he means to arouse understanding for the human shame that he exposes, there is no doubt that he is an artist of the short-story form, as description, cleverly captured dialogue, and significant climax unfold themselves.

III

We now come to writers of recent years—writers whose output, it is hoped, is far from complete.

During the 1950s a feeling grew up that writing ought to take more account of the tastes and interests of 'the man at the lathe'. This is at times unfair to writers of past generations; it also involves an old confusion between writing about the man at the lathe and writing what the man at the lathe himself wants to read. The mood of the post-war years, however, encouraged young authors to write from inside the factory lines, the adolescent street gangs, the dance halls; to demonstrate sympathy for the needy, the sickly, the violent, the criminal, as well as for the responsible.

This has had its effect on the theatre, and it has produced a lot of controversial talk, but it has not found any widespread expression in short stories. Alan Sillitoe is certainly the outstanding example of a writer who sees eccentric lone-wolf characters with intensity and who has been drawn to the short-story form. Sillitoe shows a strong, even a romantic sympathy with people of the working class who are disillusioned and resentful. His story 'The Loneliness of the Long Distance Runner' (1959) became famous as a film, and has been described as a remarkable portrait of a 'modern rebel'. Its main character, in fact its only character, as the story takes the form of a long self-centred soliloquy, is Smith, a young delinquent at a Borstal institution, who is a fine runner. Smith allows himself to be passed at the end of a race he could have easily won, by a runner who is a public school boy. His aim in doing this is that he imagines it will annoy the Governor.

Smith is certainly not inspired by any constructive social ideals. He is alone and alienated, not really a rebel at all, but suffering rather from a prolonged childishness amounting to neurosis; his notion of annoying the Governor is some sort of a delusion of revenge against society, with a touch of self-destruction thrown in. Sillitoe has a real insight and an affectionate regard for Smith's eccentricity, as he has for the sad and sub-normal lives led by other people of peculiar mentality and lack of grip, who have not half Smith's spirit and puckishness. Yet one really wants a view of the people who have been trying to help Smith. The whole affair is revealed only by way of Smith's unbalanced thoughts. How can we arrive at the truth?

In 'The Ragman's Daughter', the title story of his second book of stories (1963), Sillitoe gives us with exciting detail an insight into a more active form of criminal psychosis. This time he lets us into the feelings of an obsessional thief. Again the story is told in the form of a first-person soliloquy with a neurotic drive of 'I—I—I'. 'I' picks up a girl, who is richer than he is, and visits his back-street home. Doris shares 'I's thieving exploits, but thanks to her exhibitionist behaviour, 'I' is captured and goes to a

Borstal, while Doris escapes. While he is at his Borstal she bears him a son, and then is herself killed on a motor-cycle. 'I' comes out and sees his own son playing with the girl's rich father; he feels quite unable to approach him, yet he wants to say to him, 'Hey up, Dad. You don't know much, do you?', once again establishing in his own mind some feeling of otherness and superiority.

A good deal of this reads like an obvious fantasy—the sex, the rich girl, the thrills; yet the end is surprisingly restrained. The fantasy has vanished into the past. 'I' is settled down, married, and is working away at a steady job. A technical problem arises from the use of the first person both with this story and 'The Loneliness of the Long Distance Runner'. How did the central characters come to write or talk so brilliantly? Both of the young men think and talk in a style reminiscent of each other, and of Sillitoe. Smith tells us that he will give the story to a writer, but 'The Ragman's Daughter' is simply a first-person story without further framework. We are confronted with the problem that this kind of character does not talk or write with this degree of vivid imagery.

There is a movement among broadcasting writers to build fiction or drama out of tape-recorded material. Possibly we might say that the 'I' of 'The Ragman's Daughter' represents imaginary tape-recorded talk. In 'The Courage of His Convictions', by Tony Parker, we see the results of tape-recording the speech of a young delinquent. It certainly lacks the force and grip of a story of Sillitoe's. In fact, it lacks the literary gift that is the very thing that Sillitoe supplies. Interestingly enough, the young man in 'The Courage of His Convictions' says that Sillitoe is one of the few authors who he feels really knows and understands his point of view.

One of Sillitoe's best stories is 'To be collected', and here there is no personalized narrator. The story tells how three brothers have raised enough money to buy an old lorry with which they go scrap-collecting. The youngest brother, Donnie, who is regarded by the other two as a bit stupid, stumbles upon some sacks which contain Sten guns and ammunition. The other two brothers hasten to dump this dangerous find in a lonely pond. This annoys

Donnie so much that in a terrifying display of half-serious anger he begins shooting with one of the Sten guns.

This is a compact story; as there is no narrator the interaction of the three brothers is used to reveal their natures, rather than any intervention from a story-teller. Their waves of quarrelling, of laughter, of lying about their imaginary war service to people who are ready to help, build up an authentic picture of men who can bear a little domestication but not too much.

A saving quality that Sillitoe's leading characters seem to share is a wry sense of humour about themselves combined with the courage of their own peculiarities. Donnie thinks:

Nothing from the past was sad, no matter how awful it might have been at the time. Only the present was classifiable into good or putrid, but every incident that he could remember was laughable for the simple reason that it was past, and that he had survived it without mortal damage.

This mixture of uncooperative courage and of self-mockery is reminiscent of the Elizabethan anti-hero whom we meet in *The Hundred Merry Tales* and in the coney-catching stories; and of the sad–funny prancings of the jesters who were prepared to risk floggings and ear-severings as long as they could vent their mockery. It seems to be an old English tradition.

John Wain is a novelist and critic whose name, in the 1950s, was often linked with that of Kingsley Amis as a leading new satirist. His fondness for the short story and his especial gifts for the form are seen increasingly in his second volume, *Death of the Hind Legs* (1966). Here the amusement is compassionate rather than critical. The title story is a rare achievement: a story of Dickensian *bravura*, cast effectively in modern short-story form, brief, colourful, and controlled. Amidst the last days of a crumbling theatre, an elderly actor who, like the building, has seen better times dies on stage while playing the hind legs of a horse. This in itself could be plenty of a material for one short story; too much for many writers. In Wain's story it is by no means the climax; it is the beginning of a whole series of denouements. Quarrels turn into love affairs among the young. Courage is revived among the elderly. There is a splendid wake-party on the stage, at which pompous relations of the dead man arrive and feel themselves too refined for the merriment. This is a bold playing-up of a situation in itself full of human sentiment. There is a great deal of variety in John Wain's stories and often his art seems to look back through Stacy Aumonier and Pett Ridge. If Pritchett can be likened to Dickens in the oddity of his characters, Wain is Dickensian in the invention of emotionally bizarre human situations.

Setting aside any question of deliberate social criticism, it is obvious that, during the 1950s and 1960s, there has been a widening of theme and content. For some years two enterprising annual collections of short stories have been appearing annually: *Winter's Tales* (from 1954), edited by A. D. Maclean, and *Pick of the Year's Short Stories*, edited by John Pudney (from 1949 to 1965; the 1949 volume was called *Pick of To-day's Short Stories*).

These collections give an interesting cross-section of recent story-writing. They contain names well known since the 1920s as well as others new to print. The themes range from the polite urbanities of Noel Blakiston to the delinquent fringe of Sillitoe; they also move farther afield than formerly, beyond the scenes of the British Isles to other countries.

It is interesting, for instance, that two leading story-writers of recent years, Frank Tuohy and Francis King, who have both worked for the British Council, have also both specialized in the difficulties that arise over lack of common ground between people of different nations. Frank Tuohy's 'The Admiral and the Nuns', the title story of a book and one of the best-known stories of recent years, deals with the difficulties of a very conventionally brought-up English admiral's daughter, who has married a Polish husband. She is living with him in Argentina, remote from all forms of contact with which she is familiar. It is plain that her anchor is dragging, her background is failing her; in the end it can be only her own strength which can save her. 'But she was durable. After all she was an Admiral's daughter.' In Francis King's 'So Hurt and Humiliated', also the title story of a book, we see another English girl, this time the daughter of a widowed English colonel in Greece. She becomes entangled with an apparently charming young Greek. It is she who is hurt and humiliated, while it is he who voices a sense of grievance and says he will never understand the British.

These two stories are typical of themes which both Tuohy and King handle (though their range cannot be represented by single stories), and they both have a power of penetrating through the interest of a situation to the reality of the individual lives concerned.

In general, however, it is clear that the Chekhov influence has waned. The aim is rather different. There is less aesthetic colour, less intense visualization of the scene; communication is more linguistic, less pictorial. Stories may be penetrating and sympathetic, but they look more at the social surroundings, less closely into the heart of the individual. 'The Admiral and the Nuns', for instance, is narrated in a conversational tone by an 'I' who himself plays a small part in the story. This is the Somerset Maugham method, but the study of Barbara Woroszylski's anxious personality is far more sensitive than Maugham would have made it. The developments of short-story writing over the centuries have been absorbed so that the short-story form is now a flexible instrument available to many moods, able to shed light on many different facets of life: aware of past techniques yet cautious of portraying the intensely seen moments of the 1920s.

Doris Lessing is a writer whose novels are more than usually committed to social discussion. Coming from Rhodesia to London, she has been an intensive observer of types of behaviour and opinion. Her characters are apt to have arguments about 'your generation' and 'your class', and to display the brainwashed habits of thinking which go with such labels. Yet she is also a writer of dramatic power, of curious insights into unhappy and feverish states of mind. At times she takes a magnifying glass to the details of sex, linking erotic behaviour with character portrayal somewhat in the manner of Lawrence. She usually cuts deeper, sees more clearly when she is dealing with the African scenes of her youth, rather than portraying the artists and intellectuals of London.

Muriel Spark is a brilliantly amusing and original writer of short stories as well as novels; her stories are cleverly formed, intriguing to read, and packed with up-to-date comment. She herself is often at the reader's elbow, as a most animated conversationalist, telling all about her characters and what to think of them. Like Angus Wilson, she is an expert social analyst, but she deals with a surface of farcical glitter rather than with the severities of satire. 'The Black Madonna' is a typical story, telling of a doctrinaire, liberal-seeming couple who talk a good deal about their friendships with coloured people. The wife gives birth to, purely by psychological influence, so she insists, a coloured child—an event which is an unfair test for the husband's broad-minded theories.[5]

It is typical of the interest in public themes that Doris Lessing should also have written a story called 'The Black Madonna'. While Muriel Spark brings to the affair a surface of coruscating farce, Doris Lessing writes a passionate and unhappy story, in which an English officer and a young Italian artist, who is a prisoner of war, struggle in vain to understand each other. Their failure is a bitter personal grief.

While both Muriel Spark and Doris Lessing are prominent as short-story writers, they neither of them give the impression of being short-story specialists in the sense that some of the writers of the 1920s were. The form lies ready to their hand and on occasion they make good use of it.

IV

While themes have been ranging farther afield, it is noteworthy that they have also been coming from farther afield. In 1966 the British Broadcasting Corporation World Service in English ran a competition for short stories. It is unquestionably significant in the developing art of the short story that over 2,000 entries were received from 108 different territories.[6] New stories written in English have been coming not only from countries whose citizens descend directly from the British Isles, and whose natural language has always been English, but also from countries of completely different cultures. The Commonwealth story-writers fall into two very large groups: those from countries

---

[5] In *The Go-away Bird and Other Stories* (Macmillan, 1958).
[6] *B.B.C. Short Stories* (British Broadcasting Corporation, 1967), with a Foreword by Anthony Burgess.

that have a British ancestry and those of Asian and African inheritance, who in varying degrees must approach English as a foreign literature, even though some have been accustomed to it by generations of familiarity.

It is almost impossible to generalize even within the first group. It is probably true to say that, with the exception of Katherine Mansfield, the European influences underlying the English writers of the 1920s reached the older Commonwealth countries after they reached the British Isles; also that these countries were more subject to the direct influence of the Americans.

Is it possible to talk of any common ground among the Commonwealth countries of direct British ancestry, with their outbacks, their new cities, their own angles on the world? The natural bent has been towards a story which possesses plenty of human interest, but a core of action and everyday experience. The stories have on the whole been less probing, less interested in the inward significance of events than their English or Celtic counterparts, yet more British in outlook than American.

Such generalizations are bound to be crude, and as Dan Davin points out in his Introduction to a collection of New Zealand short stories (1953), once stories are thought of as coming from a particular country they may attract attention for their documentary interest rather than their true literary value. Who indeed can decide where one ends and the other begins? Certainly among the New Zealanders there has been a tradition of short-story creation, with Frank Sargesson, Janet Frame, and Dan Davin, as well as Katherine Mansfield. Frank Sargesson, with something of the simplicity of Sherwood Anderson, has used the art, often of the very short story, to show aspects of New Zealand life coarser than came within the range of Katherine Mansfield. He tells us with truth and integrity of lives which she approached uncertainly in such stories as 'The Woman at the Store'.

Good short stories from New Zealand and Australia have been both plentiful and interesting since the Second World War and it is impossible to discuss here the numerous new individual talents. An outstanding book of Australian short stories, *The Burnt Ones*, has come from the novelist Patrick White. His stories are most effective mixtures of subtle insight with rough appearances. 'Down at the Dump', the longest story in the book, utterly different at first glance from the world of Katherine Mansfield, challenges close comparison with 'At the Bay'. Patrick White's story tells us with intimate understanding of a loud-singing, beer-drinking family living in an unlovely tin-roofed suburb. The atmosphere is wonderfully conveyed. The family go to visit 'The Dump', a part of the beach which lies near a hideous collection of rusty metal, old tyres, and rotting furniture. Everything on the surface seems to be in complete contrast with 'At the Bay', yet the two stories are counterparts. We see the subtlety of the time movements, the completeness of this one day's activities, with its reference to hidden situations; then the lyrical happiness that suddenly wells up between the adolescents, in the surroundings of the dump itself. The author has looked into the dust and old iron and revealed the colours of human lives growing like brilliant flowers in odd corners. One cannot escape the pervasive influence of Katherine Mansfield, the influence, at least, of the kind of short story she represented.

The Indians, with their feeling for situations that are nebulous and unaccountable on the surface, yet significant within, their sensitivity to the aesthetic beauty of the world, their perception of its flickering nature, and their artistry in words, are by nature appreciative of the style of Chekhov; and some Indian authors have also made a deep response to English literature. Tagore, Raja Rao, Mulk Raj Anand, and others have made manifest a distinctively Indian personality in the art of the short story in English; Kushwant Singh has combined his often disastrous view of the human scene with a remarkable and telling precision of form.

West Indian writers, such as Andrew Salkey, Samuel Selvon, and George Lamming, have developed an especial feeling for an odd gaiety of surface, often expressing a puzzled seriousness as individuals face the strange mishaps of life, snatching comedy at moments from the edge of disaster. Many of these writers from different countries make the story as seen by Kipling seem more and more remote.

It is plain if we consider a recent collection such as *Modern African Stories*, edited by Ellis Atiyey Komey and Ezekiel Mphalele, that we are not dealing with stories that depend simply on their African background. It is the quality of creation that distinguishes the best of these stories rather than local interest. Yet the more ancient myth-making element that we see in Amos Tutuola's stories is by no means a leading characteristic. The achievement lies also in the mastery of modern form while portraying scenes from African life. In the African countries, writing in English argues by itself a certain knowledge of European culture, and the wish to communicate with a wider public; speaking in the native idiom, yet using an international art form. To take one example, Sarif Easmon's story of a clever and very self-conscious small girl could have been written only by an African; but by an African who has perfectly absorbed the art of the modern story. Here is the beginning of 'Koya'.

Koya was being groomed for stardom; in a harem. It was her birthright. And she entered upon it with a precocity that sometimes astonished and at times even alarmed her elders. She was the sole arbiter of her own dignity, a mysterious personal protocol, that decided whether *the* Koya could do this, or if Koya could not do this. Wherefore Koya was as much a problem to herself as she was a porcupine of prickly contradictions to her friends of her own age. Hardly yet a slip of a girl, she was just turned nine years.

With a grace all her own, Koya curtsied in native style as befitted a well trained Susa girl, and rose up in front of her mother, 'N'Kha Sigga, N'ga Fatmatta?' (May I go now, Fatmatta?)

Koya's day turns out to be one of childish tempers and agonies, largely of her own making. She fails to maintain her prized dignity, and all she can say to her mother at the end is 'I hate you'.

'Koya' is prose, yet it is poetry. It seems slight, yet the emotions of mothers and children are a very important part of human experience. In a sense nothing happens. Yet the whole day has been full of turbulent action from Koya's point of view; and her sensitive knowledge of life on that day becomes the reader's knowledge also.

XVIII

The American Point of View

I

We have already looked at the American theories of short-story writing that were current at the end of the nineteenth century. This chapter examines briefly the more recent moods and developments of the American short story seen partly in its relation to the British short story. There is, of course, a great deal more to be said, and the shortness of the treatment has no relation to the comparative stature of American and English writers.

Somerset Maugham once again provides a good opening argument. In his anthology *Introduction to Modern English and American Literature*, first published in New York in 1943, he said that on the whole he thought better of American short stories than English.

The short story is not an art that has flourished in Britain, but whether this is because brevity, point and form are not qualities that are natural to English writers of fiction, or whether because the outlet has not been sufficiently favourable to encourage good writers to employ their gifts in this medium, I do not know. The fact remains that during the last fifty years many more good stories have been written by American citizens than by British subjects. . . . English authors have left the best stories to the 'tec' writers. When they did write stories, the powerful influence of Henry James and their admiration for Chekhov urged them to write in the minor key and in their effort not to be melodramatic they succeeded but too often only in being namby-pamby.

This is a very revealing passage. In the first place, as we saw in chapter XVII, Maugham is very much in two minds about Chekhov and he praises him and scolds him in alternating moods.

Q

What Maugham is really saying here is that he has found among American authors more of the Maugham type of story, for he has told us clearly that the kind of short story that he likes is the kind that he writes himself. American critics, on the other hand, have often said that it is the Chekhov influence that lies behind the resurgence of American short stories in the 1920s and that this influence has continued ever since. In an anthology called *The Modern Short Story in the Making* (1964), edited by Hallie and Whit Burnett, modern American writers such as Capote and Norman Mailer refer to Chekhov and Joyce as leading influences on their own short stories; in fact, most of the authors in this anthology pay tribute to authors such as Elizabeth Bowen, Katherine Anne Porter, Katherine Mansfield, or Sherwood Anderson.

Somerset Maugham says also in his anthology that he does not think much of Sherwood Anderson; he regards his stories as 'mere sketches' and includes 'I'm a Fool' as the best of a doubtful bunch. Yet many American critics regard Sherwood Anderson as the great influence in a fresh perception not only of the short story but of all American literature. Wallace and Mary Stegner, in their Introduction to *Great American Stories* (1957), say of the years following the First World War: 'When the long drouth ended and the promises of the 1890's were fulfilled everything came with a rush, and the American short story, together with all the other arts, exploded into what history may very well call its most brilliant period.'

Austen McGiffert Wright, the author of *The American Short Story in the Twenties* (1961), bases his study on five leading short-story writers, Sherwood Anderson, Scott Fitzgerald, Hemingway, Faulkner, and Katherine Anne Porter. McGiffert Wright frequently links his chosen models and their methods with their British counterparts of the 1920s, and he tells us of his own book:

It springs from an original curiosity about the kind of short story commonly called 'modern'—the kind one finds in the collections of Hemingway and Faulkner, in Katherine Mansfield's *The Garden Party* and Katherine Anne Porter's *Flowering Judas*—that branch of the art whose ancestry is traced by most literary genealogists to Joyce and Chekhov. . . .

Why is it that stories of Winesburg, Ohio, published over forty years ago, still do not seem dated in the manner of the stories of Garlands' *Main-Travelled Roads?* Why is it that *Dubliners,* written during the first decade of this century, still seems to us in 1961 contemporary, whereas stories written by Edith Wharton in the same period do not?

He also considers that the whole conception of the stories of the 1920s lies in certain points of approach, and he stresses especially that the 'narrator' and the 'dramatic' methods are not mere points of technique, but affect the whole truth of the story. There is, in fact, much in common between the short-story writer in America and in England.

However, the American short story was certainly flourishing long before the twenties, and when E. J. O'Brien prepared his first American volume of *The Best Short Stories of the Year* in 1915, he said he had read 2,200 stories for the purpose, and added:

The American short story has been developed as an art form to the point where it may fairly claim a sustained superiority, as different in kind as in quality from the tale or conte of other countries . . . as its field of interest widens its technique becoming more and more assured and competent.

The words 'assured and competent' are unexpected, because in the long run O'Brien did not like or foster the assured and the competent, and it was he who was one of the leading spokesmen for Sherwood Anderson. Also, as he would certainly have agreed later, his words were written just before the dawn of a new period. Yet O'Brien had plenty to present in 1915 and in his Preface he comments rightly on the feebleness of the English short story in the commercial magazines at this time, and its noticeable absence from the more serious literary periodicals.

The truth is that the Americans had for generations been far more conscious of the short story as an art than the British. Poe had begun the discussion, and Hawthorne took it up. By the end of the nineteenth century American professors of literature were writing intensively about the American story. Today in America the *Best Short Stories of the Year* and the O. Henry Prize Volumes are famous, and when resident authors at universities teach creative writing, they often use the short story as a basis.

Katherine Anne Porter, Whit Burnett, Salinger, Sean O'Faolain, Frank O'Connor are among leading short-story writers who have themselves held such posts, and Mary O'Hara gives an interesting account of a creative writing class in action. She joined a summer Extension Course at Columbia in 1940—a course of two hours in the morning and two in the afternoon for five days a week, which lasted for six weeks. She was already an accomplished professional screen writer.

But there is one thing you cannot do in screen writing or radio or stage or any form of dramatic writing; you cannot indulge in author narrative because there isn't any. And this I longed to do. The only form of writing that would permit me this indulgence was short stories or novels. I did not aspire to novels.

It is interesting that she wanted 'author narrative' as a form of *indulgence*.

Mr. Burnett's method was to ask for unsigned stories, read them aloud without disclosing the author, then invite discussion.

I was indignant when, after reading a story of mine, he asked what was the matter with it, and with one voice the class answered 'too much author'.

So I argued the point, and there was a lively discussion. Mr. Burnett said 'I wouldn't want you all to write like radio writers——' but he really did. *The scene*. Write the scene. How many thousands have I done for the movies.[1]

She then submitted to the class a 5,000-word version of her famous story 'My Friend Flicka'. This was printed in *Story* and it then, so to speak, burst into flame; it was picked up by the *Readers Digest*, turned into a short novel, and then into a film.

There has never been anything like this degree of study of the form and technique of the short story in England. Yet the in-

[1] Quoted in Whit and Hallie Burnett, *The Modern Short Story in the Making* (Hawthorne Books, New York, 1964), p. 85.

tensive study may well cut both ways. While it stimulates, it may obviously involve a too pedantic approach to gifts that must flow spontaneously. One begins to founder in too much classification: the traditional story; the grotesque story; horror modified; myth and reality; the American dream. American authors have, of course, been aware of this tendency themselves, and in Salinger's *Franny and Zooey*, Buddy Glass, a character with whom Salinger partly identifies himself, makes some disenchanted remarks about his post as a resident writer at a university.

Advanced writing 24A loaded me up with thirty-eight short stories to drag tearfully home for the weekend. Thirty-seven of them will be about a shy reclusive Pennsylvania Dutch lesbian who Wants To Write, told first-person by a lecherous hired hand. In dialect.

I take it for granted you *know* that all the years I've been moving my literary whore's cubicle from college to college, I still don't have even a B.A. . . . .

This is the gloomier side of trying to stimulate creative short-story writing, and Harry Levin complains that the Joycean epiphany has been 'standardized into an industry'.[2] However, we will come back to Salinger later on after a very brief historical view of the American story.

II

In the 1820s Washington Irving, who was trained as an artist, saw his short stories as pictures, as part of a sketch-book. He tended, in fact, to 'write the scene'. Then Poe expressed the ideal of concentrated form; but his material was 'gothic'. The stories that the English know well under the title of *Tales of Mystery and Imagination* appeared in America as *Tales of the Grotesque and Arabesque*, and it is plain that Poe is far more interested in dream-like atmospheres than in human character. We must remember that Poe himself divided his stories into two types: the tales of 'ratiocination', such as 'The Gold Bug', and tales of 'atmosphere'. But it is always interesting to remind oneself just how 'grotesque and arabesque' some of his famous stories are.

[2] Levin, *James Joyce*, p. 30.

During the whole of a dull, dark, and soundless day in the autumn of the year, when the clouds hung oppressively low in the heavens, I had been passing alone, on horseback, through a singularly dreary tract of country; and at length found myself as the shades of evening drew on, within view of the melancholy House of Usher. I know not how it was—but, with the first glimpse of the building a sense of insufferable gloom pervaded my spirit.

So begins 'The House of Usher'. Now for its ending:

The huge antique panels to which the speaker pointed threw slowly back, upon the instant, their ponderous and ebony jaws. It was the work of the rushing gust—but then without those doors there *did* stand the lofty and enshrouded figure of the Lady Madeline of Usher. There was blood upon her white robes, and the evidence of some bitter struggle upon every portion of her emaciated frame. For a moment she remained trembling and reeling to and fro upon the threshold—then, with a low moaning cry, fell heavily inward upon the person of her brother, and in her violent and now final death-agonies, bore him to the floor a corpse, and a victim to the terrors he had anticipated.

The effect is that of a ritual enactment. When this dance of death is concluded, the house crashes into the tarn, to the flood-lighting of a blood-red moon, one of the most 'gothic' scenes ever portrayed, and one that has become a classic of its kind.

Hawthorne, as he tells us himself, was more interested in depicting symbolic figures than in showing the surface of things as they are. Melville talks of Hawthorne's dark obsessions, the 'great power of blackness', deriving from the sense of original sin. It has become customary in American criticism to follow tap-roots to the deeper symbolic 'realities' of Poe and Hawthorne, rather than the shallower naturalism of authors such as Bret Harte.

Meanwhile, among the humorists and others the portrayal of natural life was developing. We begin to see the fast-talking Yankee tall-story teller, shrewd yet boyish at heart, 'The early hero of our folk literature', as Ray West calls him in *The Short Story in America* 1900–1950. Though Bret Harte's stories of life in mining camps are often sentimental, his sentiment is working towards the portrayal of normal humanity. 'The Luck of Roaring Camp' shows the sentimentality of a passing emotion among crude minds; but the girls in 'La Maison de Madame Tellier' experience similar shallow feelings of an aspiring kind. Harte is sometimes too much identified with the sentimentality of his own characters. He said modestly that his predecessors had created the short-story form, and he had merely placed it in the geography of his country. Yet that in itself was a great achievement: Chekhov and Maupassant were doing exactly the same thing. Stephen Crane followed, portraying the harsh realities of city street life, as well as pictures of the Civil War. Stephen Crane's 'Maggie' makes an interesting comparison at this date with *Tales of Mean Streets*. The advantage is with Crane, who has far greater depth of insight, far less obvious piling up of calamity against his doomed characters.

Henry James can reveal both the surface and the depth of natural events, but his page-long discussions and explanations of his characters all work against the short-story form. Later, Edith Wharton produced some talented versions of condensed Henry James. O. Henry comes as the complete antidote to over-refined discussion: extremely American, the very epitome of the fast talker, fizzing with entertaining phrases, challenging the reader to a game of guessing the twist ending. Here is one example of O. Henry getting a story under way with his bright-as-a-button style, and very talkative, very personal patter. This is the opening of 'The Trimmed Lamp'.

Of course there are two sides to the question. Let us look at the other. We often hear 'shop girls' spoken of. No such persons exist. There are girls who work in shops. They make their living that way. But why turn their occupation into an adjective? Let us be fair. We do not refer to the girls who live on Fifth Avenue as 'marriage girls'.

Lou and Nancy were chums. They came to the big city to find work because there was not enough to eat at their homes to go around. Nancy was nineteen; Lou was twenty. . . . I would beg you to step forward and be introduced to them. Meddlesome reader: My lady friends Miss Nancy and Miss Lou.

O. Henry's stories contain some very real people saying some very real and amusing things. For all his surface humanity, however, he is apt to deal in ready-packaged notions, and ironies that are 'cute' rather than profound. He is an entertainer, with flashes of profundity, and he puts the stamp on the slick professional magazine story, which American writers themselves have often attacked in the last two generations, not only for being shallow but for tempting good writers away from their better selves, to play tricks at which they become all too competent.

III

In the 1920s the first new move came from Sherwood Anderson, and his early stories have been regarded as a deep influence, returning to a truer and a less cheerful vision of the lives of people who were often unhappy and bewildered in small drab towns, and introducing conceptions of the art based, as we have seen, on European models. The effect is not so much that Sherwood Anderson conveys the Russian or the French influence into the American story as that he expresses his own simplicity of outlook. In fact, although he came to have a great admiration for Chechov, and especially for Turgenev, he told Paul Cullen in a letter that the critics had spoken of the influence the Russian story writers had on him, even before he had read their work.[3] He is reminiscent of a primitive painter or a colonial period craftsman. He can be compared to Coppard in England, but on the whole he produces more of a homespun effect.

Perhaps the most widely reprinted of all Anderson's stories is 'I want to know why'. This story tells of the painful disillusion of a boy of fifteen who has seen a man whom he admired—the trainer of beautiful champion horses—making up to low-class women. Part of the point of the story is the boy's instinctive feeling for good and bad in sexual behaviour. 'Why? Why?' he asks. 'I want to know why' might be not only Sherwood Anderson's own motto, it could stand for a great deal of pained inquiry underlying the more serious American stories. Why cannot life be innocent and perfect? Why is society complex and impure? It is interesting that Hemingway, who was at first an admirer of Anderson's stories, came to believe that his simplicity of feeling

[3] Sherwood Anderson, *Letters*, edited by Howard M. Jones and Walter Rideout (Little, Brown, 1953), 2 August 1939.

was 'faked'. It is true that, like Coppard, Anderson can fall far below his best level.

'Death in the Woods' shows Anderson's art at its most effective and most serious. It tells very simply of the death of an elderly woman who has been exploited and overworked by others all her life. Stumbling home to her lonely farm one night with a bag of supplies on her back, she is taken ill, falls unconscious, and dies in the snow-bound woods. There is a strange scene in which her own and her neighbour's dogs drag the food from her sack and tear away her clothes, but do not touch her body. A boy of thirteen is among the people who see her body lying in the snow. The scene so haunts him that years later, as a grown man, he pieces her story together and sees it as a timeless whole in the moment of her death.

As we have already seen, the twenties was a rich period, Katherine Anne Porter, Robert Penn Warren, Whit Burnett, Caroline Gordon, and others following where Anderson had opened the way. Katherine Anne Porter is certainly among the finest of all American short-story writers, and in a period which was dominated by the reputations of Hemingway and Faulkner she is distinguished by her avoidance of extremes. She is sensitive in her unforced style, and sensitive to a remarkable variety of characters and lives. Her subjects range from life in the Southern States to Mexico and New York. 'Flowering Judas' is a telling portrait of a Mexican revolutionary who grew fat and flourished whatever happened, sighing unctuously amid the misfortunes and tragedies of other people. It gains, as all her stories do, from the unobtrusive way it is built up. She does not work with violence of theme or idea. At times she is a little leisurely for a short-story writer. 'A Day's Work', by way of contrast in scene, has the matter-of-fact surface and depth of feeling of James Joyce's *Dubliners*; and as it deals with an Irish Roman Catholic family in New York, and the husband's attempt to find a seedy political job, it is almost an extension of the art of James Joyce. 'Pale Horse, Pale Rider' tells of the illness and suffering of a girl hard-pressed by her work on a newspaper—harassed by the perfervid atmosphere of the American entry into the First World

War. As with all Miss Porter's work, it is portrayed with serious, but never laboured sympathy. She is a leading influence in establishing the models of the 1920s.

Of the well-known novelists, Theodore Dreiser wrote short stories, but, as he himself said, he needed length and he never used the more sharply focused methods of the short story to advantage. Faulkner and Hemingway, on the other hand, are both famed as short-story writers, and, as with D. H. Lawrence, it is hard to separate their short-story achievements from their stature as novelists.

Faulkner's stories are, in fact, a part of his novels, and they sometimes deal with the same people and scenes that appear in the novels. Sometimes his effects seem impossibly lurid when condensed into the short-story form. When the strange old 'Miss Emily' dies, the rotting corpse of her lover, who had disappeared many years ago, is found on a bed. On the adjacent pillow the print of a head is seen. It is recalled that years ago there had been a time when a terrible smell hung about the house. This seems even more grotesque than the Lady Madeline. 'Barn-Burning', which shows not so much ghoulish events as a boy's struggle of divided loyalty between his revengeful father and the ordinary claims of society, is more suited to the bounds of a short story. It depends on character and a struggle of the heart, not on a fearsome event which needs to be read symbolically as much as literally.

Hemingway is more of a short-story specialist than Faulkner, and he is often accepted as the great short-story master of this period. Unquestionably he is a master of form; especially of the vivid scene of talk and action with little narration and no comment. We know that he studied his art from James Joyce and from the French; and that with the touch of genius he transmuted Gertrude Stein to make his own stripped prose. He uses his stories not simply to look at people but to build up the Hemingway vision—of male action, of physical skills, of courage even in the face of failure—his own powerful if reiterated values.

'The Short Happy Life of Francis Macomber' is one of Hemingway's most admired stories. It shows all his skill in working up tension and climax in one swift scene. It is a story not only about bravery but about marriage. Francis Macomber is a very rich American. He is on a big-game hunting expedition with his wife, and there is a stolid English hunter, Wilson, with them. Macomber is charged by a wounded lion and is revealed as a coward. That night his wife cuckolds him with Wilson. But the next day, while shooting buffalo, Macomber finds new courage, and thus achieves that true aim of manhood. He becomes brave. The following quotation shows Wilson's view of Macomber:

It had taken a strange chance of hunting, a sudden precipitation into action without opportunity for worrying beforehand, to bring this about with Macomber, but regardless of how it had happened it had most certainly happened. Look at the beggar now, Wilson thought. It's that some of them stay little boys so long, Wilson thought. Sometimes all their lives. Their figures stay boyish when they're fifty. The great American boy-men. Damned strange people. . . . Be a damn fire eater now. . . . Fear gone like an operation. Something else grew in its place. Main thing a man had. Made him into a man. Women knew it too. No bloody fear.

But this is Hemingway himself who is talking as much as Wilson; voicing his philosophy, making his own comment in a cleverly disguised piece of 'author-narration'. Then comes the ending.

. . . and he [Macomber] did not see Wilson now and, aiming carefully, shot again with the buffalo's huge bulk almost on him and his rifle almost level with the oncoming head, nose out, and he could see the little wicked eyes and the head started to lower and he felt a sudden white-hot, blinding flash explode in his head and that was all he ever felt.

Mrs. Macomber, in the car, had shot at the buffalo with the 6·5 Mannlicher as it seemed about to gore Macomber, and had hit her husband about two inches up and a little to one side of the base of the skull.

We are very much aware of Hemingway in this story, and it is again Hemingway himself who puts the ritualistic bullet into Macomber's head. Having achieved manhood, Francis is sacrificed in his glory. He could not return to the ordinary world. Hemingway's own death makes a tragic commentary.

Frank O'Connor says in *The Lonely Voice* that the only virtue that Hemingway exalts is physical courage; that it is no use looking to him for 'mercy, pity, peace and love'; and he treats 'The Short Happy Life' with amused contempt. 'To say that the psychology of this story is childish would be to waste good words. . . . Clearly, it is the working out of a personal problem that for the vast majority of men and women has no validity whatever.'

This is greatly exaggerated. There are other qualities in Hemingway's stories, and in his sympathetic pictures of an ageing matador and boxer in 'Men without Women' we see Hemingway's feeling for men who are not simply muscular oafs but whose bravery is moral. They may be inarticulate and puzzled, but they are not insensitive: and the special character in them that Hemingway admires and captures is their integrity of purpose. They are unbribable. Surrounded by misunderstandings, double-crossings, they struggle on, faithful to their calling. The calling includes physical bravery almost as a matter of course, and this leads Hemingway on to describe violent action in detail, which is quite a large part of Hemingway's own especial calling. But in these two stories it is the character that is the underlying theme rather than descriptions of boxing and bullfighting.

'The Killers' is another of Hemingway's most praised stories, and here again one feels the author's sympathy for the outcast member of a gang, who makes no effort to avoid his death, but knowing that he has offended the code of his own tribe, 'got in bad', simply waits for them to 'get him'. One feels the author's sympathy too for the adolescent boy, who is given this insight into the relentless approach of a cold-blooded slaughter. At his best Hemingway conveys such characters with the same truth and integrity as they have themselves. Again, in reading that very famous story 'Hills Like White Elephants', one may well decide that the emotion of the story comes from Hemingway's own sense of pity for the girl who is being persuaded to have an abortion, and of despair for the state of mind of the complete cad who is going to desert her.

In *The Short Story*, Sean O'Faolain finds an extremely short and simple story of Hemingway, 'The Light of the World', 'full of unanalysable poetry' in its seemingly flat reporting of two tramps and two prostitutes talking about a man (now dead) whom one of the girls once loved passionately. In its simplicity of strong feeling this story might be compared with Hardy's 'The Tramp Woman's Tragedy', which he wrote with extraordinary concentration as a poem.

Nothing could be more different from 'Francis Macomber' than Eudora Welty's 'The Wide Net'. This story begins, too, with a quarrel between a married couple—this time young and countrified. Hazel is so preoccupied with the thought of her coming baby that she neglects her husband, William. William stays out one night with his friends and finds that Hazel has left a note threatening to drown herself. The story develops into a wonderful account of dragging the river on a long sunlit day, a grand fishing exploit. The thought that Hazel has really drowned herself vanishes. Here is the party on its way, seen for the moment through the eyes of two small boys.

On they went through a forest of cucumber trees, and came up on a high ridge. Grady and Brucie who were running ahead all the way stopped in their tracks; a whistle had blown and far down and far away a long freight train was passing. It seemed like a little festival procession, moving with the slowness of ignorance or a dream, from distance to distance, the tiny pink and gray cars like secret boxes. Grady was counting the cars to himself as if he could certainly see each one clearly, and Brucie watched his lips, hushed and cautious, the way he would watch a bird drinking. Tears suddenly came to Grady's eyes, but it would only be because a tiny man walked along the top of the train, walking and moving on the top of the train. They went down again and soon the smell of the river spread over the woods, cool and secret. Every step they took among the great walls of vines and among the passion flowers started up a little life, a little flight.[4]

Here indeed is the poetic gaze and with it a lyrical happiness that is rare in the American short story. William finds Hazel is safe and sound at home and the story ends with a youthful rough-and-tumble.

[4] In *Thirteen Short Stories* (Longmans, 1965).

'The Wide Net' is achieved in a single scene and it contains
few flashbacks or explanations—a sure sign that a story is short
in essence, and not just squeezed up. Eudora Welty's work is
varied. It can portray complex scenes and conversations, as well
as simple ones. Katherine Anne Porter has commented on the
contrast between the simplicity of her narrative method and the
complexity of her themes. Her art is, in most of its phases,
dependent on the perception of individual existence. As she herself says, 'Relationship is a changing and pervading mystery.'

IV

Eudora Welty comes at a bridge period. She is sympathetic
to the general methods of her immediate predecessors, but in
date her work takes us into the years following the Second World
War. Already, according to modern critics, the period of Hemingway and Fitzgerald is beginning to seem remote. Salinger's
character, Buddy Glass, tells us, 'The great Gatsby is my Tom
Sawyer', a remark which makes the great Gatsby seem old-
fashioned, and suggests that its values are simple and obvious in
the eyes of the new sophistication. McGiffert Wright refers to
'the charge, by now commonplace, that such seemingly tough-
minded honest writers as Hemingway and Anderson were as
sentimental in their desire to avoid sentimentality as were their
more frankly sentimental forebears'.[5]

The writers of the twenties are accused, like their English contemporaries, of dwelling on minute scenes, overworking 'the
death of a pet animal and incidents in hen houses'.

In the last twenty years there has been an extraordinary multi-
plication of short stories in America. William Peden, in *The
American Short Story—Front Line in the National Defense of
Literature* (1964), gives a list of a hundred noteworthy short-
story writers since 1940, a list which is too up to date to include
Hemingway. The general mood of the short story has turned
into one of surprising unhappiness, even of disgust. Peden distinguishes two main groups of authors: he calls one 'Jane Austens
of the Metropolis and Suburbia' and the other 'Sick in Mind and

[5] McGiffert Wright, *The American Short Story in the Twenties*, p. 374.

Body both'. There are well-known names in both groups, but even in the first group of stories there is a great deal of distress, among advertising executives, middle-aged ex-athletes, quarrelling husbands and wives, all caught up in the rat-race of drink, business worries, psycho-analysis, and suburban pettiness. John Cheevers's civilized studies of edgy days and nights in such lives provide a good example. He gives his stories force and form by much carefully compiled detail, with several recurrent themes and images in a story all moving towards a climax which is often an anti-climax, a continued suspension of his wriggling characters in the preserving fluid in which he bottles them.

In a sense this represents the dark side of Thurber's Walter Mitty. We are asked not to smile at but to magnify the pains of actually being Walter Mitty. It is remarkable how closely some scenes of the serious short-story writers from Hemingway to Salinger resemble the surface appearance of Thurber.

In the cottage the doctor, sitting on the bed in his room, saw a pile of medical journals on the floor by the bureau. They were still in their wrappers unopened. It irritated him.

'Aren't you going back to work, dear?' asked the doctor's wife from the room where she was lying with the blinds drawn.

'No!'

'Was anything the matter?'

'I had a row with Dick Boulton.'

'Oh,' said his wife, 'I hope you didn't lose your temper, Henry.'

'No,' said the doctor.

'Remember, that he who ruleth the spirit is greater than he that taketh a city,' said his wife. She was a Christian Scientist. Her Bible, her copy of *Science and Health* and her *Quarterly* were on a table beside her bed in the darkened room.

Her husband did not answer. He was sitting on his bed now, cleaning a shot gun. He pushed the magazine full of the heavy yellow shells, and pumped them out again. They were scattered on the bed.

'Henry!' his wife called. Then paused for a moment. 'Henry!'

'Yes?' the doctor said.

'You didn't say anything to Boulton to anger him, did you?'

This is from Hemingway's 'The Doctor and the Doctor's Wife', but push it on a little bit farther and it becomes very close to Thurber. Walter Mitty, the great white hunter, terror of the buffaloes, is seated on the bed. But all the time he is just a small town doctor whose wife is a Christian Scientist. Perhaps the more gentle American humorists, from Max Adler onwards, have been striking a truer balance than some of the more earnest writers.

Among writers who deal with quieter themes are John Updike and J. F. Powers. The engaging characters of Updike may be uneasy; they may find the stream of city life hard; in their sophisticated moral doubts and arguments they may become querulous, and almost invent worries, but they do not give way to horror and vice. Updike's stories are subtle, and if at times tenuous, they are both interesting and believable.

J. F. Powers has followed a vein all his own, from which he can extract true gold. He tells of the lives and thoughts of Catholic priests in the America of today—priests of the highest sincerity, priests of coarser grain, priests who fall into temptation, priests who are saintly. He sees them as if he were one of them, taking the true short-story writer's view of days or hours that reveal a life. His is a rare and quietly sustained achievement.

The second group, to which Mr. Peden gives as a chapter heading the phrase 'Sick in Mind and Body both', includes such well-known names as Capote, Carson MacCullers, and Tennessee Williams. These and some others have used their stories to convey an astonishing amount of disgust with their surroundings. Even when they are fairly restrained, they leave the impression of people whose nerves and emotions are stretched to the very limit. Tennessee Williams has said that success itself is a kind of death to an author. Thus it is not the natural disasters of life, or the brutality of an invading enemy that they feel, or memories of the despairing years of the hard times. It is the present moment, the state of life today, that causes the turmoil and in its extreme form gives the impression of feet shuffling through lunatic galleries of waking nightmare. It is not that they write bad short stories. Far from it; some of the stories show a remarkable power of imagination and many have a true understanding of the short-story form and an artist's touch with words.

Carson MacCullers' story 'The Ballad of the Sad Café' is a famous example of the modern nightmare mood. It is the Faulkner country again, the despairing South, seen in rather a different light, glimmering and yet strangely clear at moments; it is more gnome-like, more melancholy, less crudely violent than Faulkner. It tells the story of Miss Amelia, a six-foot woman of man-like strength, Lyman, the grotesque hunchback who sucks her spirit in a spider-like grip, and Mervyn Macey, the delinquent and violent dandy. After the set-piece of their public fight surrounded by peering faces, the reader is left with the feeling of an empty world echoing with horrid laughter. The controlled lucidity of the language and imagery make it all the more telling. It is a tragedy of grotesques, beautifully told; but if we think of its human meaning we begin to feel lost. William Peden writes of Mrs. MacCullers that she 'creates a compelling and nightmarish parable of love which is not love and human relations which are anti-human in their thick and clotted perversity'.[6]

Capote deals on the outward surface with more normal circumstances, but also moves into a world of symbolism and parable. Ray West, in *The Short Story in America, 1900–1950*, tells us that Capote

has pushed the modern techniques of overt symbolism and atmospheric distortion to an extreme beyond that of any of his contemporaries. With a talent sensitive to the esoteric and the grotesque in human character, his works display a boldness approaching the paintings of the surrealists or the short stories of Franz Kafka.

Mr. West compares another writer of the 1950s, Paul Bowles, to Poe, saying that his stories of far-away places, though filled with violence and cruelty, seem romantic as much as horrible because of their strangeness.

James Purdy is a writer of very short and adroit stories, each one of which is a capsule of poison. His long short story 'The Dream Palace' goes even further than Faulkner or Carson MacCullers in the grotesque and fantastic, depicting decaying houses, decaying people, drugs, bugs, sexual deviation, and the psychotic slaughter of a younger brother, whom the besotted

[6] Peden, *The American Short Story*, p. 127.

R

killer both loves and hates. A number of modern American stories, in fact, contain an almost unassimilable degree of sordid horror and despair. One hopes that what they describe is indeed no more than a symbol or overwrought dream picture.

Salinger, whom Mr. Peden places behind the banner of Jane Austen, brings us back to more usual scenes, and though his characters have their own agonies, they have also a general balance of rational behaviour. Salinger is perhaps the most famed of all American short-story writers of recent years, and the truly short and often brilliant art of his first book of stories, *For Esmé with love and squalor*, is a *tour de force*. The title story is an original picture of an American soldier in England meeting a precocious English girl of eleven and drawing comfort from her stylized and clever conversation. Little happens in Salinger's short stories. There has been action; there will be further action. He singles out true short-story moments.

Yet his best work goes deeper than the term *tour de force* suggests. The characters who reveal themselves mainly by means of their often foolish talk have a startling reality. Though they may be stupid, half drunk, or on edge with nerves, they are revealed with loving care. Sometimes it is the very inadequacy of their cliché-ridden utterance, full of 'for Chrissake', 'goddamit', and 'y'know what I mean', that reveals the pitiful seriousness of their anxiety.

There is, moreover, one suicide in this book: it comes in the story called 'A Happy Day for Banana Fish', and this deed on the part of Seymour Glass seems to have haunted the author. Around Seymour Glass, Salinger has built a whole family; and the saga of this super-subtle, highly loquacious fraternity and sorority grows book by book. As Salinger himself says, his readers may well surmise that he 'is permanently bogged down with the Glass family'.

Moreover, the long convolvulus trains of their thought have had the effect of drawing Salinger away from the short-story form. The complete absence of narrator in his early stories has turned into the complete presence of the narrator.

'Franny', the first of the two stories in *Franny and Zooey*, maintains the short-story form. It tells how Franny, the gifted college girl and famous actress of the future, keeps endlessly repeating to herself a Christian prayer; how she interferes with her young man's egotistical talk by her 'crabbing' or questioning the purity of the motives of his admired poets and teachers of literature, then how she reproaches herself for being difficult; finally, how she nearly faints through self-imposed hunger—or is it through the early stages of pregnancy? 'Franny' is a subtly appealing short story, with Franny herself an engaging mixture of the sophisticated mind and the simple heart.

'Zooey' is the sequel—a long discussion from one of Franny's brothers, also an actor, about his beloved Franny's purity of motive in her attempt at perpetual prayer. He ends with the conclusion that even if one despises the script one does not give up, but acts one's best 'for the sake of the fat lady'; and the fat lady is Zooey's private symbol for the audience—dull but suffering— the world at large; and also, says Zooey to Franny, 'Don't you know the goddam secret yet—Christ Himself.'

This is the medieval, Christian point of the story; but if ever a story was a piece of layman's theology, this is it: it is full of a personal discussion of values by which it is possible to live, and one is left hoping that Franny, now knowing what Francis Macomber never discovered, may be saved from a ritual death.

In 'Zooey' the marked personal style of narration is highly developed:

The facts at hand presumably speak for themselves, but a trifle more vulgarly, I suspect than facts even usually do. As a counterbalance, then, we begin with that everfresh and exciting odium: the author's formal introduction. The one I have in mind not only is wordy and earnest beyond my wildest dreams but is, to boot, rather excruciatingly personal. If, with the right kind of luck, it comes off, it should be comparable in effect to a compulsory guided tour through the engine room, with myself, as guide, leading the way in an old one-piece Jantzen bathing suit.

This seems as if the long-winded, parenthetical subtleties of Henry James had been brightened by O. Henry's lively wisecracks.

Is it possible to generalize among so many recent stories from so many authors? Here are at least a few impressions. There seems to be a great deal of private distress. Drink is a danger; husbands and wives tear each other to pieces, as in *Who's Afraid of Virginia Woolf?*; the job world is hateful; people are either on the verge of schizophrenic collapse or are too apt to shout their worst moments from the housetops. Perhaps this is only a shallow impression derived from recent years.

V

In longer terms we come to recognize the brilliant American talker, who is alive to everything, who wants to discuss everything. 'I want to know why,' he asks in a characteristic mixture of the sophisticated and the naïve; 'the great American boy-man', as Hemingway calls him. In their hearts the wound of life seems raw and bleeding compared with the older scar tissue of the English. And this with the American's sharp sense of form makes the short story move, as from the outset Poe moved it, towards the grotesque, the ritualistic, and the symbolically violent.

Another theme which runs through American short stories, as through much other American fiction, is the contrast between the values of art and fiction, the hoped-for ideal essence of living, and the world in which we work and marry. It can be found in Hemingway. It can be found in situation stories such as Henry James's 'The Real Thing', in which the true 'real thing' is rejected in favour of the false. The deliberations of Zooey Glass revolve round acting. What is the nature of an actor's sincerity when given a bad script? This again is one of the causes of that rhythmic emotion, that ground swell, of much American fiction: the inner sense of alienation and rejection of society, in the search for something else. Here Thoreau, Huck Finn, the Gentle Grafter, people from Hemingway, Sherwood Anderson, Faulkner, from Salinger, Purdy, and Powers seem to join hands. Walter Allen says, in *Tradition and Dream*, 'such solitary heroes dominate American fiction'.

American critics are apt to see a cause for this sense of being a 'loner' in American society itself, which they feel in some unique way forces this experience on its citizens. Caroline Gordon has a famous story of a 'loner', in 'Old Red'. Because she is not an extremist in any way, but belongs to that quieter school of acceptance and understanding which includes Katherine Anne Porter, 'Old Red' is especially worth considering; and so is the discussion of 'Old Red' in *Understanding Fiction*, by the well-known critics Cleanth Brooks and Robert Penn Warren.

'Old Red' portrays Mr. Maury, an elderly widower about whom Caroline Gordon tells us more in other stories. Mr. Maury is literary, full of ripe if rather eccentric views, and not over-fond of conventional company. Often he preferred the society of Negroes. His main idea at the moment of this story is to escape from the family and go fishing. His personality is shown to us vividly, in a single day-long scene, and at night, when Maury is half asleep, he imagines a delightful picture of himself as 'Old Red', a fox remembered from his youth, who was so cunning that the hounds always lost him. So after fishing all day, Mr. Maury snuggles down into his earth, safe and alone.

In *Understanding Fiction* the authors discuss Mr. Maury's flight from society.

Is not the story, in one sense a story about a basic conflict in our civilization—the conflict between man's desire for a harmonious development of all his faculties and a set of social conditions which tend to compartmentalize life and to make 'work' and 'pleasure' viciously antithetical? The question of importance is not whether or not we feel that Mister Maury's solution is ideal; it is rather whether Mister Maury might not have felt, in a more balanced society, that he did not need to take such drastic measures with his life in order to save himself as a human being.

This seems to me a similar process to that of taking Smith in 'The Loneliness of the Long Distance Runner' too seriously as a modern rebel. Mr. Maury and Smith may both be rebels or escapists. In Smith's position Mr. Maury might have behaved in the same way as Smith, or in some other mildly shocking way all his own. However, they are both sharply drawn, individual oddities, and it is their believable peculiarity that is the value of their stories, rather than any organized comment on American or British social shortcomings.

That people dislike the demands of work is not a state of affairs that the Americans have created for themselves. The Book of Genesis tells us that work is God's curse on Adam and Eve. It is part of the terms of life. Yet it is plain that the Americans are so anxiously aware of this conflict between the individual and the demands of society that one must treat their special feelings in this matter with respect. Their very anxiety about it seems to force the individual 'loner' and the merchandizing mob farther apart. As the closing sentence of *Huckleberry Finn* says, '... I reckon I got to light out for the Territory ahead of the rest, because Aunt Sally she's going to adopt me and civilize me, and I can't stand it.'

The wish to withdraw or to 'light out for the Territory' is self-consciously ingrained in the American; but Huck's words are far too often quoted without recalling Mark Twain's own injunction at the beginning of Huck's story, 'Persons attempting to find a motive in this narrative will be prosecuted; persons attempting to find a moral in it will be banished.' It is a very different mood from the sombre Anglo-Saxon feeling of exile. It is a loneliness that keeps on talking, that springs from frustrated hopes of an ideal citizenship. It is different again from the Celtic trauma caught in the words of Yeats in 'The Hosting of the Sidhe':

> ... Come, come away
> Empty your heart of its human dream.

XIX

Conclusion: The Question of Values

We come finally to the problem of values. It has been suggested in the course of this book that a historical view of the short story helps in itself to form a scale of values. The insights that alter from generation to generation, the changing conceptions of truth, the trying of this or that method of narration all provide a perspective by which we can realize more fully the modern art of the short story. In this long-term view the art seems to have moved towards a certain centre, poetic, unforced, truthful.

Let us first of all gather some threads. The historical study has dealt with various aspects of the short story mainly as they arise; aspects of the form itself or aspects of content, whether this consists in portraying the simplest realities of human existence, those age-old commitments referred to by Mr. Kushwant Singh; or whether it consists of expounding current moral or political notions. All these in their different ways have been ingredients of short stories.

As art forms do not develop in neat compartments, dealing with one idea at a time, or adding a convenient amount of change each half-century, it has obviously not been possible to cover the same categories in each chapter, or to write different parts of the story under separate analytical headings, such as 'Escaping the Moral', 'Change of Social Content', 'Tracing the Narrator', and so on. Nor has it seemed practical to devote a carefully proportioned space to different authors. The aim has been to trace the salient developments of the art as they occur, rather than to write a systematic guide book.

Nevertheless, there seems to have been a movement towards a point of increased value. Even with the modest art of the short story the old philosophical problems of aesthetics and literature must arise. What does the art consist of? What is good? What can it do that is not accomplished in some other way? Roughly speaking, we may answer that the modern world does not evaluate stories as religious teaching; nor as moralizing; nor, in spite'of all the arguments, as political theory; nor as the utterances of a private religion. It does, however, seem that the underlying value, which is sought for time and again from the simplest reader to the most serious author, is the value of truth. Is it *true*? Is it *real*? This is the all-important question, for if it is not true it is nothing; and all those clever devices of verisimilitude are themselves a tribute that the spinner of tall yarns pays to the need for truth.

Next, if it is true, is it important? True incidents that are more or less trivial may be piled up by the hundred. The short, single event that carries the conviction of truth, and is also memorable and of human value as a story, is very hard to come by. One can look further still and ask, has the story not merely an importance on the ordinary human scene but also a meaning that, like music, seems to arrange, to clarify, to enlighten? Such feelings may be transient, they may lead on to further vistas of unsolved speculation, yet they are in themselves of value. And beyond the thirst for truth goes the hope for some insight, some penetration through the surface of events and sensations. And here we approach closely an idea of value that is both modern and antique, that is perennially embodied in authorship, yet is free from any expository intention.

In his Introduction to a collection of modern Italian short stories, John Lehmann calls attention to a quality that he describes as 'an almost mystical fervour of realism'.[1] (Both Joyce and Katherine Mansfield speak of the 'priest of the eternal imagination'.) So we are brought back to the notion that behind the poetic truth that we may find in a short story there lies a value that we think of as religious; or that even if we are agnostics, we tend to refer to in religious terms. There is some view of the path of life itself, of the value of being human.

[1] John Lehmann, Introduction to *Italian Stories of Today* (Faber & Faber, 1959), p. 13.

Deep thinkers who may be classed as agnostic or atheist, such as Hardy or Joyce, nevertheless adopt theological positions in their intuitive feelings about the nature or absence of God. Their pictures of humanity are linked with values which have always been the ground of religious discussion. As Lord David Cecil says of Hardy, 'he must be respected for maintaining the Christian virtues without the Christian hope'. The words *good* and *bad* when applied to human actions continue to have a vital contrast which no one can avoid. If in the end they are related to a completely explicit materialism, they have of necessity to refer to a given state of affairs at a given time; and so they turn out to be only political values after all, and thus to have lost that instinctively felt contrast which is their meaning for most people.

It is the nature of good and bad in human action that the more profound creators of fiction have in mind. This is how people behave. This is what we mean by kindness. This is how people are selfish. This is how people are joyful. This is anger. This is how people make each other happy. This is how people do things that they themselves detest. This is conscience. This is a painful choice. This is how people face the solitude of separate being. These are all familiar elements in the search for truth: all everyday experiences within the ambient creation. As our spirits become anaesthetized by public and verbal creeds, religious values have in a sense moved underground. They have become the affair of millions of individuals, struggling by themselves to find the values of existing; and of authors struggling to portray their struggles.

If we turn to fiction, in what can this manifestation of value and truth consist? What is the nature of the search in which individuals are each pursuing their own tracks and their own hopes alone? To talk of an underground religion, a religion seeking some kind of a private utterance, is often a mere confusion of words. Is it possible that the work of short-story writers can contain an element to which this search for truth, this kind of language, can apply?

Let us first eliminate some of the various misconceptions that tend to arise when discussion turns to the idea of secular authorship achieving some higher significance. The touchstone is not

to be found in any of the following notions: discussions of
religious ideas among the characters of a story; the old-fashioned
apologue of orthodox religious teaching put into modern terms;
references to occult beliefs, such as theosophy, or other systems
intended for initiates; similar references to religions that have
historically gone underground, lingering on in signs of a mysterious knowledge in folklore or among gypsies; private schemes of
quasi-prophetic fervour intended to teach mankind better ways;
the deliberate manufacture of modern parables; the practice of
social satire which tends to turn people into puppets acting out
their parts in stories of virtues and vices; these are in fact also
parables, indicating a preacher in the background.

All these are on the wrong track, in fact they are on the reverse
track, since they are all forms of overt and conscious instruction,
and to suggest that the kind of truth, so anxiously sought for by
Chekhov or Katherine Mansfield, is to be achieved in any form
of deliberate admonition is obviously absurd.

To speak of parables, however, opens up the whole relationship of fiction to parable. To some minds in the Middle Ages
everything was a parable: childhood; parenthood; birth; death;
animals; tilling the soil; even getting up in the morning. Every
story was also a parable, sometimes beautiful and moving in its
application, yet sometimes uninspired. Strange morals were de-
duced from stories that never seemed intended to contain anything of the sort. Preachers became altogether too painstaking
about the world's theophany. Yet as parables partake of certain
qualities of fiction, so does fiction partake of some of the nature
of parable. Fiction is inevitably open to the discovery of inner
esoteric meanings, often unintended and unseen by the author.
Modern critics of fiction, especially American ones, are apt to
emphasize the view of fiction as symbol and metaphor; and even
without intending any very serious interpretation of his work,
the author may agree. 'The great joy of a novelist is that alone
and without restraint, using all experience, knowledge or imagin-
ings, he can create his own metaphor of the universe.'[2] This

[2] From an article, 'The Novel as Metaphor', by Maurice Edelman, in *The
Times*, 20 December 1962.

striking thought comes from Maurice Edelman, who is a novelist among his many activities. 'Metaphor of the universe' is a contemporary expression for parable or the old idea of allegory. Yet on the whole the less conscious the author is of intending a parable or an allegory, especially in a short story, the better.

What, then, remains? The world itself remains; the people in the world; and the gift of portraying them without any purposive manipulation. It is the poet's awareness that remains; the awareness that creation is its own parable. Not only can we not bear very much reality, but we are able to see only a very little reality at a time. The essential response of the poet and the artist is to portray such minute aspects of reality as he is gifted to see. He struggles to portray rather than to expound. To ask for wholesale explanations of 'the meaning of life' is simply to ask for dusty answers.

To the short-story writer the approach to truth, the theophany, is accomplished first by the gift of creative vision, and secondly by the elimination of any personal importance or any personal interpretation in the portrayal. 'Throw your own personality overboard,' Chekhov said to his brother, not in criticism of him as a moral being, but simply in advice to him as an artist. 'Part with yourself if only for a moment.' 'Lord make me crystal clear for Thy light to show through,' wrote Katherine Mansfield in her journal. In a different and cooler mood, Maupassant notes that Flaubert had told him that he never allowed himself the use of the first person—advice which might sound like a mere hint about craftsmanship. Or again, Arnold Bennett talks in his journal of an 'almost Christ-like quality of self-abnegation' needed by the writer of fiction, in entering truly into the joys and sorrows of other people.

Arnold Bennett was, of course, thinking of novels rather than short stories, but he was a student of the French theories of his earlier days. It may be possible for a novelist to create his images in a novel, and also to step aside and discuss their significance. The two elements can be separated, or may even complement each other. But within the smaller limits of the short story the comment and the vision cannot appear separately. The vision arises at that moment when the symbolic image corresponds with the natural image.

The particular domain of the short story is unique. It is a flash of insight that leads to a story; it is not a vision simply of ecstatic moments or aesthetic impressions. It is not the vision of the nature poets. It is a vision of people. Chekhov gives the writer Trigorin the thought that he is deeply moved by nature, and yet it makes him want to write about people.

The coming of these moments of insight, the flash, can be seen clearly enough in Chekhov's own notebooks or Katherine Mansfield's journals. Joyce tells us of these moments of epiphany, when it seems the veil is about to be lifted. As the 'I' in Sherwood Anderson's story 'Death in the Woods' says, 'The whole thing, the story of the old woman's death, was to me as I grew older, like music heard from afar. The notes had to be picked up slowly one at a time, something had to be understood.'

The use of the word theophany may make these considerations meaningless to some. If there is no God, there is no theophany. What, then, can be the value of 'The Bishop' or 'Death in the Woods' or 'The Doll's House'? We can still say they are rare and accurate visions of people written with depth of feeling; they are still lives in which a dimension of time is made manifest.

Two definitions of the art of the short story come to mind, both from Whit and Hallie Burnett's anthology *The Modern Short Story in the Making*. One is simply 'A glimpse through', which comes from S. G. Albee; the other from Guido Agostini, 'the accomplishment in words of a single emotional or dramatic effect which leaves the reader with the feeling of having participated in the life and movement of the world'. Both these come near success in conveying the essence of the short-story art.

If we return to the historical view of the short story we can trace throughout the generations the course of a stream, though a meandering one. Already in Anglo-Saxon times we see an inner dialogue between solitary man and his surroundings, which is expressed in clear, striking images. Then Chaucer, departing from magical and astonishing stories, portrays his characters in all their solid reality, and yet in an immortal light; *sub specie aeternutatis*, as Blake saw it; or as John Lehmann says of the Italian stories, 'an almost mystical fervour of realism'.

In due course the Elizabethans added their vigorous movement and coherence. Their novelle may tell of astonishing events, but many of them are built up in a tangible world. Then the character writers in their turn concentrate on the conception of human virtues and faults. They merge into the essay-writers, who, through their moral discussions of character in action, gradually approach the modern short story, till at length we begin to see, in the nineteenth century, the mingling of the poetic and time-dissolving vision with a short, credible narrative of human events.

It is not till this point that the perception of the solitary meditative reader as apart from the listening audience really takes effect. As the form develops, it brings with it new perceptions of human nature: it gives us evidence of increasing insights of sympathy and thoughtful understanding. Let us take any one theme, and trace it down the centuries of prose short-story tellers; the age-old theme, for instance, of marriage and of difficult relations between husbands and wives.

Perhaps the most typical husband-and-wife story of medieval times in English is the Wife of Bath's own prologue. It exhibits the whole history of her marriages as a battle; a crude contest reverberating outwards from the intimacies of the bedroom. Dame Alison is an extraordinary person; yet the picture of her married life is the epitome of a great deal that was said about husbands and wives in medieval times. The story of May and December, with the elderly man's view of his young wife mainly as a sexual instrument, and her own lack of compunction in cuckolding him in his own presence when he is blind, seems to be accepted by the pilgrims as fair game in a marriage story. Chaucer's own comment, one of the very few he makes in his own person, at the end of 'The Clerke's Tale' of Griselda, scarcely puts marriage higher than a contest of wits.

The conception of romantic love seems to exist quite apart from the realities of marriage. 'The Knight of the Tower' gives us other brutal or farcical pictures of marriage, and it seems to be beyond his range as a story-teller to see in other people the understanding he himself felt for his dead wife. He simply uses the story-telling clichés of the time.

In Elizabethan days, while Barnabe Rich can assume a tone of informal banter with his readers, and can tell at least one realistic marriage story in 'The Two Brethren', the story is still lacking in tenderness or any attempt to see the true feelings of husbands and wives. The treatment is still one of sexual infatuation, unfaithfulness, and knockabout; and the driving of the scolding wife over the edge of sanity is told with heartless relish.

With the eighteenth-century essays we find the express aim of refining manners. Steele's story of the wife who threw hysterical fits to gain her own ends is certainly more gentle and affectionate than the conception of Rich, yet its light touch makes it little more than a conversational yarn. We feel the wife could not have been happily cured of so much insincerity so easily: people who show such a degree of hysteria have a strong and sometimes indomitable force in gaining their own ends. They cause and they feel far more unhappiness than Steele allows.

In Thackeray's story 'Denis Haggerty's Wife' we enter into the true knowledge of suffering caused by an unhappy marriage. Here there is no coarse laughter, no polite amusement. It is a loosely formed story covering several years, with a number of scenes narrated by Fitzboodle, but with Thackeray showing ever more plainly and more seriously through the disguise as the story progresses. We may feel that the wife is overdrawn, but we are made to share the final passion of Denis Haggerty's sufferings.

Already we are beginning to approach the modern short story. To make a direct comparison with the stories of scolding and quarrelling that reach us from the past we might choose from the 1930s Clemence Dane's 'The Dearly Beloved of Benjamin Cobb'. It is told by a former village schoolmistress to an old pupil, and the quiet understanding between them is a convincing part of the telling. The old lady talks with compassion of the country priest, the vicar of a village parish, who married a neurotic tyrant. For many years he shields and protects her, treating her with care and charity, receiving endless bad temper and abuse in return.

Gradually the whole village learns the situation; some approve, some disapprove his tenderness; most of them bitterly condemn the wife. When after years the vicar dies, his wife becomes almost demented with grief and she rushes from the house. The villagers search for her, fearing some disaster; and later she is found lying on his grave trying to dig her way with bare hands to the man whom she really loved and desperately needed.

Here in its intensity, its insight, its conception of what needs to be told about the two protagonists, we have reached the art of the modern short story. The very fact that Clemence Dane was by no means a leading exponent of the modern short-story form, and that in some ways her narrative handling of the material is old-fashioned, makes the contrast with the stories of the past seem all the more striking. Had the author been a more complete practitioner of form, the other stories in her volume, *Fate Cries Out* (1935), would have probably succeeded with greater effect. However, 'The Dearly Beloved of Benjamin Cobb' is a modern story, and in the writing of it the developments of past generations came to her aid.

Critics at times seem to expect too much of a short story; at other times they read too much into it. I am susceptible to this modest art and have been since the days sixty years ago when I began reading Grimms' *Tales* to myself, and was struck especially by 'The Old Man and his Grandson'. At its best the short story is 'a glimpse through': even the best authors achieve it only at certain times. Yet at its best it can make lyric joy seem a mere passing intoxication and long novels an irrelevance. Among all the large, brilliantly coloured caskets it is the small unobtrusive box. Yeats may have wished to cherish within himself the feelings of angry passionate man; yet as an artist he could have been thinking of the short story when he wrote: 'Only that which does not teach, which does not cry out, which does not persuade, which does not condescend, which does not explain, is irresistible.'[3]

[3] W. B. Yeats, 'J. M. Synge and the Ireland of his time', in *Essays* (Macmillan, 1924), p. 423.

Select Bibliography

The object of the following brief selection is to provide a reading list covering the main theme of *The Modest Art*, the historical development of the written short story in English. *The Short Story Index* (mentioned below) provides a bibliography of the works of short-story writers.

(Place of publication London, unless stated otherwise)

I. *Bibliographies*

ENGLISH TALES AND PROSE ROMANCES BEFORE 1740: A BIBLIOGRAPHY, by A. J. K. Esdaile (1912). Part I, 1475–1642; Part II, 1643–1739.

THE ENGLISH NOVEL, 1740–1850, by A. Block (1939). A bibliographical catalogue including prose romances, short stories, and translations of foreign fiction.

THE SHORT STORY INDEX, by D. E. Cook and I. S. Monroe, New York (1953, with supplements in 1956 and 1960). Contains an index of 60,000 stories.

II. *A Guide to Collections of Stories and Sources before the Eighteenth Century*

THE JATAKAS, edited by H. V. Fausboll (1871).

THE IDYLLS OF THEOCRITUS, translated and edited by A. S. F. Gow (1950).

ANGLO SAXON POETRY, selected and translated by R. K. Gordon (1926). Everyman's Library Edition.

THE BLICKLING HOMILIES OF THE TENTH CENTURY, edited with a translation by R. O. Morris, E.E.T.S. (1880).

MIDDLE ENGLISH HUMOROUS TALES IN VERSE, edited by G. H. McKnight, Boston and London (1913).

LEGENDS AND SATIRES FROM MEDIEVAL LITERATURE, edited by M. H. Shackford, Boston and London (1913).

FOURTEENTH CENTURY VERSE AND PROSE, edited by K. Sisam (1921).

AN ALPHABET OF TALES, edited by M. M. Banks (1904)—an English translation of the *Alphabetium Narrationium* of Etienne de Bescançon.

EARLY ENGLISH VERSIONS OF THE GESTA ROMANORUM, edited with an introduction by R. J. H. Herrtage (1889). Early English Text Society.

THE CANTERBURY TALES, edited by A. Burrell (1908). Everyman's Library edition, partly modernized.

THE HUNDRED MERRY TALES (1526), edited by H. Oesterley (1866).

THE FRATERNITIE OF VACABONES, printed by J. Awdeley (1575), edited by E. Viles and F. J. Furnivall as *Rogues and Vagabonds of Shakespeare's Youth* (1907).

A CAVEAT OR WARNING FOR COMMEN CURSETORS, VULGARELY CALLED VAGABONES, SET FORTH BY Thomas Harman Esquire (1567), edited by E. Viles and F. J. Furnivall, as above (1907).

THE PALACE OF PLEASURE, by W. Painter (1566–7), edited by J. Jacobs, 3 vols. (1890).

A PETITE PALACE OF PETTIE HIS PLEASURE, by G. Pettie (1576), edited by H. Hartmann, Oxford (1938)

RICH HIS FAREWELL TO MILITARIE PROFESSION, by B. Rich (1581), edited by J. P. Collier (1896).

LIFE AND WORKS OF ROBERT GREENE, Volume 10, with notes by A. B. Grosart. Printed for private circulation, Huth Library (1881).

WORKS, Thomas Deloney, edited by F. O. Mann (1912).

OLD ENGLISH JEST BOOKS, edited by W. C. Hazlitt (1861).

WESTWARD FOR SMELTS, by Kinde Kit of Kingstone (1620), reprinted 1848, edited by J. O. Halliwell.

ELIZABETHAN TALES, with an Introduction by E. J. O'Brien (1937).

CHARACTER WRITINGS OF THE SEVENTEENTH CENTURY, edited by H. Morley (1891).

III. *Some Selections from Eighteenth- and Early Nineteenth-century Authors*

SIR ROGER DE COVERLEY, AND OTHER ESSAYS FROM THE SPECTATOR, edited by A. Symons (1956).

WORKS OF CHARLES LAMB, edited by T. Hutchinson, 2 vols. (1908).

THE WORKS OF HANNAH MORE, vols. III and IV (1830).

THE SHORT STORIES OF SIR WALTER SCOTT, with an Introduction by
Lord David Cecil (1934).

POPULAR TALES OF MARIA EDGEWORTH, with an Introduction by Anne
Thackeray Ritchie (1895).

SELECTIONS FROM THE WORKS OF MARIA EDGEWORTH, edited by
M. C. Selon (1919).

OUR VILLAGE: SKETCHES OF RURAL CHARACTER AND SCENERY, by
Mary Russell Mitford, with an Introduction by Anne Thackeray
Ritchie (1893); edited by W. J. Roberts (1947).

BEST SHORT STORIES OF CHARLES DICKENS, with an Introduction by
E. V. Mitchell, New York (1947).

IV. *Anthologies*

1. *General and Modern Anthologies*

THE MASTERPIECE LIBRARY OF SHORT STORIES, a thousand stories of
all times and countries, edited by J. A. Hammerton (no date).

ENGLISH SHORT STORIES FROM THE FIFTEENTH TO THE TWENTIETH
CENTURY, with an Introduction by R. Wilson (1921). Everyman's
Library edition.

SELECTED ENGLISH SHORT STORIES, XIX CENTURY (First series), with
an Introduction by Hugh Walker (1914). World's Classics edition.

SELECTED ENGLISH SHORT STORIES XIX AND XX CENTURIES (Second
Series), collected by Sir Humphrey Milford (1921). World's
Classics edition.

GREAT AMERICAN STORIES, edited by W. Dean Howells (1860–1920).

THE FABER BOOK OF MODERN STORIES, edited with an Introduction by
Elizabeth Bowen (1937).

MODERN ENGLISH SHORT STORIES, collected by Phyllis M. Jones
(1939). World's Classics edition.

TELLERS OF TALES, a hundred stories of the nineteenth and twentieth
centuries, chosen and introduced by Somerset Maugham, New
York (1939).

SOMERSET MAUGHAM'S INTRODUCTION TO MODERN ENGLISH AND
AMERICAN LITERATURE, Philadelphia (1943). Critical essays are
dispersed between the different sections.

SOUTH AFRICAN SHORT STORIES, selected by E. R. Seary, Cape Town
(1947).

INDIAN SHORT STORIES, selected and edited by Mulk Raj Amand and
Iqbal Singh (1946).

AUSTRALIAN SHORT STORIES, selected by Walter Murdoch and H. Drake-Brockman (1951). World's Classics edition.

NEW ZEALAND SHORT STORIES (First series), selected with an Introduction by D. M. Davin (1953). World's Classics edition.

MODERN ENGLISH SHORT STORIES (Second series), selected with an Introduction by Derek Hudson (1956). World's Classics edition.

WELSH SHORT STORIES, selected with an Introduction by Gwyn Jones (1956). World's Classics edition.

MODERN IRISH SHORT STORIES, selected with an Introduction by Frank O'Connor (1957). World's Classics edition.

CANADIAN SHORT STORIES, selected with an Introduction by Robert Weaver (1960). World's Classics edition.

WEST INDIAN STORIES, edited by Andrew Salkey (1960).

MODERN AFRICAN STORIES, edited by Ellis Komey and Ezekiel Mphalele (1964).

A BOOK OF MODERN STORIES, edited by Hesther Burton (1959).

AMERICAN SHORT STORIES, selected with an Introduction by Douglas Grant (1965). World's Classics edition.

2. *Some Outstanding Annual Publications*

BEST AMERICAN SHORT STORIES, Boston (annually since 1915). Edited by E. J. O'Brien till 1940; edited since by Martha Foley and David Burnett.

BEST BRITISH SHORT STORIES, edited by E. J. O'Brien (annually 1922–40).

THE O. HENRY AWARD PRIZE STORIES, various editors, New York (annually since 1919).

PICK OF TODAY'S SHORT STORIES, edited by John Pudney (annually 1949–62).

WINTERS TALES, various editors (annually since 1955).

V. *Works of Criticism*

1. *Fiction in General*

THE LIGHT READING OF OUR ANCESTORS, by R. E. Prothero (1927).

LITERATURE AND THE PULPIT IN MEDIEVAL ENGLAND, by G. R. Owst, Cambridge (1933).

ROMANCE, VISION AND SATIRE, by J. L. Western, Boston (1912).

THE ENGLISH NOVEL IN THE TIME OF SHAKESPEARE, by J. J. Jusserand, translated by E. Lee (1890).

A History of the Novel Previous to the Seventeenth Century, by F. M. Warren, New York (1895).

The Greek Romances in Elizabethan Literature, by S. L. Woolf, New York (1912).

The Literature of Roguery, by F. W. Chandler. 2 vols., New York (1899).

The History of the English Novel, by A. E. Baker. 9 vols. (1924–38). The earlier volumes are of interest.

2. *Criticism of the Short Story*

The Philosophy of the Short Story, by Brander Matthews, New York (1901).

The Short Story in English, by H. S. Canby, New York (1909)— a valuable historical account.

The Short Story, by Barry Pain (1916).

Aspects of the Modern Short Story: English and American, by A. C. Ward (1924).

The Modern Short Story, by H. E. Bates (1941).

The Short Story, by Sean O'Faolain (1948).

Short Stories, by Eudora Welty, New York (1950).

The Short Story in America, 1900–1950, by R. B. West, Chicago (1952).

The American Short Story in the Twenties, by Austen McGiffert Wright, Chicago (1961).

The Lonely Voice: A Study of the Short Story, by Frank O'Connor (1964).

The American Short Story, Front Line in the National Defense of Literature, by William Peden, Boston (1964).

3. *A Selection of Views of Short-story Writers in Separate Essays, Journals, etc.*

In addition to the introductions by Elizabeth Bowen and Somerset Maugham mentioned above, the following are of interest:

Edgar Allan Poe, article on Nathaniel Hawthorne's stories. Complete Works, New York (1902), Vol. 7.

H. G. Wells, *The Country of the Blind*, Introduction (1911).

Rudyard Kipling, *Something of Myself* (1936).

Katherine Mansfield, *Journal*, edited by J. Middleton Murry (1954).

SOMERSET MAUGHAM, *A Writers Notebook* (1949), various references.

Essays by Divers Hands (1950), Address to Royal Society of Literature.

The Complete Short Stories, 3 vols. (1951). Introduction to the three volumes.

Points of View (1958). A chapter on the short story.

KATHERINE ANNE PORTER, *The Days Before* (1953), various essays.

Index

S